THE OXFORD HISTORY OF MUSIC
VOL. IV

THE AGE OF BACH & HANDEL

THE OXFORD
HISTORY OF MUSIC

VOL. IV

THE AGE OF BACH & HANDEL

BY

J. A. FULLER MAITLAND

Second Edition

NEW YORK
COOPER SQUARE PUBLISHERS, INC.
1973

Revised edition Published 1931 by Oxford University Press
Reprinted by Permission of Oxford University Press
Published 1973 by Cooper Square Publishers, Inc.
59 Fourth Avenue, New York, New York 10003
International Standard Book Number 0-8154-0472-7
Library of Congress Catalog Card Number 72-97074

Printed in the United States of America

PREFACE TO THE SECOND EDITION OF "THE AGE OF BACH AND HANDEL."

It is not far from thirty years since the appearance of the first edition of this part of *The Oxford History of Music*; and in that time there has happened an artistic revolution at least as violent as the great upheaval of the old ideals and methods which took place, so conveniently for students' memories, about the year 1600. Like that movement, which discarded polyphony in favour of monody, and established melody as the chief factor in music, the modern revolution has thrown into the melting-pot nearly all the elements of the art, as that art was understood up to the end of the nineteenth century. Melody, harmony, counterpoint, as we knew them, have been discredited by the "modern" composers, and it remains to be seen whether any of the new compositions will be recognised as a masterpiece and thus justify so great a change of ideals. A slight reference to the earliest rumblings of the storm that began in France will be found on p. 288 of the present volume.

This is not the place to discuss modern tendencies, but a change in public opinion which does concern this part of the history has been effected in a remarkable way since the publication of the first edition. At the beginning of the century the music of Bach was held to require special gifts for its appreciation, while the execution of much of his vocal music was supposed to be beyond the powers even of the highly-trained singers. In the present day Bach is one of the most popular of all the masters of music, and the change may quite possibly be not entirely unconnected with the discredit which some of the supporters of modern music have been anxious to confer upon the strictly classical forms, as these were understood from the days of Haydn to those of Brahms.

How much Bach's position in public esteem is due to the work of Bach enthusiasts who have succeeded in establishing

a weekly broadcast performance of his church cantatas it is
impossible to guess ; whether such performances have created
the taste, or whether the widespread love of the music caused
the plan to be tried, the fact remains that Bach's name is a
most powerful attraction for the general public, not merely for
a company of fanatics.

The Bach literature has been enormously enriched by the
indefatigable researches of Professor C. Sanford Terry, among
whose valuable contributions to the subject may be mentioned :

Bach : a Biography. 1928.

Edition of Forkel's Biography. 1920.

The Origin of the Family of Bach Musicians. 1929.

Bach's Cantata Texts. 1926.

Sir Hubert Parry's masterly book on Bach, published in 1909,
and Albert Schweitzer's Biography (1908), translated by
Ernest Newman, in two volumes, 1911, must also be referred to.
It is obvious that none of these could be mentioned in the first
edition of this book, as they did not then exist.

If the Handel literature has been less fortunate, yet it is
worth mentioning the life of the master by Newman Flower,
1923. The experiment has been tried in Germany, and on
one occasion in England, of reviving some of Handel's operas
on the stage. In a less ambitious way the discovery and
publication of a fairly large number of keyboard pieces hitherto
unknown, and containing very interesting illustrations of the
way in which Handel employed the two manuals of the
harpsichord, was due to the late William Barclay Squire,
M.V.O., who obtained some twenty-five volumes of MSS.,
which he presented to the King's Music Library permanently
on loan to the British Museum.

.The little " ground " in C minor, referred to on p. 157 as by
Purcell, is undoubtedly by William Croft ; it exists in two MSS.
only, and in both Croft's name, or initials, appear as those of
the composer.

The reference to " God save the King " on p. 347 has been
amended, as a fortunate discovery has enabled us to set back

its antiquity as a familiar expression of loyalty. In a catch by Purcell (*Purcell Soc. Publications*, vol. xxii, p. 12) the words " God save the King " are associated with four notes identical with the opening of the tune we know. As the catch celebrates the return of the Duke of York (James II) from Scotland in 1680, and as the words in question are used as a quotation from something well known, it is pretty clearly established that it was used as a national song, and in honour of the House of Stuart, at some date very much earlier than 1740, when its documented career is held to have begun.

A record of the discussion on the whole question, together with the music and words of the catch, will be found in the *Proceedings of the Musical Association*, 43rd session, 1916–17, p. 123, and in the *Musical Times*, June 1917, pp. 268–270.

In the many references to Grove's *Dictionary* it must be remembered that in 1902 only the first edition of that work was in existence.

PREFACE

Two of the great giants of music dominate the period that roughly coincides with the first half of the eighteenth century. Though the movements and tendencies of the age of Bach and Handel are to be traced with a fair amount of certainty in their works, the consideration of which necessarily occupies a large proportion of the following pages, yet from the music of their contemporaries in various countries it is possible to illustrate, even more definitely than from their own, the changes that were . passing over the art of music, whether in the actual music itself, or in the attitude of musicians and the public towards the art. In the short space of fifty years almost everything connected with music underwent a striking change in all the countries of Europe; and the transitions are but various tributaries to the main stream of musical development. The central change in the structure of music, and one which gives the key to all the rest, may be defined as one from counterpoint to harmony. At the beginning of the eighteenth century, while the laws of strict counterpoint were held as still binding, in all music of serious pretensions the treatment of harmonic progressions, independently of counterpoint, was tentative and uncertain, and it is clear that the greater number of composers had not acquired the power of conceiving their ideas upon a harmonic basis. At the end of the period here described, the attitude of composers had completely altered; the movement of solid masses of harmony had succeeded to the movement of interweaving parts, and the way had been prepared for the advent of modern music, with its wealth of emotional expression. Melodic invention had become of greater importance than before, and as a consequence more stress was laid upon the dynamics of music, upon the means of varying the volume of tone produced. The structure of instruments and the balance of different sections of the orchestra were gradually improved; and the wealth of tone-colour put at the disposal of the musician enabled him to present his ideas with a very remarkable degree of variety. In the course of the transition from a contrapuntal to a harmonic way of regarding music, certain curious weaknesses of style are to be traced in many of the masters of the second order, who preferred melodic platitudes to the rich sonorities of a former age, and found easy and lucrative employment in copying from one another certain formulae, mere tricks of the pen as meaningless as the flourishes of a writing-master. In no department of music are these conventionalities, which are often to be found side by side with passages of real beauty and solid worth, more strikingly displayed than in operatic music. With the exception of Reinhard Keiser's work at Hamburg early in the eighteenth century, opera seemed for the time to have lost all connexion with dramatic truth. The music of the stage was in all countries the most artificial, cold and formal that has ever existed: beautiful as some individual operatic songs might be, very few if any of them were capable of conveying real dramatic expression, and in theatrical music the period before the reforms of Gluck must count as the darkest hour before the dawn.

J. A. FULLER MAITLAND.

CONTENTS

LIST OF AUTHORITIES

GENERAL

HISTORIES—

BURNEY, Dr. Charles.

History of Music, 4 vols., 1776–1789.

The Present State of Music in France and Italy, 1771.

The Present State of Music in Germany, the Netherlands, &c., 2 vols., 1773.

HAWKINS, Sir John. History of Music, ed. 1853.

NAUMANN, Emil. The History of Music, translated by F. Praeger (the additional chapters by the editor, Sir F. A. Gore Ouseley, on Music in England, are of especial value).

DICTIONARIES—

BAKER, Theo. Biographical Dictionary of Musicians, 1900.

BIOGRAPHIE UNIVERSELLE.

DICTIONARY OF NATIONAL BIOGRAPHY.

FÉTIS. Biographie Universelle des Musiciens, 1837, with supplement by Pougin, to 1880.

GROVE, Sir George. Dictionary of Music and Musicians, 1878–1889.

MENDEL, H. Musikalisches Conversations-Lexicon, 1870–1883.

RIEMANN, Hugo. Musik-Lexicon, 1882 (Eng. transl., 1896).

WALTHER, J. G. Musikalisches Lexicon, 1732.

MUSIC, PRINTED AND MS. In the British Museum, the
Royal College of Music, the Fitzwilliam Museum, Cambridge, and other collections.

SPECIAL

BACH—

FORKEL, J. N. Ueber J. S. Bach's Leben, Kunst, und
Kunstwerke (1803).

MOSEWIUS, J. Theodor. J. S. Bach in seinen Kirchen-
Cantaten, 1845.

PIRRO, A. L'Orgue de J. S. Bach, 1895.

PREFACES in the edition of the Bach-Gesellschaft.

SPITTA, Philipp. Life of Bach (Eng. transl., 3 vols., 1884).

HANDEL—

BURNEY, Dr. C. Commemoration of Handel.

CHRYSANDER, F.

G. F. Händel (biography still incomplete), 1858–1867.

Supplemente, enthaltend Quellen zu Händel's Werken.

MAINWARING, J. Memoirs of the Life of G. F. Handel,
1760.

MONTHLY MUSICAL RECORD. Articles by Prof. Prout,
in November and December, 1871, and April, 1894.

PREFACES to edition of the Händel-Gesellschaft.

ROCKSTRO, W. S. Life of Handel, 1883.

THEORY OF MUSIC, FORM, ORNAMENT, &c.—

ADLUNG, Jacob. Anleitung zur musikalischen Gelahrtheit, 1758.

AVISON, Charles. Essay on Musical Expression, 1752.

BACH, C. P. E. Versuch über die wahre Art das Clavier
zu spielen, 1753–1762.

DANNREUTHER, Edward. Musical Ornamentation, n. d.

FUX, Johann Joseph. Gradus ad Parnassum, 1725.

GALLIARD, J. E. Translation of Tosi's treatise (see below), as Observations on the Florid Song, 1742.

HEINICHEN, Joh. David. Der Generalbass in der Composition, 1728.

KIRNBERGER, F. Wahre Grundsätze zum Gebrauch der Harmonie, 1773.

MALCOLM, Alexander. Treatise of Music, 1721, &c.

MARPURG, F. W.

    Abhandlung von der Fuge, 1753-1754.

    Der kritische Musikus an der Spree, 1749-1750.

    Historisch-kritische Beyträge zur Aufnahme der Musik, 1754, &c.

    Kritische Briefe über die Tonkunst, 1759-1763.

MATTHESON, Johann.

    Critica Musica, 1722, &c.

    Das beschützte Orchester, &c., 1717.

    Das forschende Orchester, &c., 1721.

    Das neu-eröffnete Orchester, &c., 1713.

    Der musikalische Patriot, 1728.

    Der neue göttingische Ephorus, 1727.

    Der vollkommene Capellmeister, 1739.

    Grosse Generalbassschule, 1735.

    Grundlage einer Ehrenpforte, 1740.

    Kern melodischer Wissenschaft, 1737.

    Kleine Generalbassschule, 1735.

MIZLER, Lorenz Christoph.

    German Translation of Fux's Gradus, 1742.

    Neu-eröffnete musikalische Bibliothek, 1736-1754.

MONTÉCLAIR, Michel Pignolet de. Méthode pour apprendre la Musique, 1700.

PROUT, Prof. Ebenezer.

    Applied Forms, 1895.

    Fugue, 1891.

QUANTZ, Johann Joachim. Versuch einer Anweisung, die Flöte traversiere zu spielen, 1752.

THEORY OF MUSIC, FORM, ORNAMENT *(cont.)*—

RAMEAU, J. P. Nouveau système de Musique théorique, 1726.

SCHEIBE, Johann Adolf. Der critische Musikus, 1737–1740.

SHEDLOCK, J. S. The Pianoforte Sonata, 1895.

SMITH, Rev. Robert. Harmonics, 1758.

TOSI, Pier Francesco. Opinioni de' Cantori antichi, &c., 1723.

WINTERFELD, C. G. A. von. Der evangelische Kirchengesang, 1843–1847.

THE OPERA—

ALGAROTTI, Francesco. Saggio sopra l'Opera in Musica, 1763.

ARTEAGA. Le Rivoluzioni del Teatro Musicale Italiano, 1785.

BITTER, C. H. Die Reform der Oper durch Gluck und Wagner, 1884.

BROWN, John. Letters on the poetry and music of the Italian Opera, 1789.

BURNEY, Dr. C. Memoirs of Metastasio, 1796.

CHASTELLUX, Chevalier F. J. de. Essai sur l'Union de la Poésie et de la Musique, 1765.

CROCE, Benedetto. I Teatri in Napoli, a series of articles in Archivio Storico per le Province Napoletane, anno XIV, XV.

FLORIMO, Francesco. Cenno Storico sulla scuola musicale di Napoli, 1869–1871.

LINDNER, E. Otto T. Die erste stehende deutsche Oper, 1855.

MARCELLO, Benedetto. Teatro alla Moda, 1720.

MARX, A. B. Gluck und die Oper, 1863.

MATTHESON, Joh. Der musikalische Patriot (see p. xi).

MILLAN, Don Luis Carmena y. Crónica de la Ópera Italiana en Madrid, 1878.

MUSICAL TIMES, 1899, p. 241–3.

NEWMAN, Ernest. Gluck and the Opera, 1895.

PLANELLI, Ant. Dell' Opera in Musica, 1772.

PREFACES to the volumes of ' Chefs-d'œuvre de l'Opéra Français.'

RAGUENET, l'Abbé. Parallèle des Italiens et des Français en ce qui regarde la musique et les opéras, 1702.

ENGLISH TRANSLATION of the above (anon.), as A Comparison between the French and Italian Music, 1709.

RIVISTA MUSICALE ITALIANA, 1900, art. by G. Roberti on ' La musica in Italia nel Secolo XVIII, secondo le impressioni di viaggiatori stranieri.'

THE SPECTATOR, Nos. 18, 231, 235, 258, 278, 405.

THE TATLER, Nos. 4, 115.

THE WORLD, Nos. 98, 171.

WIEL, Cav. Taddeo. 'I Teatri musicali Veneziani del Settecento' first appeared in the ' Archivio Veneto ' 1891–1897, and in book-form in the latter year.

GERMANY—

BURNEY, C. Tour, referred to on p. ix.

KADE, Otto. Die ältere Passionskomposition, bis zum Jahre 1631. 1893.

MATTHESON's Works, referred to on p. xi.

TAYLOR, Chev. J. History of Travels and Adventures, 1751.

ITALY—

ADDISON, Joseph. Remarks on various parts of Italy, 1705.

BUSI, Leonida. Benedetto Marcello, 1884.

DE BROSSES, le Président. Letters published as ' L'Italie il y a cent ans,' 1836.

ITALY (*cont.*)—

    DE LALANDE, J. J. le François. Voyages d'un Français en Italie, 1769.

    DORAN, Dr. 'Mann' and Manners at the Court of Florence, 1876.

    MONTAGU, Lady Mary Wortley-. Letters.

    MONTESQUIEU. Voyages, published by Baron Albert de Montesquieu, 1894.

FRANCE—

    BLAMONT, François Collin de. Essai sur les goûts anciens et modernes de la musique Française, 1754.

    BONNET, Jacques. Histoire de Musique et de ses Effets, 1715.

    DE LA BORDE, Jean Benjamin. Essai sur la Musique ancienne et moderne, 1780.

    POUGIN, Arthur. Rameau, sa vie et ses œuvres, 1876.

    ROUSSEAU, J. J.

        Dictionnaire de Musique, 1767.

        Lettre sur la musique Française, 1753.

ENGLAND—

    BEDFORD, Rev. Arthur. Great Abuse of Musick, 1711.

SPAIN—

    ESLAVA, Don M. H. Lira Sacro-Hispana, 1869.

THE

AGE OF BACH AND HANDEL

INTRODUCTION

THAT part of musical history of which Bach and Handel
are the chief ornaments is, even apart from them, a momentous
period. In every branch of the musician's industry it is
equally true that nothing remained at the end of that period
exactly as it had been at the beginning; and the changes
through which each branch of the art had to pass were such as
affected its whole being and essence. Perhaps no half century
has seen such radical alterations in ideals, in methods,
both creative and interpretative, and in the relations between
musicians and the outer world, as that period which roughly
coincides with the first half of the eighteenth century. Stated
in terms of the lifetime of one or two men, the rapidity of
the changes seems remarkable; but when it is remembered
that the death of Henry Purcell was only separated from the
birth of Mozart by an interval of sixty-one years, it is easier
to realize how extensive a phase of development had to be
passed through in a space of time which, in any other history,
would seem impossibly short for any transition less momentous
than an actual revolution. And none of the great artistic
revolutions fall into this period; that sudden substitution of
the monodic style for the polyphonic which affected all

countries alike, coincides, most conveniently for students' memories, with the junction of the sixteenth and seventeenth centuries, and the operatic reforms which we associate with the name of Gluck lie just past the middle of the eighteenth. These crises, the two nearest in time to the lifetime of Bach and Handel, must each of them be kept in mind if we would study the influences and tendencies of the period that lies between them; for even a century after the old art of the motet and the madrigal had been superseded by the simpler yet more expressive methods of musical utterance, men were still far from realizing all that the change involved, and were as yet in a comparatively hazy condition as to the functions of the new style; while in the latter years of the period under consideration, we are compelled to study the gradual progress of that operatic convention from which Gluck set the world free.   Between these two revolutions there is a strange parallel, which has often enough been pointed out; for the ground won for the expressive functions of music by Monteverde had to be conquered again by Gluck, and the truths which were dimly apparent to the earlier of these two reformers, and were only fully appreciated by the latter, were precisely the principles which Wagner found it necessary to restate in after years.

The two giants who dominate the earlier half of the eighteenth century had little or no direct and conscious connexion with either of the revolutions referred to, although Handel had a good deal to say to the process by which opera was so conventionalized as to require complete reform.   It was only in a slight degree that the various structural changes in music concerned the two greatest composers of their time.   Each, so far as his own work went, remained contented with the forms in which his predecessors had expressed themselves, and to each the discoveries or inventions of contemporary theorists or musical instrument makers were mainly interesting as affording new opportunities for the expression of their ideals.

Both, however, may justly be regarded as the epitomes of the period in which they lived; it is true of each, but in very widely different senses, that he embodied in himself the whole of the music of his age. For Handel, the older composers and his own contemporaries existed as a treasure-house from which he might appropriate the ideas he was too busy to invent for himself; the circumstances of his career made him acquainted with the styles of all countries, and nearly all periods, and enabled him to form a style in which could be assimilated with equal success his own inventions and his adaptations from other men. Bach, with a far narrower range of musical literature at his command for purposes of study, entered far more deeply into the spirit of those he knew, and, grasping the essential principles upon which the older masters had worked, rather than the external features of their work, he attained to a style entirely his own, a style which in some points has never been superseded in all the years that have passed since his death.

The genius of the two men worked in exactly opposite directions; and if in studying Handel we seem to have our eyes turned always towards the past, in Bach we are continually brought face to face with idioms and turns of expression which are so much of the essence of modern music, that the student is tempted to imagine that the art has made no progress since Bach. Handel sums up the eighteenth century, and in studying all but a very few exceptionally inspired pages of his works, we remain conscious of the full-bottomed wig, the lace ruffles, and all the various other details of his costume. It is only here and there that Bach brings a corresponding image of himself before our minds, so constantly does he make us feel the presence of a spiritual, immortal beauty over which time itself has no power. The historical attitude of mind, that in which we take an interest in a past period and its productions solely because they are antique, is wholly unsuitable in approaching the works of Bach, who is for ever startling us by some touch that we have been used to think of as essentially modern, and whose compositions are sometimes felt to be less definitely belonging to a bygone day than many things by Mozart or Haydn. Many amateurs, unversed in musical history, have been heard to dismiss a specimen of Purcell or of Corelli with the remark that it is very like Handel in style, while upon the same class Bach's music nearly always makes an impression of being particularly modern.

The various parallels and contrasts between the lives of Bach and Handel, and the methods of their work, which will claim our notice more urgently in later chapters, have a peculiar significance, since with these masters began that supremacy of German music which lasted without a break from the year in which both were born down to the date of the death of Brahms, a period of 212 years. Of the various European nations in which musical activity has been manifested from time to time, each has had its own period or periods of efflorescence lasting for a longer or shorter space of years; the student of history watches the sceptre of musical supremacy passing, as it were, from England to the Netherlands, and so to Italy, from Italy back to England, and by another medium, to France; the firm establishment of the art in Germany was accomplished later than the flourishing periods in the other countries, but when it once took root, there was no further interruption to the succession, so that at any moment between 1685 and 1897, the greatest composer of the time would have been found among German musicians. It is this continuity, more than anything else, which has given Germany its position in the world of music, a position only to be compared with that held by Italy in the world of painting from the time of Cimabue to that of Paolo Veronese. During the shorter periods in which one art or the other prospered in the less favoured countries, there may have been great moments of artistic excellence, but the mere continuance of the tradition strengthens it with each decade that passes, so that with the

Germans of the seventeenth to the nineteenth centuries, music has become a second nature, just as the instinct for pictorial art must have existed in the Italian race from the thirteenth century down to the end of the sixteenth.

The German supremacy once begun, we shall not go far wrong if we seek henceforth among German musicians the best illustrations of the various tendencies which swayed the world of music during this period. The development of the most important forms, for example, could be clearly traced by referring only to German compositions; and, by taking Germany as a centre, we shall obtain a more definite idea of the growth of the art than would be possible in any other way. All forms and all materials of music, as has been pointed out already, were in a state of fusion during the lifetime of Bach and Handel; two alone of the whole number attained, in this period, their full growth and that point of their development beyond which no further progress was possible. These two forms are the fugue and the oratorio; and the two, by something more than a mere coincidence, are inseparably connected with the names of Bach and Handel respectively. Bach's position in regard to the fugue is precisely that of Beethoven towards the sonata; that is to say, the form attained, in his hands, to an eloquence, a directness of expression, and a vitality, which gave the crowning touch to the structure upon which so many other hands had laboured. Yet as the student of sonata-form would be required to study a more conventional type of sonata than Beethoven's in order to assimilate the strict rules by which that form is governed, so the laws of fugue can be more clearly deduced from the works of the older, more conventional masters, than from those of Bach, whose wealth of ideas impelled him to frequent departure from the established code, and with whom the essential import of the composition was of greater consequence than the manner of its treatment. It is perhaps a logical consequence of the freedom which these illustrious masters introduced into forms

that were becoming stereotyped at the time they wrote, that
their utterances in these forms should have been in some degree
the final expression, as well as the highest, of their possibilities.   Here and there, since the time of Bach, a fugue has
been produced which strikes us as a spontaneous creation,
and there are sonatas of the post-Beethoven period which have
a value of their own; but the great majority of modern fugues,
and a good many modern sonatas, suggest that the writers
are deliberately adopting the costume of an earlier day, that
they are in fact posing in fancy dress.

In much the same way the oratorio found its highest and
ultimate expression in the maturest work of Handel; the later
masters have indeed used the form, and in some instances with
marvellous success, but these are exceptions to the general rule,
and it is generally held that the last great writer of oratorios,
as well as the first, was Handel.

With all the other forms of music the case was different;
the sonata, as has been said above, had to wait for a far later
date before its perfection was reached under Beethoven; in
the history of the opera our period is one of cold convention,
without any kind of organic life; church music had many
further stages of development to attain which were unguessed
at by the men of Handel's days; and even the suite, which,
to a cursory student, may appear to have found its ideal
development under Bach and his French contemporaries,
showed, when it passed into the serenades and 'cassations'
of Mozart's time, that it had a new life of its own; and in the
present day, it may be doubted if it have not a truer life than
the more highly organized form of the sonata.

To glance for a moment at the theoretical side of music, a
side which must occupy our minute attention later on, one
of the most momentous changes which was taking place all
through the lifetime of Bach and Handel was the transition
from the strict counterpoint of their predecessors, to the free
part-writing of their followers.   There never was a happier

definition than that which makes it clear for us that the older
music was regarded from the horizontal point of view, the
newer from the vertical. That is to say, the older writers held
the even flow of each part for its essential quality, and the
most complicated score would always be capable of being
resolved into so many real parts; notes which served no other
purpose than to fill up the harmonies were virtually unknown,
and even if they were used as a makeshift in arrangements
for the lute or the like, the composition was never looked
upon as built upon a series of chords in a harmonic progression.
It is interesting to see how gradual the transition was from
the one system to the other, and how far the old traditions
were felt to be binding even on the writers who were seeking
their way to the freedom of a later date. With greater licence
in the manipulation of various parts or voices, came an ever-
increasing sense of individuality. The well known and universally felt difficulty of discriminating between the styles of
the old masters is sometimes accounted for by saying that we
stand too far from their times to see the differences, just as
the inhabitants of distant countries seem indistinguishable from
one another until a nearer acquaintance allows us to perceive
personal idiosyncrasies as well as racial resemblances. But
as a matter of fact, the older schools of music show few or
none of those marks by which the work of the early painters
or poets can be ascribed with tolerable certainty even where
documentary evidence of origin is wanting; individuality, as
a thing to be sought for itself, would seem, in music at least,
to be a far more modern object than would be generally
supposed.

In a period when all the accepted forms of music were in
a state of fusion, when the greatest of them all was only dimly
apprehended, and when so many were found insufficient for
the ideas the composers had to put into them, it seems almost
paradoxical to point out that the period was marked by the
utmost conventionality on the one hand, and on the other by

rebellion against conventionality. In an age when manners, dress, and ideals, were artificial to a degree that has never been exceeded it is not perhaps surprising that music, or at least those branches of it which were intended to minister to the pleasure of people of fashion, should have become as artificial as themselves, and indeed it would have been inexplicable if it had remained free from artificiality. But, while the other arts were old, music was still in its most vigorous youth, and its inborn energy could not but impel its devotees to the discovery of new vehicles of expression, and to the development of fresh principles of construction. The contrast between the artificiality of the eighteenth century with its wigs, ruffles, and furbelows, and the dewy freshness and naturalness of the music in vogue at the time, has often been pointed out; but it is really quite analogous to the discrepancy between what may be called the decrepitude of society at the time, and the virile adolescence of the youngest of the arts. While the conventional surroundings of the period did much to hamper the free outpourings of natural genius, and to encourage the formalism which is the bane of all art, it is to be remembered with gratitude that a whole series of the changes above referred to, whether in the structural forms or the outward materials of music, were due in the first instance to the patronage of music by the fashionable world, which did more than anything else, first, to create the profession of executive musicians whose function was purely interpretative of other men's work; secondly, to stimulate the production of music whose primary object was to give opportunity for manual or vocal dexterity; and thirdly, to make those demands for great sonority, which brought about a complete reformation in the manufacture of instruments and the training of the human voice. Considered solely as ends in themselves, these objects, or at least most of them, might well be regretted, since to a certain extent the opportunities for individual display which now arose did much to obscure, for performers and hearers alike, the true spirit and ideal purpose of music; but in after times the greatest masters of all must have come short of perfect ease and fullness of utterance had they possessed no vehicles better calculated to arrest the attention of the public than those which were in use at the end of the seventeenth century. And it cannot be doubted that the modern orchestra, the most complete vehicle of musical expression yet devised, could not have reached its present beauty of proportion or the perfection of its component parts, without that passion for virtuosity as an end in itself, which is one of the leading characteristics of the period now to be considered.

A few words may not be out of place concerning the arrangement followed in treating the history of the period of Bach and Handel. At first sight, the division of music into sacred and secular may seem like a return to a purely arbitrary and unscientific system of division, such as would be unworthy of a serious contribution to the history of an art. But until quite modern times, the worlds of sacred and secular music were separated by a great gulf; this was the case, not merely in the different character of the words employed for vocal music, or in the obvious contrasts of a solemn with a lighter style, but still more unmistakably in structural forms and in disposition of materials. Here and there, as in the *sonate da chiesa* of the Italians, the secular forms obtained an entrance into church music, but as a rule, and for the greater part of this period, the two classes remained totally distinct, owing, no doubt, to the fact that there was little or no opportunity for purely instrumental music apart from more or less elaborated dance-forms, while the great development of secular vocal music, as apart from opera, was a product of a far later day.

In dealing successively with the chorale, the cantata, the vocal music of the church, and the oratorio, we shall trace many of the principal elements in the artistic development of the greatest composers of their time; passing next to a review of the condition of the musical instruments of the period, we must study the course of those transitions which were to result, after the close of this age, in the completion of the sonata-form; and a short survey of the rise of virtuosity will lead us to the history of opera and its various conventions. Within the limits of our survey falls the darkest hour of operatic conventionality, which preceded the dawn of a new era of musical eloquence in the mature works of Gluck. Finally, the condition of things in each of the four countries most actively represented in the art is considered separately, in order to include the names of many composers who, though meritorious in themselves, yet had little or no influence on the general development of music; and to obtain a general idea of the way in which the ordinary musicians, the rank and file of the profession, came into relation with the men of their time.

CHAPTER I

In studying the rise of that German supremacy in music which began with Bach and Handel, we are justified in assigning a particular importance to the national inheritance of the Chorale. No other country can show an artistic possession of equal value, or one that so perfectly fulfils the definition of a national treasure. Allied on the one side to the *canto fermo* of the Latin Church, from which indeed it derived many of the germs of its melodic structure, and assimilated on the other side, in its rhythmic definiteness, to the folk-songs preserved in popular tradition, it had attained, by the middle of the seventeenth century, a place in the hearts of the whole German race, in which love and reverence had an equal share. For the words and tunes of the Lutheran hymns had acquired by this time an authority, even a sanctity, which ensured them against alteration; yet both were, so to speak, in the vernacular, and there was no hindrance to their popularity such as would arise from archaisms in verbal or musical phrases. There had not been time since the Reformation for the enthusiasm of the people to cool towards their hymns, which remained as the outward and visible signs of the religious liberty won by Luther for the German race. Brought up upon melodies the simplest and most beautiful that have ever been created, it was little wonder that the whole nation should have become musicians; and it is curious to see at how many points the characteristics of the chorales seem to have suggested expedients which have resulted in the development of artistic forms of lasting value. The survival, in many of the chorale melodies, of the influence of the ancient ecclesiastical modes, gave the musicians of Germany a greater freedom in the manipulation of harmonic relations than was possessed by any other nation after the decisive supplanting of the modes by the modern scales. The fact that, unlike the plainsong of the Catholic Church, the Lutheran melodies were at once rhythmical and congregational, rendered it necessary to wait at the end of each line of the hymn until the tardy singers in the body of the church had reached the same point as the choir; and this expedient, at first a mere makeshift to get rid of a practical difficulty, brought about the filling up of these pauses with instrumental interludes, a practice which not only gave new scope to the invention of the organists, but which eventually suggested the form of those cantata-choruses in which some of the greatest music of the world has found expression. Another peculiarity common to almost all the chorale melodies, is their fitness for imitative or fugal treatment, in which they rival, if they do not surpass, the plainsong of former years.

Again, the chorale treated in four-part harmony involved the liberation of harmony, and no doubt hastened the day when the older rules were to be relaxed. Although it is hardly correct to speak of the chorale as belonging, as strictly as the plainsong melodies belong, to the ecclesiastical modes, yet they conform in many respects to the conventions of the modes, and in none more uniformly than in the scheme of the final cadence, in which the final of the mode, or the key-note, is approached by one descending step. In the earliest dawn of harmonic treatment the tonality was marked—for there must always have been a desire for its definition—by the practice of allowing one other part to approach the key-note from one step below, thus making a third or a sixth with the penultimate note in the modal part. This pair of parts made up what was called the 'clausula vera,' and its normal disposition was this:—

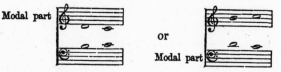

Modal part   or   Modal part

In all modes except the Phrygian and its plagal counterpart the descent upon the final was by a whole tone, and the other part, which must rise to the final by a semitone whether the mode naturally contained a semitone here or not, combined to form a rudimentary harmonic progression, which, to modern ears, conveys the idea of a passage from the dominant to the tonic harmony. Long before the days when such progressions were viewed harmonically, the madrigalian writers had developed their cadences from this harmonic germ, letting the bass fall from dominant to tonic, except in the very rare instances where the bass is the modal part. In almost every work of the madrigalian period, this form of cadence will be found, not necessarily at the very end, but within a few bars of the close. It is clear that if the two parts shown in the example coincide on the key-note or its octave, and the bass also falls to the key-note, two more parts are required if the tonic harmony is to be completed; this is, I take it, a main reason for the great preponderance of five-part compositions in the sixteenth century and later. In disposing the chorales of his nation in four-part harmony, as he did in a long series of cantatas as well as in the set of 371 published after his death, a collection which includes many of the cantata settings, Sebastian Bach made an innovation which must at the time have seemed revolutionary; he allowed the part which held what is now called the leading-note to break the rule of rising to the key-note, and to fall either to the dominant or the mediant of the key. This occurs with hardly an exception in those chorales, and they are by far the most numerous class, which form their cadence by descending one degree upon the key-note.

In considering what may be called the spiritual ancestry of Bach, it would be impossible to lay too much stress on the influence of the chorale upon his training. And in the history of his family, too, it played an all-important part. It is a fact unique in the history of music, that for many generations before the birth of Sebastian Bach, his ancestors, direct and collateral, had so greatly excelled in the art of music, that in Thuringia the family name came to be used as a synonym for 'musician.' The comprehensive review of the works of the elder Bachs contained in the first book of Spitta's *Life of Bach*, shows most plainly that the sacred music of the time in Germany consisted, largely if not almost exclusively, in arrangements or adaptations of chorale-themes in one form or other. Cantatas, motets, instrumental fugues, and the like, were founded on melodic germs taken from the hymn tunes, and nearer still to the original chorale stood the form of chorale-prelude, or chorale-variation, two forms of the utmost importance in the work both of Bach and of his ancestors.

Johann Sebastian Bach, born in March[1], 1685, at Eisenach, therefore inherited the art of the chorale as a birthright, and it is not surprising that we should find a series of 'chorale-partitas' enumerated among the works which Spitta attributes, on internal evidence, to the period when he was still employed in the choir of the church of St. Michael, at Lüneburg. The half-brother who became his guardian on the death of his father had been a pupil of Pachelbel, and the organist of another church at Lüneburg, Georg Böhm, had learnt his art from Reinken of Hamburg. It was mainly through these two channels that the influence of the great masters of North Germany reached Bach at a time when he was most open to artistic impressions from without. The pilgrimage undertaken by Bach to hear Reinken play at Hamburg is one of the most

---

[1] The day of his birth is not known, but he was baptized on March 23.

familiar stories of the great composer, and the apparently
miraculous discovery of the money he so sorely needed for his
return journey in the herrings' heads thrown out from an inn
window, is one of the most picturesque incidents in his early
career. In Böhm, Reinken, Vincentius Lübeck, Pachelbel,
and Buxtehude, we have a group of composers all of whom
influenced the young Bach, while all devoted themselves with
peculiar zest to the composition of such chorale arrangements
as have been referred to. The word 'partita' in Bach's early
works already spoken of, points strongly to Reinken's influence,
for the sets of variations on the chorale tunes which were so
entitled were his special province. If Spitta is right in tracing
the influence of Böhm on Bach's arrangement of the chorale,
'Erbarm' dich mein [1],' and therefore in assigning it to an early
period of the composer's career, we are brought face to face
with the phenomenon of a pupil attaining in his earliest years
a level undreamt of in the world before [2]. For this arrangement
has a poignancy of grief, a power of emotional expression,
quite beyond anything existing at the beginning of the
eighteenth century, qualities that are generally supposed to
mark only Bach's maturest productions. Throughout his long
life, the love of his country's special form of sacred music
remained with Bach, and innumerable are the instances in
which he took the suggestion of his compositions from the
chorales; his use of the chorales in various arranged forms
in church cantatas, and for the organ, which will be discussed
in later chapters, is one of the chief characteristics of his
personality, and it is not without significance that his last act
on earth was to dictate from his deathbed to his pupil and
son-in-law, Altnikol, the amended form of an organ chorale
arrangement, originally inscribed 'Wenn wir in höchsten

---

[1] See edition of the Bach-Gesellschaft, xl. p. 60.

[2] A remarkable similarity exists between this and a movement in one of
Kuhnau's *Bible Sonatas*, describing the combat with Goliath. (See J. S. Shedlock,
The Pianoforte Sonata, p. 54.)

'Erbarm' dich mein, O Herre Gott.'   J. S. Bach.

Nöthen sein,' but now adapted to the hymn ' Vor deinen Thron tret' ich hiemit.' So closely was the love of the chorale interwoven with the art of Bach that it gives us a key to his whole nature; and the more constantly the influence of the chorale upon him and upon the best of his contemporaries is kept in view, the more thoroughly we shall understand his manner of expressing himself in music.

CHAPTER II

THE CANTATA

As the direct outcome of the German chorale, the church cantata, a form exclusively confined to Germany in its original inception, deserves consideration in the next place, both on its own account, and in view of its large employment by Bach throughout his life.

The normal design of the church cantata is rooted in the chorale. Its stricter forms retain the actual melody and words of the chorale in the successive numbers; the poems to which many of the specimens are set form a kind of meditative commentary on the spirit of the hymn, or on the passage of scripture from which the hymn is taken; and, with hardly an exception, the simple delivery of the chorale, in four-part harmony, brings the work to a close. This form was recognized and used before Bach's time, by his uncles, Johann Christoph and Johann Michael Bach, who left among their so-called 'motets' many compositions which conform rather to the type of church cantatas, though perhaps they are as a rule more polyphonic in style than these.

In a freer form of the cantata, the hymn-tune appears as the groundwork of the opening chorus, and is referred to vocally or instrumentally in some, if not all, of the intermediate sections for solo voices. The opening chorus is often built, too, on the scriptural text by which the hymn is suggested; three of the vocal parts, it-may be, confine themselves to these words, while a fourth brings in the successive lines of the hymn-tune with its associated words. The musical theme of each line gives the suggestion of the instrumental interludes by which the lines are separated, just as the lines are separated in singing the hymn in the Lutheran churches; the final verse of the hymn is sung as it would be in the church service. If, as often happens in the works destined for the greater festivals, the cantata is in two great divisions, a simple chorale-verse generally ends each division, the space between the two parts being occupied, in performance, by a sermon. Thus the cantata is almost as closely bound up with the service of the church as the chorale itself; as to the part taken by the congregation in the simple chorales at the close, we are not very clearly informed, but, whether the people actually sang or not, one thing is certain, that the whole was regarded as a symbolic act of devotion. As a rule the solo portions are in a contemplative style, set to verses written newly around the central idea, in the so-called 'madrigal' form [1]. Occasionally they are a paraphrase of the biblical text, but more often they are supposed to be the utterance of the individual soul in acceptance and application of the teaching of the scripture.

Thus it will readily be seen that the cantata is very unlike the type of oratorio to which we are accustomed in the present day. The oratorio, as we shall see in a later chapter, is a

---

[1] It may be well to point out that the word 'madrigal' as used in connexion with German poetry has little or nothing to do with the beautiful form of vocal music practised in the sixteenth century; yet the secondary meaning is derived directly from the first, as appears in the title of the first German book in which the word was employed, Caspar Ziegler's *Von den Madrigalien, einer schönen und zur Musik bequemsten Art Verse, wie sie nach der Italiäner Manier in unserer deutschen Sprache auszuarbeiten, nebenst etlichen Exempeln,* Leipzig, 1653. Ziegler, who no doubt obtained his knowledge of Italian madrigals from his brother-in-law, Heinrich Schütz, defines the poetic structure of the poetry as being unconfined to any particular number of lines; the lines must not be of equal length, and rhymes, though permitted, were not enjoined. It is necessary for musical readers to bear in mind that the distinctively German use of the term refers only to the words, not to the music. (See Spitta's *Life of Bach,* Eng. transl. i. p. 469.)

quasi-dramatic form of art, and its occasional lapses into a meditative style are comparatively rare, and do not strictly belong to the type. The cantata never loses sight of the devotional or religious purpose, and for this reason it must always find its complete realization, and fulfil its highest object, in connexion with a church service, while the oratorio is primarily intended for the concert-room or even the theatre. In the oratorio, too, the incidents belonging to the story chosen must all be clearly presented in dramatic or narrative sequence; in the cantata it very often happens that only a passing allusion is made even to important circumstances.

The 'pietistic' leanings of many of Bach's contemporaries found expression in various mystical poems in which the exaggerated sentimentality of the style becomes almost absurd; but the fashion of viewing everything in its symbolic aspect had no little influence on Bach's choice of words, and he not infrequently pursues an idea to the verge of what a less imaginative generation than his own might well deem childish. In his hands, however, and when allied to the highest kinds of music the world has known, it is not difficult to excuse the occasional naïveté of some of the cantatas. In passing some of the most prominent of the long series under review, it will be seen what an important place the cantatas hold in the mass of Bach's work, and how closely he adhered to the form throughout his life. It will be well briefly to enumerate the divisions in Bach's career to which the four main groups of the church cantatas are assigned by Spitta, whose conclusions, based upon the most careful examination of the internal and external evidence, may be taken as accurate in all instances. (1) The Arnstadt and Mühlhausen period (1703–1707); (2) the Weimar period (1708–1717); (3) the Cöthen period (1717–1723); and (4) the Leipzig period (1723–1750).

The first part of the first period, while Bach was organist at Arnstadt, has only one cantata assigned to it by Spitta, as his creative activity at this time was applied mainly to

the works for organ, which will come under consideration in
a later chapter. In 1707, his position at Arnstadt apparently
having become irksome to him, as a not unnatural consequence
of his escapade to Lübeck and his serious prolongation of
the leave of absence granted by the Arnstadt consistory, he
obtained the pos of organist at the Blasius-Kirche at Mühlhausen, and about the same time he married his first wife,
his second cousin, Maria Barbara Bach. The principal works
ascribed to this period imply that the master was unconsciously
making studies for those cantatas in which his greatest thoughts
were to be expressed; they are two cantatas, on sacred words
indeed, but both connected with secular events, one in celebration of the 'Rathswechsel' or change of councillors, the
other in honour of a wedding. With his appointment as court
organist and 'Kammermusicus' to the Duke of Weimar, in
1708, Bach was brought more closely than heretofore into
connexion with instrumental music, since his duties included
playing the first violin in the ducal band. It was only natural
that his attention should have been for a time diverted from
the cantata-form, in which he made only three essays during
the first four years of his tenure of the post. One of these
was, however, the famous 'Gottes Zeit ist die allerbeste Zeit,'
in which a very remarkable departure may be observed from
the usual scheme, the choral and solo portions being much
more closely interwoven, and the continuity of the work as
a whole far greater. The work is one of the best known of
the cantatas, and one in which the emotional design and
doctrinal intention of the form can best be studied. It does
not belong to the stricter class of chorale-cantatas, since not
one chorale, but three, are introduced in its course, while
none of them appears in any form in the first chorus. An
exquisitely pathetic and melodious adagio for instruments (may
we not see a trace of Bach's newly-formed acquaintance with
Italian music in the title 'Sonatina' prefixed to it?) leads to
a series of three short choral movements, and these pass,

without a break, into solo passages for tenor and bass, bearing on the subject of preparation for death and resignation to the Divine will, since the cantata, or 'Actus tragicus' as it was commonly called, had a memorial purpose. The chorus which follows these numbers is the most important part of the work ; the three lower vocal parts carry on a fugue on the words ' It is the old decree: man, thou art mortal,' while the soprano part, on an independent subject, utters the words 'Yea, come, Lord Jesus.' Meanwhile, the tune of the chorale 'Ich hab' mein' Sach' Gott heimgestellt' (I have cast my care upon God) is given out by the flutes and viol-da-gamba, the whole combination giving us, as it were, a complete sermon on death, and at the same time a piece of music of perfect beauty. An alto and bass solo embody Christ's promise to the penitent thief, and the two voices are combined at the close, the alto singing, against the more declamatory passages of the bass, the chorale 'Mit Fried' und Freud' fahr' ich dahin,' a hymn always associated with the idea of death. The work ends with yet another chorale for choir, set much more elaborately than in the majority of the cantatas, where, as already said, four-part harmony of the simplest kind is the rule. It is set merely to the words of a doxology, but the melody is that of the chorale 'In dich hab' ich gehoffet, Herr,' so that the thoughts of the listeners, to whom all these chorales were as familiar as any part of the appointed liturgy, would be constantly directed towards a meditation on the subject chosen.

In about 1712, Bach became acquainted with the religious poems of Erdmann Neumeister, and in the next year or two used five of them for the cantatas which he was required to produce at regular intervals. On the model of Neumeister's work a great many cantata-texts were written by Salomo Franck, and set by Bach about this time; the year 1714 saw 'Ich hatte viel Bekümmerniss,' and by 1717, some thirteen more had been written. Two more, apparently composed during the period of his residence at Cöthen, or about 1720, are all that precede the splendid time of his creative activity in Leipzig. The Cöthen period, as it is called, brought Bach so much more closely than before into connexion with secular and instrumental music, that it will be best studied in subsequent chapters; the master's appointment as Cantor of the Thomas-schule in Leipzig, in 1723, gave him renewed opportunities in regard to church music, and accordingly we find his maturest and sublimest choral works dating from this period. It has been calculated that Bach wrote in all 295 cantatas, since Mizler in his *Necrology*, p. 168, states that he composed five 'year-books' for the church festivals and Sundays, and there were fifty-nine days in the ecclesiastical year when music of this kind would be required. Deducting the twenty-nine compositions which were undoubtedly written, as we have seen, before he went to Leipzig, we get the remainder 266 as the number written in Leipzig itself. Enormous as this number seems to us, it was considerably less than was achieved by some of Bach's contemporaries, and it must not be taken as evidence of over-production, since the composition of the works was spread over a long period. Of the 295 cantatas, Spitta estimates the number actually preserved as 210, but this includes the six cantatas of the *Christmas Oratorio*, as well as various fragments. Now, the edition of the Bach-Gesell-schaft includes 191 complete cantatas, five fragments, and four doubtful compositions, which, together with the six of the *Christmas Oratorio*, only make up the number to 206.

It is clearly impossible to analyse the whole body of the cantatas that have come down to us; to describe the most important of them, or even to enumerate them by name, would far exceed the space that can be devoted to them. But in-asmuch as some personal traits in Bach's character, some points of difference by which this class of compositions is distinguished from another in some ways similar to it, are illustrated in certain examples, it is necessary to study these in detail. Bach's realism and the quaint literalism of his treatment, have been before referred to; in one of the finest of all the cantatas, we have a most instructive example. 'Wachet auf, ruft uns die Stimme' is founded on the hymn beginning thus, and deals, as the hymn does, with the subject of the parable of the wise and foolish virgins, connected with the mystical marriage between Christ and the Church. The plan of the work is perfectly symmetrical, the three verses of the hymn being divided by two duets, each preceded by a recitative, and entirely independent of the chorale-tune. While the numbers in which the chorale occurs deal with those who are represented by the wedding guests (the middle section of the work, in which the tenor voice or voices sing a description of the wedding festivities, while the festivities themselves are naïvely represented by a bourrée, is of quite exquisite beauty), the two duets can only be described as love music, differing hardly at all in style from what might appear in a dramatic work. In a dramatic oratorio of the Handelian or Mendelssohnian type, such a definite identification of the Christian Church with an individual singer possessing a soprano voice would be unspeakably disturbing to reverential feelings, to say the least of it; here, where all is on a plane of mysticism, and the whole is to be regarded as approaching very near to an act of worship, we feel that the literalism is fully justified.

We shall notice a precisely similar piece of literalism in the soprano song with echo in the *Christmas Oratorio*, and in passing, reference may be made to another emotional or religious motive which occurs with remarkable frequency in the cantatas. It is the expression of the devout Christian's longing for death, and the suggestion of tolling or chiming bells with special reference to the idea of a knell. In a cantata written during the Weimar period, 'Komm, du süsse Todesstunde,' and in the Leipzig work, 'Liebster Gott, wann werd' ich sterben?' the imitation of the passing bell is contrived in the same way, by pizzicatos on the strings, and reiterated high notes on the flutes. And in the fine cantata for alto solo, 'Schlage doch, gewünschte Stunde,' an actual bell is introduced into the score. We are enabled to see the bent of the master's mind in another instance, since of all the chorales on which the cantatas are based, one only occurs as the groundwork of three separate compositions—'O Ewigkeit, du Donnerwort,'—a circumstance from which it is not unfair to assume that the stern and vigorous piety of the composer was often engaged in the contemplation of the Four Last Things. That he took a grave view of many of the brightest Christian festivals is clear again from the fact that his Easter cantata, 'Christ lag in Todesbanden,' treats the solemn chorale in such a way as to heighten its severity, and in fact with an almost forbidding sternness of character throughout. In the last division of the *Christmas Oratorio*, too, we find the chorale that we should least expect used as the culmination of a work intended to be festal,—the chorale that is most intimately associated with the Passion of Christ, from its frequent occurrence in the settings of the Passion Music.

It has been often debated whether the *Christmas Oratorio* should be regarded as a single work, or as a collection of six church cantatas. The latter view is justified by the fact that the six parts were intended to be performed on the successive days of the festival, ending with the Epiphany. Whether we conceive of it as one organic whole, or as made up of six short works, one thing is certain, that the name 'Oratorio,' though given by Bach himself, is a misnomer, more especially when the later developments of the Handelian oratorio are taken into account. It was written in 1734, after the series of Passion settings, and it conforms, far more strictly than they do, to the type set in the church cantatas. The great choruses indeed, which are spread over the six parts, are none of them founded, as in the bulk of the cantatas, upon any hymn-tune, and in largeness of design they approach nearer to the colossal forms of the B minor Mass than to any that we know in the cantatas. But there is no attempt at impersonation, no imitation of dramatic methods. The solo parts are individualized only so far as the expressions of the emotions vary; a terzetto in part V, for example, may be supposed to be sung by two devout but timid souls, waiting for salvation, while a third, more hopeful than they, reassures them with the words 'Peace, for this is surely He.' The nearest approach to the dramatic treatment is in the question of Wise Men 'Where is the new-born king?' but here the inquiry is given to a whole chorus, and is answered by a soloist, in the words 'Seek Him within my breast,' which show that the plane upon which the work is treated is a purely mystical one. The famous cradle-song suggests that the person of the Virgin is in a manner represented, but the words are less suitable to the character than to the typical Christian soul.

It remains to speak of the six motets of undoubted authenticity[1]; the form of these differs from that of the cantata mainly in being without accompaniment; the most beautiful of the series, 'Jesu, meine Freude,' is for five-part chorus, and has several trio-numbers, the words of Johannes Franck's hymn are set in their entirety, and the chorale-tune appears in the middle as well as at the beginning and end. There are four colossal works in eight parts, 'Singet dem Herrn ein neues Lied,' 'Der Geist hilft unsrer Schwachheit auf,' 'Fürchte dich nicht,' and 'Komm, Jesu, komm'; the four-part motet, 'Lobet den Herrn, alle Heiden,' has a *basso continuo* accompaniment, showing that the organ must have been used. A special interest attaches to these works, inasmuch as their tradition went on in Leipzig, through all the years when Bach's great compositions were neglected. Even finer than any of these is the single eight-part chorus 'Nun ist das Heil,' which with orchestral accompaniment, which Spitta considers to have

---

[1] The beautiful *Ich lasse dich nicht*, which long passed as a work of Sebastian Bach's, is almost certainly the work of his uncle, Joh. Christoph Bach.

belonged to some Michaelmas cantata, the rest of which is lost, or possibly was never written. The mighty swing of the theme, and its solemn fervour of triumphant expression, make it one of Bach's most sublime creations, worthy to stand on a level with the massive choruses of the B minor Mass. In the whole range of the church cantatas there is nothing of quite equal grandeur.

CHAPTER III

THE PASSION MUSIC

THE various settings of the Passion own, as their direct source, a form of church music quite apart from the chorale, and therefore have a less close connexion with the cantatas than is shown, for example, in the *Christmas Oratorio*; but as there is, still less real similarity between them and the actual church music of the period, or the oratorio form as we know it, it will be best to pass in review the principal works in this form that have survived in Germany, among them the masterpieces of Bach, and some important early compositions of Handel.

The practice of reciting the history of the Passion at vespers during Holy Week was one of those which the Lutheran Church adopted from the Catholic, and the Germans of the sixteenth and seventeenth centuries contributed largely to the number of musical works intended for use at this service. Dr. Otto Kade[1] enumerates and analyses nearly sixty works of the kind from the time of Obrecht down to Heinrich Schütz. Of the composers represented in his list, fourteen are German, and among the writers of other nations may be mentioned Cyprian de Rore, Claudin de Sermisy, Orlando di Lasso, Tommaso Lodovico Vittoria, and our own William Byrd. In the earliest specimens, as the liturgical reading of the gospel for Palm Sunday in the Roman Church was distributed among three ecclesiastics, the narrative is divided into three parts, repre-

[1] Die ältere Passionskomposition bis zum Jahre 1631, Gütersloh, 1893.

senting respectively Christ, the Evangelist, and the people
(Turba). But originally none of these was taken by a single
voice; and for some time after the introduction of single voices,
the words were sung by the representatives of Christ and
the Evangelist to recitative passages closely modelled on the
plainsong of the Church. As late as the time of Schütz there
was nothing but the biblical narrative, except, indeed, such
introductory words as 'Passio Domini nostri Jesu Christi
secundum Matthaeum,' or 'Erhebet eure Herzen, und höret
das Leiden unsers Herrn Jesu Christi.' The reflective numbers
and the interspersed chorales were alike a later innovation.
It was apparently not until 1672 that entirely original music
was used throughout the Passion service by Sebastiani of
Königsberg, and in 1704 Menantes' poem, 'Passions-
Dichtung des blutigen und sterbenden Jesu,' seems to have
been set to music by Reinhard Keiser, and performed at
Hamburg [1].

In the same year there appeared in the same city one of
the earliest important works attempted by Georg Friedrich
Händel, who was then nineteen years of age. Born on Feb. 23,
1685, just a month before his great contemporary, Bach,
Händel [2] was the second son of Georg Händel, town-surgeon
of Giebichenstein, a suburb of Halle, by his second wife,
Dorothea Taust; his musical genius found its opportunities,
in spite of the indifference of his parents and relations to
music, in the possession of an old clavichord which he smuggled
into a garret in the roof of the house. In early childhood,
knowing that the court of Sachsen-Weissenfels was more or
less a centre of music, and that his father was summoned
thither, he undertook to run behind the carriage, begging his
father to let him go with him. Happily the surgeon relented,

---

[1] The statement rests on the authority of W. S. Rockstro, who tells us, in his
Life of Handel, p. 31, that the absence of the chorale-element, and of the actual
words of scripture, drew down upon the work the censure of the Lutheran Church.

[2] The English form of the name, always used by the composer in his later life,
is here adopted.

and allowed the boy to accompany him; and when the child's
wonderful talents were discovered by the court organist and
the members of the duke's band, the duke himself persuaded
the father to give up the idea of making his child a lawyer,
and to let him devote himself to music. F. W. Zachau,
organist of the Liebfrauenkirche at Halle (1663–1721), was a
perfectly competent master for him, and under his guidance
Handel made astonishing progress, so that by 1701 he was
already famous, and in 1702 was appointed, on a twelve-
months' probation, organist of the Cathedral of Halle. During
this time he was a student at the university. His settlement
in Hamburg in 1703 brought him into a circle of musicians
who were active in all branches of music. His adventures
in connexion with the opera will be referred to in a later
chapter; we are now concerned with his early Passion-music,
called 'Ein kleines Passions-Oratorium,' arranged from the
gospel according to St. John, with no chorales, but with
contemplative airs, &c., set to words by Wilhelm Postel. The
meditative numbers begin with a soprano air following immediately upon the recitative of the Evangelist; the chorus
is in five parts almost throughout, soprano, alto, first and
second tenors, and bass. The important part of Pilate is set
for an alto solo, those of the Evangelist and Christ for tenor
and bass respectively. The 'ecce homo' passage is declaimed
to a more elaborate accompaniment than is usual in recitative,
and further on, the scriptural words, whether of Pilate or
the other characters, are expanded into set airs. There is
a fanciful little duet 'Schauet, mein Jesus ist Rosen zu gleichen,'
and some vigorous choral writing at the passages 'Crucify,'
and 'If thou let this man go.' The soldiers casting lots for
the vestment are represented in a fugato chorus for alto, two
tenors, and bass. There are two long duets for soprano and
bass, a bass aria 'O grosses Weh,' in the course of which,
at a reference to the Saviour's words 'Es ist vollbracht' the
full string band is suddenly introduced into the accompaniment.

This introduction of a more elaborate accompaniment at important points is a foreshadowing of the device so happily used in the St. Matthew Passion of Bach, where, in the recitatives, Christ's words alone are accompanied by the orchestra.

It is difficult to understand why Handel's work should have been bitterly censured by Mattheson as long after its performance as 1725; the second part volume of his *Critica Musica*, published in that year, begins with a dialogue headed 'Des fragenden Componisten erstes Verhör über eine gewisse Passion'; the plan of beginning with a recitative, the frequent repetition of important words, the introduction of a long run (*passaggio*) on the word 'scourged,' are most severely criticized, and although the composer's name is not mentioned, there can be no doubt as to the reference, for long quotations are given from the words.

A new stimulus was given to the composition of passion-settings by Brockes' poem, 'Der für die Sünde der Welt gemarterte und sterbende Jesus,' which was set no fewer than thirty times between 1712, the date of its publication, and 1727. The first setting was by Reinhard Keiser, and was performed in Holy Week in 1712 and 1713, a selection of the favourite numbers from it being published in 1714 under the title of *Auserlesene Soliloquiae*. The instrumentation was for two violins, violette (i. e. violas), two flauti dolci, two oboes, flauto traverso, three 'Bassauni' (*sic.* probably trombones), violoncello, and cembalo. The published portions are simply the meditative numbers with the recitatives for the Evangelist interspersed. The form of the work is far nearer to the oratorio pattern than anything we have studied as yet; the meditative portions are allotted to an imaginary 'Tochter Zions' or a 'Gläubige Seele,' as though the dramatic element were gradually creeping into the form. The two airs of St. Peter, the vigorous 'Nehmt mich mit,' and 'Schau, ich fall' in strenger Busse,' represent Keiser at his best; the former is carried out with a good deal of skill, and the second is really expressive. Two more passion oratorios by Keiser are in existence, one incomplete and of doubtful authenticity; one is set to the narrative in St. Mark's gospel, and is chiefly memorable from the fact that Sebastian Bach wrote out the separate parts of it with his own hand. More important than these was Keiser's setting of König's poem, 'Der zum Tode verurtheilte und gekreuzigte Jesus,' composed in 1715. The usual selection was published from this, under the name of 'Seelige Erlösungs-Gedancken,' in which the impersonal 'Gläubige Seele' is almost dispensed with, the meditative portions being divided among such personages of the narrative as Mary Magdalene, the disciples, the Virgin, and Mary Cleophas, the two latter of whom have a duet. The scene with the penitent thief is very simple and pathetic.

Among the most prominent of the thirty settings of Brockes' poem was that of Handel dating from 1716, the same year in which Telemann's version saw the light. It was composed at Hanover, whither Handel returned in attendance upon the Elector, our George I. The story of Handel's loss of favour at the English court, and his reconciliation through the 'Water Music' belongs to a later part of this book; by this time he was not only fully reinstated in the royal estimation, but he had already modified his style of writing very considerably under the influence of the English composers of the past, and particularly of Purcell. In speaking of the German Passion, W. S. Rockstro says [1], 'The choruses are expressive, or vigorous, in accordance with the nature of the words; but none exhibit any very striking form of contrapuntal development; nor do they ever rise to the grandeur of the *Utrecht Te Deum* or *Jubilate*. It would almost seem as if the composer, having once set English words to music, could nevermore identify himself with the school he had forsaken, or do his best in connexion with German poetry.' It must not be supposed from this, that the style of the work has anything

---

[1] *Life of G. F. Handel*, by W. S. Rockstro, p. 101.

in common with the later English oratorios; it conforms to
Keiser's model almost exactly, and as compared with Telemann's bland and empty strains, or indeed with the work of
Keiser himself, it reaches a high level of expressiveness,
although it cannot be compared with the great compositions
of Bach which were soon to be given to the world. The
choruses are founded on chorales, for the most part, with
simple ritornels or interludes; and as the meditative portions
are identified with a 'Daughter of Zion,' it is difficult to
dissociate the plan from that of oratorio. There is a vigorous
air for Christ, 'Lo! I will smite the shepherd,' and as usual
this part is sung by a baritone. John and James are represented by two altos, and they join in a duet, 'Awake ye now!'
Peter, a tenor, has two fine airs, and another tenor song,
allotted to a 'Believer,' is introduced by a long violin solo
of the most rococo style. The remorse of Judas is expressed
with a quaint dramatic emphasis which almost recalls the
methods of the opera. The soprano air with choral accompaniment, 'Haste, ye souls,' foreshadows a form afterwards used
by Bach in both the famous Passion-settings; the choral
interruptions, 'Come where?' are effective in a measure,
though the idea is never developed, as it is in Bach, into a
beautiful and integral part of the musical creation. The duet
between Christ and the Virgin could hardly fail to strike
listeners in the present day as overstepping the bounds of
reverence, and the smug airs sung by the 'believers' during
the crucifixion are far from giving the impression of a sublime
tragedy.

At a time when Passion-settings were so greatly in vogue
it would have been strange if so self-centred a person as
Mattheson had refrained from trying to outdo his contemporaries in the composition of a work of the kind; in the
first volume of his *Critica Musica*, published in 1722, he gives
notice that in March, 1723, a 'neue und besondere Passion'
of his own will be performed in the Cathedral at Hamburg;

it is to abound in harmonic and contrapuntal devices of every
kind, and the author explains that he has employed them not
because he attaches much importance to such feats of musical
erudition, but in order to give evidence of his own skill. To
approach such a theme in such a spirit was thoroughly
characteristic of the man.

As Bach wrote five complete 'years' of church cantatas,
we have good reason to believe that, as Mizler, his biographer
says, he wrote also five Passion-settings. Of these it seems
that three came, after his death, into the hands of his dissipated son, W. Friedemann Bach, and disappeared; while
the other two, falling to Carl Philipp Emanuel Bach, were
carefully preserved, and are the two great works which we
know as the St. John and the St. Matthew respectively.

A St. Luke Passion, undoubtedly in the handwriting of
Sebastian Bach, was long considered to be spurious, or at least
doubtful; Mendelssohn would have none of it, and, in writing
in 1838 to the owner of the autograph or transcript, Franz
Hauser, points out the great inferiority of a certain chorale
to all known works of Bach. Still, the weight of documentary
and other evidence led Spitta to regard the work as a genuine
composition of Bach's Weimar period[1], and when it was
published, at first in a pianoforte score, and subsequently in
the edition of the Bach-Gesellschaft, the great majority of
German authorities were convinced of its authenticity, although
it is evidently a very early work.

If we are warranted in accepting the St. Luke Passion as
a genuine work of the Weimar period, it must be nearly
contemporary with Keiser's, Handel's, and Telemann's works.
We are struck with the great preponderance of chorale-verses
over reflective solos; there are thirty-two of the former, and
only seven of the latter, in the course of the whole work. The
single instrumental movement, too, is the chorale, 'Ich hab'

---

[1] *Life of Bach* (Eng. transl.), ii. 508 ff.

mein' Sach' Gott heimgestellt,' played in simple four-part
harmony on wind instruments, before and after the singing
of a verse of the same hymn. By a stroke of genius which,
as Spitta says, is a strong evidence for the authenticity of
the work, the same tune, with the same disposition of instruments, interrupts the course of the pathetic tenor air, 'Lasst
mich ihn nur noch einmal küssen.'

Such musical meditations on the biblical text seem to have
gained in importance as time went on. One of the most
striking points in the comparison between the two great and
well-known Passion-settings of Bach is the relatively small part
which such numbers play in the earlier of the two, that
according to St. John. It may have been, as Spitta is careful
to say, that the poem of Brockes, from which Bach took most
of the non-scriptural words of the first part, was unsuited to
his purpose for the second, so that he was compelled to write
the words for himself; but it is also possible that the element
of devout reflection upon the events of the story assumed an
ever-increasing importance in Bach's mind. Certainly the
reflective numbers of the St. Matthew Passion are both more
numerous and of greater beauty than the corresponding portions
of the St. John; while in the latter, the utterances of the
crowd, the priests, the disciples, and, in short, all the persons
who could be represented by a chorus, are far more elaborately
set than they are in the St. Matthew Passion, being longer
and more organic in structure. Such a series of magnificent
choruses as 'We salute Thee,' 'Crucify,' 'We have a law,'
'If thou let this man go,' 'Away with Him!' 'Write thou
not,' and 'Let us not divide,' finds no exact counterpart in
the St. Matthew Passion; but their place is there taken by
the duet with chorus, 'My Saviour Jesus now is taken,' with
its dramatic sequel, 'Have lightnings and thunders in clouds
disappeared?' which are obviously of the same mystical
character that was referred to in speaking of the cantatas.
There are points in both works where the plan of structure

is seen to suggest almost conventional numbers; each has at least one of those solos on a freely invented subject, accompanied or interrupted by a chorale or chorale-like chorus, the pattern of which was set in the St. Luke Passion, by the tenor solo already mentioned; and the same motive of a valedictory chorus sung to Christ in the grave is employed at or near the close of each. Just before this final chorus of the St. Matthew Passion, the theme of which has recently been found in a sarabande from a suite in C minor published in B.-G., xlv. 1, we find a very beautiful arioso for four solo voices answering one another, with choral refrains; and the same type of composition appears in the corresponding place, just before the last chorale of the Christmas Oratorio.

In the St. John Passion, which was performed for the first time on Good Friday, 1724, we find no attempt made to distinguish between the words spoken by Christ and those of the other persons of the history; but in the St. Matthew Passion, first performed on Good Friday, 1729, the master adopted the expedient of giving the accompaniment of Christ's words to the orchestra, and leaving those of the others supported only by the bass, the harmonies being filled up at the discretion of the harpsichord or organ player. This alternation of tone-colour gives the most beautiful contrast that can be conceived, and the solemnity which it adds to the utterances of the Saviour is one of the most impressive elements in the work. In each of the compositions, the formal announcement of the source of the history, quoted above as the opening words of almost all the older settings of the Passion, has been expanded into elaborate introductory choruses, and that which opens the St. Matthew Passion is one of the greatest creations of the master. The motive, which no doubt grew out of the chorale-interruptions already referred to, of letting a chorus break in upon the long smooth flow of a solo with brief interrogations, had been used by Handel in the work above mentioned, and by Bach himself in the St. John Passion, where in the bass solo, 'Haste, ye deeply-wounded spirits,' the word 'Come' suggests the choral interruption 'Come where?' a device which in less sacred surroundings might provoke a smile, but which, as used by Bach, is pre-eminently suggestive and beautiful. Although he uses it again, at pre-cisely the same point of the narrative (the mention of the word 'Golgotha') in the alto solo, 'See the Saviour's outstretched arm,' Bach was not afraid of discounting its effect by anticipa-tion; the introductory chorus of this latest of his Passion-settings is divided into three bodies of singers, the first of which, in a flowing, plaintive measure, expands the motive, 'Come ye daughters,' while a second choir breaks in upon the first with the single words 'Whom?' or 'What?' As if this were not enough, a third chorus, of sopranos only, gives out the first verse of the hymn, 'O Lamm Gottes, unschuldig,' the whole forming one of those monumental compositions in which Bach has had no peer.

In both the great Passion-settings, the recitatives of the Evangelist and of Christ are marvellous in their emotional power; that the solemn utterances of the Saviour should inspire a great religious writer like Bach to his sublimest thoughts is perhaps less surprising than that he should have found varying expressions for the words of the Evangelist, and have fused, as it were, the conventional endings of reci-tative into phrases that must strike every hearer as giving the exact musical equivalent of a narrative told with the utmost simplicity, yet with the most complete and affecting sympathy. Never before or since has recitative been raised to so high a value of expressiveness, whether we consider the *recitativo secco* of the narrative portions (note the exquisite little cadenza in which the bitter weeping of St. Peter is described), or the more elaborate numbers with accompaniment, such as 'O blessed Saviour,' 'Although my heart and eyes,' 'The Saviour low before His Father bending,' or 'At evening,' all in the Matthew Passion. If recitative has never been so eloquent,

surely some of the airs surpass all the musical outpourings
of the human spirit in intensity of melodic utterance; 'It is
finished,' and 'Consider, O my soul,' of the St. John Passion,
and 'Have mercy' of the St. Matthew, have no rivals in the
range of art. The width of Bach's sympathetic insight into
human nature is wonderfully shown in the circumstance that
in the later of the two great Passion-settings, the meditation
on the betrayal, in the soprano solo 'Bleed and break,' and
the splendid air in which the remorse of Judas is expressed,
are not less emotional, not less vividly treated, than the
repentance of St. Peter. Often too, in both works, but oftener
in St. Matthew, the obbligato instruments which are introduced
so frequently in the airs are given a directness of utterance
which makes them more eloquent than the sung words they
accompany. This is especially the case with 'Have mercy,'
where the violin obbligato is even more emotional than the voice
part; and in 'Come, healing cross,' the viol da gamba becomes
the chief interpreter of the meditation.

It is not unsuitable that at this point we should consider
the character of Bach's writing for the voice, as exhibited in
the long series of works intended for the Lutheran Church.
Throughout these, two widely different styles of treating the
voice will be perceived by every one. On the one hand, the
form of the vocal phrases in the recitatives, and the structure
of the subjects in the choruses allotted to the disciples or
the Jews in the Passion-settings, are mainly declamatory;
they are always suggested by the natural accent of the words
as they would be spoken, and although in the choruses the
subject may be expanded into a flowing melody, it is in the
first instance dictated by the words. In both these classes,
expression is the primary object of the composer, and neither
here nor anywhere else can we find Bach choosing a phrase
that was inexpressive because it happened to suit the convenience of a singer. For this reason, the vocalists who are
nothing else, have in all times eschewed the music of Bach,

leaving it for the artists who aim at perfection of the interpretative art. The other side of Bach's vocal writing is displayed
in the chorale-choruses, and in the meditative airs; in the
former the vocal phrases are thought of as making a flowing
contrapuntal accompaniment to the chorale-tune which serves
as the *canto fermo*, and the ideal is not very different from
that of the composers of the previous century, although the
manner of treatment has nothing in common with these. The
airs are often accused of being too instrumental in design,
and to a certain extent the charge is not ill-founded. To Bach,
as to all the greatest masters of the art, the chief interest of
what is called 'abstract' music was in the themes themselves
regarded as sequences of ideal sounds, unconnected with any
special quality of tone; adopting the common analogy from
painting, Bach was first a draughtsman, and a colourist only
in the secondary sense. For this reason, his vocal melodies
lose little by being played upon instruments, and indeed their
beauty is sometimes enhanced by such a change. For though
they are beautiful and melodious in the highest degree, they
are not always very 'grateful' to the singers; and it must
be owned that in the cantatas there are not a few numbers
which seem as if Bach had a special detestation of the tenor
voice as well as a low opinion of the intellectual capacity
that generally accompanies it. For the abounding difficulties
of many of the tenor airs can hardly be explained unless we
assume that Bach was not unwilling to set before his singers
tasks of mere virtuosity which could never be perfectly accomplished. Nor would he ever countenance any slightest
alteration of the musical text; his strictness with regard to
this went so far that he adopted the convenient plan of writing
out the exact notes of the recitatives as they were to be sung,
departing from the custom of his contemporaries and predecessors, who had a whole code of conventional closes and
cadences represented by notes altogether different from those
intended to be actually performed.

In the same way his arrangement of the syllables in airs and choruses is thoroughly characteristic, and to alter it in any way is to sacrifice much of the point and vigour of Bach's ideas. A well-known instance is in regard to the beautiful air, 'Mein gläubiges Herze,' from the cantata 'Also hat Gott die Welt geliebt.'

The arrangement of the syllables in the opening phrase gives
a sense of energy, of spiritual elation, which is entirely lost
when the common change is made to—

And at the same time, the final drop of a seventh at the
end of the air is generally translated into the commonplace
rise of one note, because it is a little easier to sing. The
beginning of this air has been quoted at length, since it
illustrates a marked characteristic of Bach's airs. When the
voice first enters, it sings not the whole of the first strain,
but only half of it; the whole strain is not given in this case
until bars 9–12. The space between the half-strain, and the
repetition which is completed, is filled by two bars of the
ritornello which has already been heard, bars 7–8, a literal
repetition of bars 3–4. In examining the whole number of
airs scattered through the cantatas and elsewhere, this exact
pattern occurs so continually that it must surprise the student
of Bach who has been accustomed to consider him as the
least conventional of all the composers of old time. It is
indeed strange that so original a master should have used a
purely conventional formula to such an extent as he has done;

and it is still more strange to find that it is of commoner
occurrence in the later cantatas written at Leipzig, than in
those which date from the Weimar period. Whence could
have come, we may ask, the influence which led Bach to write
in a more conventional style in later life, if only in this one
respect? The formula is certainly not of his invention, for
it occurs before the date of Alessandro Scarlatti, in whose airs
it is used almost universally. The explanation of the pattern
is probably this; that the proper structure of the air begins
at the point where the first strain is sung in its entirety (in
the above instance at bar 8, last quaver). The opening
ritornello is as usual a mere introduction, and between this
and the air itself, comes what we may regard as a passage
partaking of the nature of a second ritornello, partly vocal
and partly instrumental. It is not impossible that it may
have had its origin in the desire to incorporate in an idealized
form the title of the song, or its opening words, before the
air itself was started. From a point of development at which
the singer may have been in the habit of announcing to his
hearers what he was about to sing, it is no long step to
embodying the title in the introductory portion of the air.
(Compare the expansion of the sung title of the older Passion-
setting, 'Passio secundum Matthaeum,' &c., into the sublime
opening choruses of Bach.) But whatever its origin, it is at
least not unlikely that Bach may have acquired and assimilated
the habit of using this formula during the secular part of
his career, the Cöthen period, when he was brought into
contact with the music of other countries more closely than
at any other part of his life. There are signs that he did not
consider the formula as worthy of his most dignified and
important work; in the Matthew Passion there is only one
example, in the bass air near the end, 'Make thee clean, my
heart, from sin'; in the St. John Passion the first treble
air is the only number in which it is strictly adhered to; and
the last treble air, 'Dissolve, O my heart,' shows it, but in

a modified form, the repetition not being quite literal. In the B Minor Mass it may be traced in the rhythmic structure of the bass air, 'Et in Spiritum Sanctum,' but nowhere else; and this work moreover contains a most interesting number in which Bach has adopted an air from one of the cantatas, but has changed its structure in such a way that this formula, though prominent in the cantata, disappears altogether from the later version. The alto air, 'Agnus Dei,' of the Mass is a remodelled version of 'Ach, bleibe doch, mein liebstes Leben,' from the cantata 'Lobet Gott'; while the general course of the opening section follows that of the cantata-air, the bare repetition of the first phrase is avoided, partly by interchanging the parts allotted to the voice and the violins, and partly by the addition of the beautiful little phrase to which the words 'Agnus Dei' are first sung. The middle section of the cantata-air is also left out altogether, another change which supports the surmise that in this greatest work of his life, Bach was anxious to depart from the conventionalities of his time in every way that was possible.

The history of the Passion-settings after the time of those of Bach is one of growing sentimentality. In this, as in all other branches of music, solidity and grandeur, massive effects, and the solemnity of piled-up harmonies, were sacrificed to a gentle, not to say effeminate style, which aimed solely at stirring an amount of emotion which could be indulged without transgressing the limits of good breeding. What had been dignified became merely pompous; and for the poignant expression of Bach, the later composers gave soft inanities which were occasionally plaintive, but never pathetic. The tendency to this weaker style came undoubtedly from the opera, which, in all countries, was under the same influence. And the last of the German attempts to treat the subject of the Passion in music, or rather the last we have now to consider, came from the two most popular of the German opera-writers, Hasse and Graun, whose careers must be more fully dealt with in a later chapter. A comparatively small quantity of Hasse's works has been preserved, but among them one of the most important is the oratorio, or so-called 'Passions-Oratorium,' *Die Pilgrimme auf Golgotha*, or in Italian, *I Pellegrini al Sepolcro*. The evil traditions of the opera, and the silly sentimentality that was their consequence, here reach the very limits of the absurd. Four pilgrims, provided with male names, although all four voices are soprano, are conducted to the sacred hill of Calvary by a 'Führer' (bass), and their pious ejaculations, conveyed in a long series of trite airs, with an occasional concerted number in the most meagre style of harmony for two sopranos and bass, make up the whole plan of the work. At the end of the whole is a four-part chorus with imitative entries, 'Uns, die hier als Pilger wallen,' which, with the overture, is the most considerable thing in the oratorio.

In scheme the famous 'Tod Jesu' of Graun evidently belongs to the meditative or rather sentimental treatments of the subject; and the style tells of a time when massive workmanship in choral writing was still admired by technically educated musicians, although the more meagre setting of comparatively simple melodies had already begun to be preferred by the general public. While the choruses in 'Der Tod Jesu,' such as the first, 'Sein Odem ist schwach,' the joyful 'Freuet euch alle,' or the final 'Hier liegen wir,' have something of Bach's dignity and much of the solid grandeur of the best eighteenth century work, the smooth airs, with their leanings towards vocal display and an almost operatic style, seem almost like a foreshadowing of the earlier works of Haydn. The structure of the airs is entirely formal, and every number that is not a fugue, a recitative, or a chorale, is in the *da capo* form. The soprano is indeed more highly favoured than the other soloists, but there are tenor and bass airs, and the latter voice has two very fine numbers. The chorales are all in the broadest four-part harmony, and in one number, 'Ihr Augen weint,' a chorale-theme is taken by two sopranos, above a bass solo, 'Weinet nicht.' The dialogue-form of this, and the words and style of the final chorus, illustrate the conventionalities of the Passion-music of which we have traced the course from Keiser's day onwards.

Although there seems to be no record of its ever having been given in England, Graun's 'Tod Jesu' has been kept before the German public by the fortunate circumstance that in consequence of a bequest it is still annually performed in Berlin during Holy Week, and has thus acquired the place of a recognized classic, quite apart from its intrinsic merits. Considerable as these are, the work has not the strength and vitality which have given *The Messiah* its unique position in the affections of the Anglo-Saxon race, or which obtain ever more and more widely-spread recognition for the Passion-settings of Bach.

CHAPTER IV

LATIN CHURCH MUSIC

BEFORE completing our survey of Bach's choral works by
an examination of the great Mass in B minor and the other
compositions set to Latin words, it will be well to turn our
attention to the state of church music outside Germany, in
order to obtain a standard of comparison from the works of
the principal composers of music primarily intended for the
service of the Church. In this respect the only country that
had a large and living influence upon the art of the time was
Italy. The English anthem-writers of the generation that
followed Purcell were of very small account, and their works
naturally had no vogue outside the walls of the English
cathedrals; the best and most typical of the French productions in this kind, Campra's motet—'à grands chœurs et
symphonies'—'In convertendo,' is a fine piece of six-part
choral writing, with strings generally in unison with the voices;
solo voices are used, oboes are introduced, and the strong
influence of Lully is apparent throughout, so that it has a
strange likeness to the accompanied anthems of Pelham Humfrey
and Blow, and even of Purcell. The composers of Spain were,
like the rest of the world, influenced by the Italians, and more
especially by those of the Neapolitan school, just as the
Viennese were by those of the Venetian. Naples, it must be
remembered, was at this time under the dominion of Spain,
as Venice and a great part of northern Italy was under that
of Austria; and although the Spanish composers never managed

to establish a school of European celebrity, such as that which gave Vienna the supreme place among European capitals for so long, they left a number of church compositions which will claim our attention in a later part of this chapter.

The successors or pupils of Carissimi, Legrenzi, and Alessandro Scarlatti, whose works are almost, if not altogether, exclusively vocal, are less famous than their contemporaries whose skill on the violin marks an epoch alike in virtuosity and in composition. To understand the position of these less renowned writers in the development of their art, we must review very briefly the course of musical events during the preceding century. For almost a hundred years after the revolution of 1600, when monody superseded polyphony, and the ideals of musical composers were completely altered, one musician after another had borne his part in the reconstructive process which was necessary in order to bring a well-ordered art, a cosmic whole, out of the chaotic condition into which music had been plunged by the innovators with Monteverde at their head. In process of time, a large measure of skill had been attained in the new surroundings, and a kind of polyphony had been shown to be possible, even though the motion of a single melody was henceforth to be recognized as the primary object in music. The interweaving of many voices into a smooth fabric in which no one part should be more prominent than another, was no longer held up as an end desirable in itself; rather was it the composer's ideal to allow now one, now another part, to hold the supreme position in. the expansion of one melodic idea. In considering the church compositions of Durante, Leo, Caldara, and in fact the great bulk of Italian vocal writers down to the date of Jommelli, we are often puzzled by finding numbers in which a magnificent idea of vocal sonority goes hand in hand with constructive ability and polyphonic resource, set in close juxtaposition with portions whose triviality of style, thinness of texture, and poverty of invention, seem to us in the present day so out of keeping with what has gone before that another authorship might be suspected, were not the phenomenon too common to admit of such an explanation. Not seldom does one of their choruses begin with a massive fugal section, conceived on the broadest lines, and worked with masterly ability and address in regard to the imitations and the intertwining of the voices; without a moment's pause, perhaps in the middle of the same number, we find ourselves listening to a couple of soprano parts pursuing each other in thirds above a dull bass without the slightest intermediary support from the inner parts. It is not at all easy to account satisfactorily for the incongruity. The facts will not allow us to suppose that in Italy in the eighteenth century there were two antagonistic parties, as with our own public in the present day, the one able to admire what was complex, the other only capable of grasping the simplest and least original strains that could be put before them. Nor is it more likely that the increasing demands of solo-singers for passages meant to show off their voices were the cause of the poverty of certain sections as contrasted with the rich beauty of the neighbouring divisions of the work. The practice is far too nearly universal to be explained on grounds as accidental as these. The true explanation seems to be that the Italians, although possessing all the skill of treating many parts, all the feeling for massive harmonies and sonority of effect, were yet far behind their contemporaries in Germany and England in respect of the form into which a great choral work should be cast. Fugal composition seems to have been easy to them, but apart from fugue and its kindred forms, they were at a loss for an effective means of obtaining relief in any manner that could be called truly choral. During the reconstructive process already referred to, the Germans, even before the days of Bach, had discovered that their own chorales could be used according to the older methods of a past day, as *canti fermi*, or in other ways as a groundwork for large choruses; and Handel was

not slow, on his arrival in England, in studying the characteristics which had given Purcell his position as a writer of
choruses.   The Italians had no such opportunity, and were
compelled to seek variety in complete contrast.   It is difficult
for us who have outlived the vogue of Rossini's 'Quis est
homo,' and Bellini's 'Mira, o Norma,' to realize the extraordinary fascination which two-part writing of a certain kind
exercised upon the Italians down to the date of those compositions, without a break from the time when the Abbate
Steffani (1655–1730) first won popularity by his chamber
duets.   These, of which the style is faithfully reproduced by
Handel in his series of twelve chamber duets, and in the duet
'O death, where is thy sting' in *The Messiah*, contrive to
give an effect of richness, and even of elaboration, with means
almost the simplest that could be devised.   In Clari's (1669–
c. 1745) works of the same class we find a growing preference
for easy flowing melody, for the sake of which a certain amount
of thinness of effect is allowed.   It is clear that the combination
of two sopranos, or soprano and contralto, above a bass, could
not always have been considered as bald as it would be in
the present day, for its popularity lasted down to the days
of Callcott and the English glee-writers generally.   In the
days of which we are speaking, too, it must be remembered
that intricacy and involution were falling into disregard; and
that, as time went on, music in Italy became ever simpler
and simpler in structure; and although the Italians themselves developed no new forms upon their simplified music, it
was the clearness of outline, and the prominence given to
smooth melodic motion, which prepared the way for the advent
of Haydn and Mozart.

In order to understand the state of music in Italy we must
bear in mind the three great schools of Venice, Bologna, and
Naples, the glories of which, in a former generation, had been
respectively Legrenzi, Colonna, and Alessandro Scarlatti.   The
first of these schools produced Lotti, Gasparini, Caldara,

Marcello, and Galuppi. From Bologna came Clari, Bononcini, and Martini; and in some ways the Neapolitan school is the most important of the three, since it contains the names of Astorga, Durante, Porpora, Leo, Cafaro, Pergolesi, and Jommelli.

The first of the great Venetians of our period, Antonio Lotti (c. 1667–1740), is a man whose attitude and ideals it is hard to understand. It may be that his connexion with St. Mark's, of which church he became a chorister in 1687, principal organist in 1704, and maestro (after his return from Dresden) in 1736, gave or strengthened his taste for the older music. It is very difficult to ascertain the chronological sequence of his compositions, as he published nothing but a collection of 'Duetti, terzetti, e madrigali' in 1705. As compared with the true madrigals of the sixteenth century his compositions so called fall very far short of perfection; but it is clear that both in his attempt to write any kind of music in a form that was by this time voted out of fashion, and in his liking for polyphonic music generally, he was far more in sympathy with the solid style of the past than with the increasing delight in what was trivial.

It has been suggested by more than one historian that this severe style of music was that in which he chiefly delighted, and that he was induced by the claims of a frivolous public to write as he did in his operas, which indeed scarcely ever rise above the prevailing style of the period. But this can hardly be an accurate summary of the case, for it happens not seldom that we find the two styles in close association with one another. His sacred works show a great and in fact almost unaccountable variety of style, ranging from the most severe polyphony to a brilliant and far more modern style of which an incomplete Mass[1] (the Kyrie beginning in G minor, and the Gloria ending in F major) is a typical instance. In

---

[1] Brit. Mus. Add. MS. 24,297.

its course a brilliant solo, 'Laudamus,' leads into a 'Gratias agimus' for chorus, in homophonic style with very distinct rhythm. The orchestration is of a very rudimentary kind, and is generally confined to instrumental repetitions of what has just been sung. It is difficult to believe that the same hand can have written this, and such uncompromisingly austere music as the mass for four voices unaccompanied, given in vol. i. of Proske's *Musica Divina*, the four-part *Magnificat* published by Breitkopf and Haertel, or the two versions of the 'Crucifixus' that are contained in Rochlitz's *Sammlung vorzüglicher Gesangswerke*, vol. ii. Between the two in that book stands a 'Qui tollis' in an entirely inappropriate *siciliano* style with an undoubtedly effective, but sadly irreverent accompaniment. The 'Crucifixus' for eight voices has a fine opening in imitation, and the other, in six parts, has an ending so curiously like Sebastian Bach's setting of the same words in the B minor Mass that it seems worth quoting for purposes of comparison [1]. These are the last fourteen bars of the piece:—

[1] For other examples of the influence of Lotti upon Bach, see Spitta's *Life of Bach* (Eng. transl.), ii. 638, 9; iii. 28.

. . pul . . . . tus est, pas-sus et se-pul-tus est.

et se-pul . . . tus est, pas-sus et se-pul-tus est.

et se-pul . . tus est, ... et se-pul-tus est.

. . . pul . . . . . . tus est, pas-sus et se-pul . . . tus est.

. . . pul . . . . . . tus est, pas-sus et se-pul . . . tus est.

. . . pul . . . . . . tus est . . . .

The resemblance is far less one of notes than of general
character, for the actual motive of the three descending notes
is more like the 'Qui tollis' of Bach's mass; but the mood
of the two compositions is practically identical, although Lotti's
rather dull close cannot compare for a moment with the
wonderful harmonies at the end of Bach's chorus. Still if
this, or the other 'Crucifixus,' were what Burney heard in
St. Mark's, we need not wonder at his being moved to tears
by the impressive effect of the music[1].

Another pupil of Legrenzi, Antonio Caldara (1678–1736),
like so many of his contemporaries, spent a great part of his
mature years abroad, being vice-capellmeister under J. J. Fux
of Vienna from 1716 until his death. He was a marvellously
prolific writer, and as a natural consequence, his works have
passed almost out of remembrance. Yet while his well-known
song, 'Come raggio del Sol,' gives an idea of the dignity of
his melodic writing, a *Crucifixus* in sixteen vocal parts[2]
shows complete mastery of the contrapuntal problem, and an
eight-part *Magnificat*[3] is of sterling value; the Dorian mode
is handled with a knowledge rare at this date. The same MS.

[1] Burney, *Tour in France and Italy*, p. 145. [2] Brit. Mus. Add. MS. 32,389.
[3] Add. MS. 31,550.

contains a fine setting of the Psalm *Confitebor* for ‘obuè,’ two
violins and a four-part chorus with soprano solo. The oboe part
is written a note lower than the rest, which is in the key of A.
The solo voice is used in various numbers, both alone and with
chorus, with great skill, in a fairly florid style, with which such
a number as the following chorus contrasts rather oddly :—

et ter - ri - - - bi - le, et ter - ri - bi - le, ter -

. . . . ter - ri - - bi - le, et ter - ri - bi - le, ter -

- ri - bi - le, ter - ri - - bi - le, et ter - ri - bi - le, ter -

- - ri - bi - le, ter - ri - bi - le nomen e - ius, et ter - ri - bi - le, ter -

- ri - bi - le no - men e - ius, San - - ctum

- ri - bi - le nomen e - - ius, San - - ctum

- ri - bi - le no - men e - ius, San - - ctum

- - ri - bi - le no - men e - ius, San - - ctum

In the library of the Royal College of Music are twelve
motets for two and three voices (two sopranos and bass would
seem to be a favourite combination), as well as three masses
(one, for five voices and strings, has only a Kyrie and Gloria).
The mass for four voices and strings in D minor contains some
of Caldara's best work.

Of the compositions of Francesco Gasparini (c. 1668–1737)
there is none that has the slightest importance in the present
day; he was a pupil of Corelli and Pasquini in Rome, and
went to Venice as music teacher of the Ospedale della Pietà,
where he had for his most distinguished pupil Benedetto
Marcello (1686–1739), who was also a pupil of Lotti's. Marcello
was of noble family and held various official and legal posts,
so that he was what we should call in modern times an amateur.
None of his operas, oratorios, or masses, attained anything
approaching the success of his setting of the first fifty Psalms
in the paraphrase of Girolamo Ascanio Giustiniani. The eight

volumes which appeared between 1724 and 1727 were frequently reprinted, and MS. copies are not uncommon. Beginning with a whole volume of compositions in two parts (chorus and solos) with a *basso continuo* for the only accompaniment, the settings become more elaborate as they go on, and the longest, as well as one of the finest of the series, is the last Psalm l (our Psalm li), a *Miserere* for three parts, alto, tenor, and bass, with obbligato parts for two violette (violas). All the settings, whether simple or elaborate, display great skill and knowledge of good effect, and one reason of their wonderful popularity must surely be that the composer is a master of the art of contrast and variety; solos or duets are interspersed with the choral portions, and are for the most part in a far more suave and flowing style than these; though far less austere than Lotti's sacred works, the Psalms show no lack of solid workmanship, and the handling of the contrapuntal parts shows much skill.

The sacred music of Baldassare Galuppi (1706–1785) need not detain us, as it is far less famous than his operatic or instrumental works. And in this division of the history the school of Bologna need not be gone into very closely; the two-part compositions by which Clari's name is best known have already been referred to; of Bononcini much will have to be said in connexion with the opera and the English surroundings, and the deservedly great name of Padre Giambattista Martini (1706–1784) rests upon his skill as a teacher and an authority on the history of the art rather than on his own compositions, though a book of 'Litaniae' was published, and the Liceo Filarmonico at Bologna possesses three oratorios by him. Beside the world-wide influence he exercised on musicians, which made Bologna a kind of central point of the musical world during his later years, his greatest works were the *Storia della Musica*, of which three volumes were brought out (1757–1781), and the *Saggio di Contrappunto* (1774–1775).

Turning now to the school of Naples, the eldest of the generation who claims to rank as its pupil is Astorga, who is assumed to have studied with Francesco Scarlatti at Palermo, but who spent the time of his musical education in the convent of Astorga in Spain, to which he was sent by the kindness of the Princess Ursini, maid of honour to the wife of Philip V. At ten years old he had seen his father, a Sicilian nobleman, the Marchese Capece da Roffrano, expiate on the scaffold his unsuccessful revolt against the power of Spain. The horror of the occasion was intensified by the fact that the child's mother died at the same time, and we may well believe what has been often stated, that the poignancy of the sorrow which breathes from every page of his best-known work, the great *Stabat Mater*, is to be traced to the influence of that tragic scene. In this, which has rightly been regarded as the most important work of its nation, there is not a trace of conventionality; it is throughout sincere and noble, and alike the choral and solo portions are expressive, solemn, and appropriate. Yet the artist who wrote his masterpiece in a strain of almost monastic piety was at the same time a singularly prosperous man of the world, who, after obtaining the title of Baron d'Astorga by the interest of the Princess, was sent on a diplomatic mission to the court of Parma, and thence, after an unsuccessful love affair with the daughter of the duke, Elisabetta Farnese, despatched to Vienna, where again he charmed every one at the court by his beautiful singing. An interesting record of his stay in Austria is the fact that he acted as godfather to Caldara's daughter in 1712[1].

Francesco Durante (1684–1755) was an almost exact contemporary of Bach and Handel; he learnt his art from Alessandro Scarlatti, Pitoni, and Pasquini. As the second of these is chiefly famous for the fact that he wrote a mass in sixteen vocal parts, we may surmise that it was from him

---

[1] Grove, *Dict. of Music and Musicians*, s. v. Astorga.

that Durante gained the ease and fluency in polyphonic writing
for which he is remarkable. The strictures pronounced upon
the music of this period, which apply more nearly to the
Neapolitan school than to the other schools of Italy, are less
appropriate to him than to many of his contemporaries, and
his works show a good deal more unity of design than is
apparent in some of theirs. In a *Tantum ergo* for five-part
chorus, strings and organ, he uses the two soprano parts
together in opposition or antiphony to the rest almost throughout, and the device is a kind of foreshadowing of that system
which, as has been already said, remained in vogue in Italy
far into the nineteenth century, and in England nearly as
long. There are not wanting signs that the average musical
person of the period thought little of the balance of parts,
or of massive solid harmonies, in comparison with the brilliance
that is undoubtedly gained by the association of two soprano
parts, whether in duet or chorus. In the earlier instances of
this association, such as the chamber duets of Steffani or Clari,
the two are treated as of equal importance, and cross one
another with beautiful intertwinings, above a solid instrumental bass. It was not till later on that the practice arose
of letting one be always subordinate to the other, a practice
which ultimately degenerated into an uninteresting sequence
of thirds and sixths, depending for its effect upon uniformity
of phrasing and delivery, rather than upon a fair balance of
timbres. This conventional treatment of the two soprano
voices is one of the most salient features of the tendency
which is commonly called the ' Zopf,' a term of which
both the meaning and origin require some explanation. Why
German historians of the arts should have selected this word
to denote what it does, it would be hard to say, unless the
idea of a pigtail or peruke conveyed to their minds, by chronological coincidence, the style of art which prevailed at the
time these were most commonly worn. There are certain
characteristics in the eighteenth century that may help us

to understand the tendency which, for all its affectation, was of enormous importance in the development of the art of music. Perhaps the best definition of the 'Zopf' would be the assumption of simplicity by courtly persons who had become artificialized, and wanted a new sensation. For it was never an honest turning from what was elaborate to what was really simple; in all its aspects there was a strong element of falsehood, of make-believe, and of the charm that comes to some people from pretence of all kinds. Closely allied to this assumption of simplicity is the love for a superabundance of ornament as distinguished from solid workmanship — in architecture for stucco roses hiding a wall of rubble, and, in music, for stucco melodies hiding a poor and ill-wrought harmonic fabric. Of the influence of the solo singers in aiding this tendency, we shall have to speak at length in a later chapter; here it must suffice to draw attention to the movement which, consciously or unconsciously, was beginning to spread over the whole of Europe in one form or other.

In an eight-part *Requiem* of Durante[1], the very arrangement of the parts on the pages of the score is an illustration of what has been said above concerning the use o° the two soprano parts together. The three lower parts of each choir— alto, tenor, and bass—are arranged as is usual in music for a double choir, but above them stand the two soprano lines next each other, so that at first sight it looks as if the composition were intended for two soprano solos, accompanied by a double choir of six parts. The internal evidence of the music shows that it is not so, but that the two soprano parts fall in with the others in the ensemble, although holding a far more elaborate course of their own, very often moving in passages of thirds. The work is furthermore remarkable for the somewhat naïf attempt to depict the terrors of the 'Dies irae'

[1] Brit. Mus. Add. MS. 31,611.

by interspersing the vocal phrases, at perfectly regular intervals, with scales on the violins and basses, which not even the adjective *spaventoso*, added in writing above them, can make in the least alarming. It is also noticeable that the theme of the chorus, scales and all, returns at various points after solo numbers, one of which, in its repetition of the soprano solo, 'Quaerens me,' to the same music sung by an alto to the words 'Juste Judex,' may be due to the same desire for variety which prompted the now usual change of singers in 'He shall feed His flock' in *The Messiah*. The resumption of themes previously introduced is a practice again adopted by Durante in a mass[1] in G for five-part chorus, accompanied by strings, two oboes, and two horns. The theme of the Kyrie recurs as that of 'Cum sancto Spiritu'; there is a fine fugue at 'Christe eleison,' and a florid trio at 'Domine Deus,' with trumpets added to the accompaniment. A *Dixit Dominus* for two sopranos and bass in the same MS. shows a complete abandonment of the massive style of much of Durante's choral writing for a trivial thin effect, not unlike that of the English glees of a later date. Rochlitz[2] gives another fine *Requiem* for four-part chorus in G minor with violin accompaniment, as well as a chorus, 'Regina angelorum,' from a rather flimsy Litany; the chorus chosen is almost Haydnesque in style. Durante excelled in the invention of obbligato parts, and the two violin parts of his (printed) *Magnificat* are as successful in their own way as the brilliant passages of his well-known song 'Danza fanciulla.' In another *Magnificat*[3] he leads off with a soprano against a flowing bass, in a kind of *canto fermo*, with the other voices joining in presently in a way that is very familiar in some of Handel's choruses, such as 'Immortal Lord of earth and skies' in *Deborah*. The same theme recurs at the 'Sicut erat.'

[1] Brit. Mus. Add. MS. 31,610.
[2] *Sammlung vorzüglicher Gesangswerke*, vol. ii.
[3] Brit. Mus. Eg. MS. 2,453.

The fame of Niccolò Antonio Porpora (1686–1766) both
as an opera writer and as the most successful vocal teacher
of his time is very great, and in most of his masses and other
sacred works the triviality and superfluous ornamentation
about which so much has been said are carried to an extreme.
One work of his, a volume of six duets on the Passion[1], is
but another instance of the ever-recurrent puzzle concerning
the contrast of styles in the Italian composers of this
time. For all are dignified, superb in harmony and melody
alike, while one of them, 'Tanquam Agnus immolatus,'
must be placed among the noblest pieces of sacred music
in existence.

Born ten years after Durante, but dying ten years before
him, Leonardo Leo (1694–1746) was a greater man, since he
had a far greater degree of vigour and broad effect, while his
ease of manipulating many parts was at least as conspicuous.
The three settings of the Psalm *Dixit Dominus* are the works
by which he is best known, and they undoubtedly possess very
remarkable dignity and originality. They, with two masses
and a number of other sacred works, are contained in the
Fitzwilliam Museum at Cambridge, and specimens of a good
many are in Novello's Fitzwilliam Music. Professor C. V.
Stanford has edited the splendid *Dixit* in C for eight-part
chorus, and the setting for five-part chorus in A has also
been printed, but the one for ten-part chorus in D is only
represented in print by the extract in Fitzwilliam Music. The
most available of these, the work in C, is as typical a specimen
of the best Italian eighteenth century work as could be found.
The opening for the two sopranos in unison over a flowing
bass on a *canto fermo* reminds us of Durante's *Magnificat*.
The writing for soprano solo, both in 'Donec ponam' and in
'Virgam virtutis,' in which it is combined with the two choirs
with brilliant effect, is excessively florid, and there are very

---

[1] Published by Breitkopf and Haertel.

few singers of the present day who could do it justice. The opening theme returns at the close to the words 'Sicut erat,' where the original key is resumed after a series of modulations in the successive numbers that is most seldom met with in this period. As in the setting of the Psalm in A the 'Tu es sacerdos' is set to a fine double fugue, so here it is set to a triple fugue of great dignity and impressiveness. In his *Miserere*, which dates from 1743, Leo seems to have gone for his model as far back as to the famous work by Allegri; for the antiphonal idea which is so striking a part of that is here turned into a kind of dialogue between two choirs on the one hand, and the soloists, one by one, on the other. These sing the alternate verses successively as recitatives, and after a time, the first choir takes the recitative verses in antiphony with the eight parts together.

The church music of Pasquale Cafaro (1708–1787) has little to distinguish it from the other works of the Neapolitan school; he was Leo's pupil, and his powers were better fitted in writing for the stage, or in oratorio of an operatic kind, than in music intended for the service of the Church. There is an 'Amen' for five-part chorus in Novello's Fitzwilliam Music.

In his short life of twenty-six years, Giovanni Battista Pergolesi (1710–1736) made himself a name which is far above all his near contemporaries among Italian musicians. He was a pupil of Greco, Durante, and Feo, at the Conservatorio dei Poveri, having been taken to Naples from his birthplace, Jesi, in the Roman states, to learn the violin under Domenico de Matteis. It was his power of inventing passages for his instrument, and the originality he displayed in so doing, that induced his teacher to place him under the masters of composition already mentioned. It may perhaps be a result of his violin studies that his use of the orchestra, even of the strings alone, as in his most famous work, the *Stabat Mater*,

produces an effect of being really an integral part of the
composition, not a mere mechanical support to the voices,
which was allowed on occasion to play *ritornelli* between the
various sections. He is almost the first of the Italians of his
day whose orchestral accompaniments make the hearer feel
that they are indispensable. One of his two masses for double
choir of five parts each, and double orchestra, is said[1] to
have been commissioned for a special occasion after the de-
liverance of the city from an earthquake, and to have drawn
expressions of delight from Leo, who, as the head of another
conservatorio in the same city, would not have been impelled
to exhibit an enthusiasm he did not feel. A *Dixit Dominus*
for the same combination as these two masses is given in
Novello's Fitzwilliam Music, and, although the ten vocal parts
are not employed in strict polyphony, there is a wonderful
knowledge of the effects to be gained by opposing the two
masses of sound to each other. In him, too, is felt a nobility
and grace, not merely in the manipulation of the melodic
phrases, or the alteration of various media of sound, but in
the art of design; each section is carefully planned from the
beginning, and reaches its logical ending by steps that have
been clearly foreseen from the first. Pergolesi's career as an
opera-writer must come under consideration later; even there,
though his *Serva padrona* was destined to revolutionize the
French stage, and to set a pattern from which no departure
was allowed for many years, its success at first was not very
remarkable, and his *Olimpiqde*, his last theatrical work, was
unsuccessful at Rome. The preparation of the last-named
work interrupted the composition of his *Stabat Mater*, which
was only finished a few days before the composer died of
consumption. This work was commissioned by the confra-
ternity of San Luigi di Palazzo, and we shall not be far wrong
if we regard its expression of poignant sorrow as the fruit

---

[1] Grove, *Dictionary of Music and Musicians*, ii. 687.

of the bitter disappointments of the last years of the master's life.

The vogue of writing for two female voices was no doubt partly, if not mainly, accountable for the arrangement of the *Stabat Mater*, which is set out for soprano and contralto voices alone, whether in solo or choral parts. Strings and organ are the only accompaniment of the work in its original condition, although Paisiello added wind instruments not long after Pergolesi's death, and, in modern times, it has been scored for full orchestra. In spite of the limited means at his disposal, Pergolesi never loses sight of the massive dignity of the subject; his vocal treatment is flowing and natural, yet he never yields to the temptation of writing for the sake of the singers, or of allowing the vocal phrases to obscure the musical idea. The astounding variety of effect, the almost fugal impression the hearer receives from such a number as ' Fac ut ardeat,' and the extreme beauty of every page, make it one of the salient sacred works of all time.

No greater contrast could possibly be imagined to the sad life of Pergolesi than the brilliant career of Niccolo Jommelli (1714–1774), who was a perfect type of the successful composer of his day. As he was first a pupil of Durante's at the Conservatorio di San Onofrio, and went from there to be under Leo at the Conservatorio della Pietà, he may be said to unite in himself the two main branches of Neapolitan training. He played an important part in the transmission of the current Italian style into Germany, and in this way had some share in the artistic ancestry of Haydn and Mozart. His career as a composer began with several operas, performed at Rome and Bologna; at the latter place he profited not a little by association with Padre Martini, and after a visit to Vienna, was appointed assistant chapel-master of St. Peter's, in Rome; in 1754 he became chapel-master to the Duke of Würtemberg, at Stuttgart, a post he retained for fifteen years. While he was in Germany he wrote some of his most important works,

among them a so-called oratorio of the Passion, and the
Requiem of which the opening number, 'Kyrie eleison,' was
printed as Haydn's in some editions of the latter's mass in
E flat. The former work is a series of more or less brilliant
musical meditations allotted to the characters of Mary Magdalene, John, Peter, and Joseph of Arimathea; it shows skill,
smoothness, but no inspiration, and its lack of unity in style is
illustrated in the fact that the fine, solid fugue, 'Quanto costa,'
is interrupted by a duet in thirds that is almost worthy of
Bellini at his worst. This same fondness for the device so
often mentioned already, of allowing two treble voices to follow
one another in thirds or sixths indefinitely, is further illustrated
in a 'Sicut locutus est' for three female voices. But he was
not always in this trivial vein, even when writing for two
female voices alone; his *Miserere* for two soprano soli and
string accompaniment, said to be his last composition, is not
very far inferior to Pergolesi's *Stabat Mater*, and as in the
case of Pergolesi, the composer had been bitterly disappointed,
at the time when he wrote it, with the want of success his
maturest operas received in Italy, where they were considered
too German in their style. A mass in D[1] contains a foreshadowing of a plan that came into vogue long after this time,
of connecting the various sections by similarity, not to say
identity, of themes.

Concerning the church music of Spain, the monumental
collection of Eslava[2] contains examples of what are pre-
sumably the finest compositions of all periods of Spanish sacred
music. From an examination of this, it may be inferred that
the gradual transition in style from a pure polyphony to the
manner of the 'Zopf' took a good deal longer to accomplish
in Spain than elsewhere. If we are justified in accepting
the theory strongly insisted upon by Naumann[3] and others,

---

[1] Published in Paris about 1800.

[2] Miguel Hilarion Eslava, *Lira Sacro-Hispana*, Madrid, 1869.

[3] *History of Music* (Eng. transl.), i. 537 ff.

that the transition in Italian music was due to the reaction
after the shock of the Reformation, we shall have a clue to
the slowness with which the new style made its way in Spain;
the power of the Catholic Church, defended by the tremendous
agency of the Inquisition, had been far less shaken in Spain
than in Italy, and there was no need to counteract the influence
of German Protestantism by introducing new fashions into
the service of the Church.   Down to the middle of the seventeenth century under Pontac and his contemporaries, pure
polyphony was still practised just as if the artistic revolution
of 1600 had not taken place; and when the change of fashion
began to make itself felt, the antiphonal style, which employed
two or even three four-part choirs, had obtained a firm footing.
The two styles were successfully worked together, as in the
beautiful twelve-part 'Lamentations' of Teodoro Ortells,
maestro de capilla in the cathedral of Valencia (fl. 1668).   It
was at Valencia that the Spanish antiphonal style seems to
have had its origin; the practice of employing three complete
choirs at one time must have spread to other parts of Spain,
as it is exhibited with comparative frequency in Eslava's
collection.

The various motets of Don Juan Garcia Salazar (d. 1710)
have the essential features of the sixteenth century poly-
phonists, in respect of the invention of the musical ideas,
with the formal or conventional pattern of a later day in
regard to the figured bass for the accompaniment.   Here is
the end of his 'Mater Dei,' a very expressive five-part motet,
with soprano solo:—

The sudden change from the chord of D to that of B flat in the second bar, and the style of the cadences, breathe of the sixteenth century, and the only thing in this example that tells of its later date is the progression of the tenor part in the last bar but one. A remarkably impressive motet, 'Audite universi populi,' for twelve-part chorus and contralto solo, is by Pedro Rabassa, who was maestro de capilla of Valencia in 1713, and of Seville in 1724. He was the author of a 'Guia para los que quieran a aprender composicion,' a text-book which had a great celebrity, and he died in 1760. Francisco Vicente, another Valencian organist, and Francisco Valls of Barcelona (1665–c. 1743) wrote in a severe and truly ecclesiastical style, as did Cáseda (d. c. 1723) and Antonio Líteres, who flourished in the first half of the eighteenth century. It is with Pascal Fuentes (d. 1768), who was appointed to Valencia in 1757, that the style of the 'Zopf' first shows itself; the duet for soprano and tenor in his 'Beatus vir' proceeds in a series of the most bland thirds above an eight-part chorus of very little interest. Fray Benito Juliá, who studied at the monastery of Montserrat, taking the habit

there in 1745 and dying in 1787, wrote in a fairly modern
style, but had evidently a strong feeling for the old. His
fellow-student at Montserrat, Fray Antonio Soler (1729–1783),
was the author of church music of a severe style, in conscious
imitation of the ancients, and in strong contrast to the style
of his twenty-seven harpsichord sonatas, dedicated to his pupil,
the Infante Don Gabil. With Josef Nebra (d. 1781) and
Antonio Ripa (1720–1795) we pass into a more modern manner
of writing; the former is represented in Eslava's collection
by a *Requiem* for Queen Barbara, his patroness, for eight-part
chorus, two flutes, and string accompaniment. The 'Dies
irae' has some quite modern effects, and a florid violin figure
in the 'Lacrimosa' is worth noticing. Ripa is represented
by an eight-part mass with strings and trumpets, and a very
solid *Stabat Mater* with organ accompaniment.

From the many church compositions of the Italian and
Spanish composers, set to Latin words, of which those referred
to are but isolated examples, it is a curious change to turn
back to Germany and to consider once more the work of
Sebastian Bach, whose stupendous mass in B minor, beside
the compositions lately considered, is not unlike a magnificent
Gothic cathedral, full of mystery and confusion to the un-
accustomed eye, with its distances lost in a perplexing maze
of interwoven arches, and aisles dim with incense-smoke, beside
the typical church of the Italian Renaissance, where everything
is definite, bright, and hard, and where smoothness of surface
in pavement, walls, or columns has evidently been the builders'
first object. Bach set the words of the mass five times in all;
four of these compositions are short, and many of their numbers
are rearranged from cantatas [1]. The greatest of the five, as
well as by far the longest, was the only one in writing which

---

[1] For an account of the Latin masses set by Bach, and a detailed analysis of the
B minor Mass, the reader must be referred to Spitta's *Life of Bach* (Eng. transl.),
iii. pp. 25–64; and a reference will be found to the use of Latin words in the
Lutheran services, in vol. ii. p. 263, of the same work, and elsewhere.

Bach seems to have contemplated its use in connexion with the Roman ceremonial; he took the first two divisions of it in 1733 to Dresden, and presented them to the Elector Augustus III, soon after his accession. There is no trace of its having been performed in Dresden, and it seems hardly likely that even the master himself should have imagined that, when completed on the same scale of grandeur, the whole could possibly fit in with the Catholic office. Still, fortunately for the world, he did complete it, his last work on it being assigned by his biographer to the year 1738. The qualities which entitle it to rank among the supreme masterpieces of music, and in particular to be counted with Palestrina's *Missa Papae Marcelli*, and Beethoven's Mass in D, as one of the three greatest of all masses, are to be found rather in the choruses than in its solo numbers. Not even in his settings of .the Passion had Bach revealed anything like such a wealth of massive conceptions, every theme of which is not only noble and expressive, but individual; from the broad vocal harmonies of the opening 'Kyrie,' which precede the instrumental introduction to the fugal chorus, down to the end of the 'Dona nobis pacem,' set to the same music as the 'Gratias agimus,' in the course of which, after the gradual rising of the imitative entries from voice to voice, the trumpets in their highest register soar upwards, like the very symbol of prayer and thanksgiving ascending to the throne of God, the whole of the choral numbers have a beauty of material, a splendour of intricate treatment, and a propriety in regard to illustrating the words, that are surpassed in no music of earlier or later date. From the exuberant 'Gloria' with its exquisitely tender change at the word 'pax,' and the unspeakably satisfying cadence at 'bonae voluntatis,' we pass, by way of various solo numbers, to the 'Gratias' already mentioned, to the 'Qui tollis,' a wonderful series of enchained suspensions of the boldest kind, and to the brilliant 'Cum sancto Spiritu,' built on a theme which seems at first too spontaneous for the extraordinarily elaborate fugal treatment it afterwards receives. The vast *Credo* begins with the ecclesiastical intonation given out by the tenors, and imitated by the other four voices—for it should be said that the majority of the choruses are in five parts; the 'Crucifixus,' exquisite in expression, is startling even to ears accustomed to modern music, so daring is its harmonic progression over a ground bass thirteen times repeated; the joyful subject of the 'Et resurrexit' is given a tone of menace in the quasi-solo for the bass chorus, 'Et iterum venturus est'; and in the 'Confiteor,' than which the literature of music contains no nobler example of every kind of canonic device happily treated, we meet again with a fragment of plainsong, first introduced in the bass part, and then taken up in augmentation, i. e. in notes of double the original length by the tenors. The 'Sanctus' in six parts, and the 'Osanna' in eight, are the perfection of rapturous devotional utterance; and in this part of the work occur the two most beautiful solos—the 'Benedictus' for tenor and the 'Agnus Dei' for contralto—the latter altered, as already stated[1], from a song in a cantata, with the best possible result.

In setting music to Latin words, the fact that Bach altered his style considerably need not be demonstrated, as it is obvious to every one who has ears. But the wide gulf between the essentially German settings of the Passion or the cantatas for the Lutheran service, and the great mass, with its world-wide significance and universal appeal, is in some measure bridged by certain compositions to Latin words, in which the characteristics of the best Italian music of the day are adopted. The words of the *Sanctus* were used in the Lutheran church on various festivals, and Bach set them, exclusively of the setting in the great mass, four times; that in C, for four-part choir and full orchestra, is less individual than the work in D, in which the four-part choir is accom-

[1] See p. 44.

panied by violins in unison above a figured bass[1]. But both
here and in the great setting of the *Magnificat* for five-part
choir, solos, and full orchestra, there is clearly a recognition
of the beauty and fitness of the best Italian style, and even
such mannerisms as the setting of the two treble parts in
opposition to the rest may be traced, as well as the habit of
writing for these two mainly in thirds. This, and the most
elaborate of the settings of the *Sanctus*, are ascribed by Spitta
to Christmas 1723[2].

The structure of the opening chorus is referable to the
concerto rather than to any other form, the choir taking the
part of the solo instrument, or the *concertino* of the *concerto
grosso*, while the orchestra supplies the accompaniment in
a manner not at all unlike the accepted type of accompaniment in the concertos of the day. A point of special beauty,
and one which throws some light on Bach's attitude towards
what may be called impersonation in sacred music, is seen in
the air in F sharp minor, 'Quia respexit,' where the soloist
(first soprano) is interrupted at the words ' omnes generationes '
by the whole choir, the voices of which successively enter on
a phrase of four repetitions of the same note; the order of
the entries in the imitative phrase, is, after an introductory
bar, in which the bass has the theme, soprano 1, on the high
F sharp, followed by soprano 2, alto, tenor, and bass, not
alternating the tonic and dominant of the key but all entering
on C sharp; then still at the distance of half a bar from the
last entry they begin again, from the F sharp of the altos,
and proceed by one note higher at each entry—thus : alto
F sharp, soprano 2 G sharp, soprano 1 A, bass B, alto C,
tenor D, soprano 2 E, and soprano 1 F sharp. The uncon-
ventionality of these entries gives, as perhaps nothing else
could, the suggestion of the whole human race all down the

---

[1] The Sanctus in C appeared in the *Bach Choir Magazine*; all four settings are
in vol. xi. of the Bach-Gesellschaft edition.

[2] Spitta, *Life of Bach* (Eng. transl.), ii. 369 ff.

ages of the world, uniting to call the Virgin blessed. Another chorus, 'Fecit potentiam,' in which the fugal parts are accompanied by the rest of the voices for just two bars after their start, foreshadows the 'Patrem omnipotentem' of the *Credo* of the great mass, and the treatment of the words 'dispersit superbos' is not unworthy of the style of the mass. The lovely trio-chorus for female voices, 'Suscepit Israel,' leads into the chorus 'Sicut locutus' and on to the 'Gloria,' in the course of which, at the words 'Sicut erat in principio' the brilliant theme of the opening chorus returns.

If we had nothing but the work itself to guide us to the nationality of the composer of this *Magnificat*, we might pardonably guess it to be a compendium of all that was best in the Italian masters of the time, for if we must choose a work to be its parallel in conception and general effect, we can find none nearer than Leo's eight-part *Dixit Dominus*, although the execution and the originality of genius are lacking in the Neapolitan, and could not be kept out of the German's work.

CHAPTER V

THE ORATORIO

WE have now before us the means of tracing the pedigree of the most important and elaborate art-form that was brought to perfection in the time of Bach and Handel. For the early stages of development of the oratorio, the reader must be referred to the preceding volume of this series. When Handel went to Italy in the early years of the eighteenth century, the form had already begun to show the strongest possible affinity for the conventions which governed operatic composition, and it is not too much to say that the average Italian oratorio of this time was distinguishable from opera merely by the character of its words. And, after all, the affinity is not without reason, for the ideal of oratorio is far more widely separated from music that can be called 'devotional' than from the music of the stage. All church music worthy of the name, whether the mass of the Roman communion, the cantata of the Lutheran church, or the anthem of the Anglican, has for its primary and acknowledged object the desire of stimulating devotion, if the congregation be not actually encouraged to regard it in itself as an act of worship. But the common distinction between the words 'congregation' and 'audience' exactly fits the distinction between the two classes of works; the oratorio is performed before an audience, and realizes its purpose in the concert-room or theatre, while the natural sphere of all the other forms is the church. Beyond all

dispute, the oratorio reached its culmination in the series
of works written by Handel for the English public, and we
may most fitly study the progress of the form, by noting the
successive influences under which the composer passed.   He
possessed, as we have already seen, and shall see often again,
the power of assimilating and really making his own all
that was best in the music of those with whom he came in
contact, and of those countries in which he took up his
abode ; and the two oratorios which he composed during
his sojourn in Rome in 1708-9 are at least not unfavourable
examples of the Italian style, as practised by the school of
composers whose works were discussed in the last chapter.
Like them, Handel had tried his hand on Latin words before
this, and his settings of certain psalms prove him to have
grasped the principles of the Italian masters of the time.   His
Laudate pueri for five voices begins with that device associated
with the name of Alessandro Scarlatti which consists in stating
the first phrase, and then dividing it from the complete
delivery of the melody by an instrumental introduction ; and
in the *Dixit Dominus* for five voices and orchestra, written
in Rome in 1707, the way in which the words 'Tu es sacerdos'
are employed as a kind of *canto fermo* against 'secundum
ordinem Melchisedech' is thoroughly Italian.   The choruses
which conclude each part of *La Resurrezione* are each of
them led off by the soprano, and answered by the rest of the
voices in obvious, simple harmonies, in the way which we
noticed in Durante's *Magnificat*[1].   Alike in this and the
next oratorio, *Il Trionfo del Tempo e del Disinganno*, the
score of *Agrippina*, an opera produced shortly before at
Venice with the greatest success, was laid under contribution.
For example, the famous bass air, 'O voi dell' Erebo' is
identical with 'Col raggio placido' from *Agrippina*, with the
single exception that the long scale-passages in the accompani-

[1] See p. 64.

ment are peculiar to the oratorio, where the whole scene in
which it occurs, between Lucifer and an angel, is conceived
with great dramatic power. In another number of the
work, it is not quite in accordance with modern ideas that
one and the same air, words and music alike, should have
been held to suit the character of Mary Magdalene in the
one work, and of Agrippina in the other.

The *Trionfo del Tempo* dispenses with the chorus altogether,
and its four characters take part in an ensemble. The chief
interest of the work is that it was twice revived in the later
part of Handel's career, when he made a great number of
alterations, such as opening the work with a chorus, shortening
the instrumental introductions to some of the airs, and im-
proving the workmanship in different ways. Here is an
example from an air accompanied by oboe, where the
monotonous figure of accompaniment in the first version is
changed into the spirited passage of the second.

It was in the course of a rehearsal of the overture to the *Trionfo del Tempo* that an amusing scene between Handel and Corelli took place; the overture contains some very florid writing for the violins, such as Handel may well have put in when he knew that so great a player as Corelli was to undertake the office of leader; and Corelli found the passages so difficult that Handel was obliged to snatch the violin from his hand to show how he wished them played; upon which Corelli gently said, 'Ma, caro Sassone, questa musica è nel stile francese, in ch'io non m'intendo.'

The oratorio developed but very little in Italy during the years of Handel's residence in England, and such a work as Leo's famous *Sant' Elena al Calvario* shows scarcely any advance upon the two works of Handel just mentioned. There is the usual bass air, with the accompaniment in unison with the voice almost throughout, as in 'O voi dell' Erebo' and many other of Handel's oratorio songs; there is a certain amount of choral work, and one of the choruses, 'Di quanta pena è frutto,' included in Vol. iii. of Rochlitz's collection, is a fine example of the more elaborate choral writing of the time.

Handel's first visit to England, which preceded the accession of his patron, the Elector of Hanover, to the throne as George I, was merely transitory, and connected with the production of his early operas; the Serenata for Queen Anne's birthday, 1713, and the *Utrecht Te Deum*, written in the same year, date from that prolongation of his Hanoverian leave of absence which cost him the favour of the court after the change of sovereign. These two works, but especially the latter, show that by this time the composer had absorbed the prevailing English style, as embodied in the *Te Deum* and *Jubilate* of Purcell; it was from Purcell's music that Handel learnt to use simple means to obtain massive effects; and while he adopted the Englishman's bluff style of expressing himself, he did much to smooth away the bold progressions that were typical of Purcell's individuality, and to unite his strength with an Italian sweetness. The years that passed between this time and the creation of his first English oratorio were taken up with the composition and production of various operas, with the reconciliation associated with the Water Music, the journey to Hanover in the King's suite, and the fulfilment of his duties as director of the music at Cannons, the gorgeous residence of the Duke of Chandos. It was here that the series of twelve Chandos Anthems were written, which, beside their intrinsic importance, have the additional interest of serving as studies for the branch of composition that was to be the greatest achievement of Handel's career. At Cannons, too, the first oratorio of the series, *Esther*, was written and performed in 1720, Handel receiving £1000 from the duke as his reward.

In considering the curious fact that twelve years elapsed before Handel had anything to do with an oratorio again, we must remember that those twelve years saw the foundation and collapse of the operatic scheme called the 'Royal Academy of Music,' the management of which, together with the production of a large number of operas for it, would have fully taken up the time of any ordinary person. The idea that oratorio could be made to pay does not seem to have entered into Handel's business-like head until after his first work, *Esther*, had been revived with action, scenery, and costume, by the children of the Chapel Royal at their master's house in Westminster, twice repeated at a tavern in the Strand, and lastly presented, without authority, at a charge of five shillings a head at 'the Great Room in Villar's Street, York Buildings,' on April 20, 1732. It was as a counterblast to this piece of sharp practice that Handel announced that *Esther* would be performed at the King's Theatre on May 2, 1732, by 'a great Number of the best Voices and Instruments.' The theatrical presentation of the work in regard to scenery and acting had been forbidden by the Bishop of London, so the advertisement announced that 'There will be no Acting on the Stage, but the House will be fitted up in a decent Manner, for the audience. The Musick to be disposed after the Manner of the Coronation Service. Tickets will be delivered at the usual prices[1].' There were several new numbers added to the score of the work, in order, no doubt, to present a greater attraction than the pirated performance could offer; in the air 'Watchful angels' we have a reference to *La Resurrezione*, and 'My heart is inditing' from the Coronation Anthem appears in this revised version. Whether from the private nature of the former performances, by which curiosity would have been stimulated, from the publicity given to the entertainment by the pirated performance, or from the circumstance that Handel's undertaking was largely patronized by royalty, the fact remains that there were more applicants for admission than the theatre would hold, and that six performances in all took place. The success of this experiment led Handel to compose, for the Lenten season of the next year, 1733, a far more important oratorio on the story of *Deborah*, by means of which he hoped to recoup himself for the losses on the operatic year, a period that marks the height of the dispute between the partisans of Handel and Bononcini. His plan of doubling the usual prices of admission had the reverse of the desired result, for only a very small audience was present. The Passion Music set to Brockes' words was largely used, as was. also the Coronation Anthem, but the famous eight-part chorus 'Immortal Lord of earth and skies,' in which, by the way, the start for sopranos alone recalls another habit of the Italian composers, is one of the finest of all Handel's creations.

In *Athaliah*, first performed at Oxford on the occasion of the 'Public Act,' in 1733, together with *Esther*, *Deborah* and *Acis and Galatea*, we find Handel using almost the form of

---

[1] Advertisements in the *Daily Journal* of April 19, 1732, and subsequent days.

the German chorale-cantata in the eight-part chorus 'The Mighty Power in Whom we trust'; he diversifies the form with an alto solo, and repeats the last section at the end of the work.

His next oratorio, *Saul*, was written in July and August, 1738, and brought out in January, 1739, after the pecuniary failure of his Italian operas, and his severe illness, an attack of paralysis from which he was cured by drinking the waters at Aix-la-Chapelle in 1737. The composer's ardent panegyrist, W. S. Rockstro, calls this work 'the first great oratorio in which he himself seems to have felt that he was doing all that could be done[1].'

A calmer judgement must admit that there is about *Saul* a unity which allows us, for the first time in speaking of the Handelian oratorio, to discuss its merits as a whole. This same unity distinguishes only some seven out of all the oratorios of Handel; in the rest, single numbers may be found which are as fine as anything in the best of the series, but between the solos and the choruses, or between the choruses themselves, there is little congruity, and it is impossible to feel that the whole has been created or conceived by a single effort of the imagination. It is for this reason, more than for any other, that the great majority of the series are never heard as a whole in their entirety even in England, in spite of the boundless admiration of the English public for Handel. In *Saul*, from the overture to the final lamentation, we follow the sequence of the story as a continuous whole; and while the two great choruses 'Envy, eldest born of hell!' and 'O fatal consequence of rage' are of the finest order of Handelian choruses, the lament of David 'In sweetest harmony' and the associated numbers are deeply expressive. The curious passage for organ solo in the overture is explained by the practice, first adopted in a revival of *Esther*, in 1736,

---

[1] W. S. Rockstro, *Life of Handel*, p. 215.

of the composer playing organ concertos between the parts
of his oratorios; it may have been from a feeling of the greater
unity of this oratorio that he wished to define the limits of
such additions to the entertainment. The introduction of
a 'carillon' into the processional music is another peculiarity
of the work.

The next of the oratorios, *Israel in Egypt*, written in
October, 1738, performed in April, 1739, brings us to the
climax of Handel's work, as well as to a problem in musical
history that is of surpassing interest. Not only is there the
same unity that was mentioned in regard to *Saul*, but the
general plan of allowing the chorus to be the protagonists
in the drama is as daring as it is successful. The great
eight-part numbers sweep the hearers onward with irresistible
force, and in the description of the plagues in the first part,
and in the jubilation of the second, there is a grandeur and
a kind of expressiveness that are nowhere paralleled in Handel's
works. There is good evidence to prove that the original
design was to set the 'Song of Moses' alone; for what now
is the second part of the work was undoubtedly written first,
in the space of eleven days. The first part occupied Handel
for an even shorter time, for the autograph is dated at the
beginning '15 Octobr.' and at the end 'Octobr. 20.' No good
reason has ever been alleged for the terrific hurry which these
dates imply, for the work was not brought out till six months
later, when it was found too severe for the audience, and at
the repetition of it it was announced as 'shortened and inter-
mixed with songs.' The rate of speed at which it was prepared, however, is the only cause that has been assigned for
the fact that Handel's most imposing work is a mere *pasticcio*,
consisting to a great extent of the work of other men. Out
of the thirty-nine numbers into which the oratorio is divided,
in no fewer than sixteen is the work of others employed;
that is not, of course, including Handel's own organ fugues,
which appear in 'They loathed to drink of the river' and 'He

smote all the firstborn.' A serenata by Stradella was laid
under contribution in 'He spake the word,' the Hailstone
chorus, 'But as for His people,' and 'And believed the
Lord.' In Stradella's work, the antiphonal effect which was
no doubt useful to Handel, is provided by the two orchestras
which are supposed to arrive on the scene of action in two
coaches, as representing the music provided by the two lovers
of the same lady. No good purpose could be served by
quoting long passages from each of the sources of Handel's
work; the extent to which use is made of the different pieces
varies considerably, from the employment of a single theme
or phrase which is subjected to different treatment, to the
quotation of an entire movement, such as the organ fugue
of J. C. Kerl, which appears, with only the minutest alterations possible, as the chorus 'Egypt was glad when they
departed.' The most instructive instance of Handel's dealings
with the work of others is in the chorus 'But as for His
people,' where, as already stated, the phrase 'He led them
forth like sheep' is taken from a solo in Stradella's serenata,
though not note for note. But in Stradella it remains in the
key of C throughout; Handel, after starting his chorus with
a strain that seems to point distinctly to the key of D,
although the signature is that of G, gives the Stradella phrase
first in G, and then in C, falling, as it were, from one sub-
dominant to another, in a way which gives the exact reflection
of the pastoral idea. In reversing the treatment of the repetitions of the phrase, so as to get back to the original key,
Handel adds the little group of five notes, which carries us

He   led   them forth

first from C to G, then from G to D, for the resumption of
the opening strain as it was at first.

In the second part the appropriations are all, with one
exception, from a single work. The exception is that the

'dotted' figure of accompaniment in the duet 'The Lord is a man of war' comes from a *Te Deum* by Francesco Antonio Urio, a work which had been used with some freedom in *Saul*, and was destined to further employment in the *Dettingen Te Deum*. In the vocal parts of this, and the greater part of eight other numbers of the second part of *Israel*, Handel made copious use of a *Magnificat* by a composer otherwise unknown, Don Dionigi Erba, whose work is preserved in two copies, one of them in the library of the Royal College of Music, the other, in Handel's own hand, and without mention of Erba as the author, in the Buckingham Palace collection of Handel's sketches and fragments. As in the first part, the quotations vary in the use made of them, from such literal transcriptions as 'Thou sentest forth' and 'The earth swallowed them,' to an identity of thematic material, or the literal quotation of a part of one of the movements. But the curious fact is that, in the quotations from Stradella and Erba alike, the sequence of the originals is preserved almost intact; in the *Magnificat*, the various sections adopted by Handel appear in the order in which he used them[1].

From time to time, since the discovery of these originals was made, various attempts have been made to discuss the problem they present in such a manner as to present Handel, in spite of all of them, as a man of the utmost artistic probity. It has been said, for example, that it was the common custom of the time to adopt the themes or the treatment of other

---

[1] For the convenience of Handel students, a series of ' Supplemente, enthaltend Quellen zu Händel's Werken' was issued by Dr. Chrysander for the subscribers to his edition of Handel's works. Erba's *Magnificat* is No. 1 of the set; No. 2, Urio's *Te Deum*, seems not to have been included in the series, but it had been issued much earlier, in 1871, as one of the Denkmäler der Tonkunst. No. 3 is Stradella's *Serenata*; No. 4 a volume of duets by Clari; and No. 5 Gottlieb Muffat's harpsichord pieces, 'Componimenti musicali.' Those who wish to pursue the subject further may be referred to the *Monthly Musical Record* for November and December, 1871, where the works quoted in *Israel* are fully discussed and analyzed by Professor Prout. Kerl's organ fugue may be seen in Hawkins's *Hist. of Music*, ch. cxxiv.

composers, with or without acknowledgement; and those who take this view point to the subject of the fugue 'They loathed to drink of the river' which, with only a very slight alteration, re-appears in the *Wohltemperirtes Clavier* of Bach, the 'Cum sanctis tuis' of Mozart's *Requiem*, and many other places. But in this case, and in others of a similar kind, it is only the subject which is taken; the treatment it receives is different in every instance, and there is no doubt that this and some other fugal themes, have usually been regarded as common property. But to follow every entry in a fugue, to copy every device with the most absolute fidelity, as Handel has done with Kerl's fugue in the chorus 'Egypt was glad,' is going a good many steps further; and when the case is not single, or even rare, we are driven to some other means of defending Handel, more especially when no other of the great, or even of the little composers, of that or any other time, has been found out in anything like the same extent of appropriation. Besides, if it was the general custom, we may well ask how it was that Bononcini was driven from London in ·disgrace owing to the detection of his fraud in passing off Lotti's madrigal, 'In una siepe ombrosa,' as his own?

Another defence against the most flagrant part of the charge, and, be it noted, against that alone, is that the 'Rd. Sigr. Erba,' whose name appears upon the Royal College copy of the *Magnificat*, was not the composer, but only the possessor, of the ·work[1], and that Handel was himself the author of it, and had therefore every right to adapt his own creation as he pleased to a new libretto. But Dr. Chrysander, in his preface to the edition of the work, makes it clear that this theory will not hold water; and even if it did, we are left with an overwhelming amount of evidence of Handel's fairly constant practice in such matters. The theory will not cover the allegations concerning Urio, Stradella, and Kerl, to take only the names of those quoted by Handel in *Israel*.

[1] Rockstro, *Life of Handel*, ch. xxvii.

Another argument is that in the obscurity of such composers as Erba and Urio, we have a proof that they could not have achieved such great things as the choruses in *Israel* and the other works with which they are credited.   If, say the supporters of the theory, there were men upon the earth at that time who could create music of this splendour, why not displace Handel from his pedestal, and reverence instead a small group of composers hitherto regarded as nobodies?   But surely this is pressing the accusation further than it will bear; a close examination of the whole of the sources only reveals rarely a case of close and literal transcription, such as that of Kerl's fugue, and some of the Erba numbers; in the great majority, some such process as was described in the case of 'But as for His people' has taken place, and even in numbers where all the thematic material must be assigned to other hands, its treatment shows a masterly skill that is Handel's own. The duet 'The Lord is a man of war' is an example of two quotations so happily welded together that they seem always to have belonged to one another; yet the figure of accompaniment comes, as before stated, from Urio's *Te Deum*, the voice parts from Erba.   Still, when we have made every excuse that the circumstances will allow, it is impossible to acquit Handel altogether of the practice of adopting for his own use materials from the works of other composers.   In the vast majority of the instances, there can be no suggestion of unconscious plagiarism; the appropriations were intentional in practically all cases, for the adoption of the parts quoted is literal, as far as they go.

While it is not true that there was any recognized community of musical ideas which would completely excuse Handel's proceedings, the men of his time were very far from having established any kind of moral copyright in their inventions, and granted the identity of a certain theme, Handel's instincts would naturally lead him to treat it according to the patterns of those Italian composers who had written the kind of music

in which he himself excelled.   One other plea that has never,
so far as we know, been set up in his defence, is that it is
at least possible that his illness of 1737, while it had not
permanently affected his mental well-being in the least, may
have caused him to forget the source of some of the MSS.
in his possession, and he may have mistaken the unnamed
copy of Erba's *Magnificat* for a work of his own, when he
wanted materials for *Israel*.   It is true that, in order to
establish this theory, we shall be obliged to modify Rockstro's
conclusions as to the date of the copy, and to ascribe it, as
earlier critics did, to a date anterior to his visit to Aix-la-
Chapelle.

Many special difficulties beset the path of the modern writer
who attempts to express a carefully-weighed opinion as to
The Messiah, the crowning achievement of Handel's career,
a work upon which a space of only twenty-four days was
spent by the composer, since the evidence of the autograph
score in the Buckingham Palace collection gives August 22,
1741, as the day of commencement, and September 14 as the
date at which the 'filling-up' of the orchestration was completed.   It cannot be supposed, however, that a work of this
importance was actually conceived as well as written down
in so short a time; it is more probable that the scheme was
prepared, and that some at least of the ideas were matured,
before the moment at which the process of writing was begun.
But the rapidity of committal to paper is not one of the
difficulties alluded to.   Since the day when, in 1789, Mozart
prepared parts for wind instruments to replace the organ part
for a performance at Vienna in a room where no organ existed,
various well-meaning persons have taken upon themselves to
add to the accompaniments, and the public at large, with the
directors of the choral societies at their head, have agreed to
accept all the accretions as part of Handel's original plan,
and this in spite of the indubitable fact that, to name but
one instance, the trombone parts of a person named Smithies

fit so ill with the directions of Handel's score, and with the additions of others, that a cacophony of almost incredible kind would be heard and realized by every musical ear, were it not that the sound produced by our large choruses is enough to drown any detail of orchestration. This practice of organizing 'monster' performances of Handel's works, culminating in the triennial Handel Festivals at the Crystal Palace, has done at least as much harm as good to the appreciation of the master by the more intelligent class of Englishmen; the disproportion between the voices and the accompaniment, the ponderous style of phrasing which is absolutely necessary when so great a number of singers is employed, and the violent contrasts of tone in which the public delights, have given the majority of hearers quite a wrong idea of Handel, and, while on the one hand the fashion has had the result of raising him into a kind of national fetish with the ignorant public, on the other his reputation has suffered with those who are obliged to hear, or to take part in, *The Messiah* at frequent intervals, to the exclusion of almost every other work of Handel's. They have naturally lost the power of judging it, and from mere weariness at its constant repetition at the provincial festivals, and elsewhere, have formed the habit of speaking as if it were less than superlatively fine. A whole host of evil traditions has been allowed to remain in ordinary usage, as a natural consequence of the pecuniary advantages offered by the familiarity of the work and the consequent rarity of anything like a general rehearsal of it. One of the earliest of these traditions, which seems to have arisen soon after Handel's death, is that of allowing the two stanzas of 'He shall feed His flock' to be sung, the first by a contralto, the second by a soprano; it is quite true that Handel altered in many points the disposition of his solos, 'Every valley' and 'Comfort ye' being available for either tenor or soprano, 'But who may abide' for either alto or bass, and so forth; but to combine the two versions of 'He shall feed His flock'

in the way that is almost universal in modern times is to
present a distortion of Handel's idea not less serious than it
would be for the first part of 'But who may abide' to be
sung by a contralto who should be supplanted by a bass at
the words 'For He is like a refiner's fire.' While the composer's directions as to taking the first bars of 'Glory to God'
softly are persistently disregarded, the practice obtains of
beginning 'For unto us a child is born' in a whisper in order
to emphasize the outburst at 'Wonderful'; on a par with
this is the allotment of the two little choruses, 'Since by
man came death' and 'For as in Adam all die,' to a solo
quartet[1]. But all these untoward circumstances, many of
which after all have had the result of bringing Handel's masterpiece home to the English public as to no other in the world,
must not blind those who regret them to the manifold beauties
of the work itself. It is impossible to imagine anything more
sublime than the scheme of the work, with its gradual un-
folding of the plan of redemption, from the prophecies,
becoming more and more definite as the fact of the Nativity
is approached, to the ineffable expressiveness of the so-called
'Passion music,' the words of which are wholly taken from

[1] It is only right to record the excellent work done in recent years in the way of
restoring Handel's original creation in public performance; the first attempt to
get rid of the evil traditions was at the Birmingham Festival of 1885, at which, in
spite of the retention of both Mozart's and Robert Franz's additional accompaniments, the other points noted above were restored by Dr. Richter. The change was
not received with universal approval, for the great public does not really care much
about Handel's intentions, but prefers what it has always been accustomed to.
As a practical result of an article by Professor Prout in the *Monthly Musical Record*
for April, 1894, a performance was given at King's College, Cambridge, in June of
that year, under Dr. A. H. Mann, when advantage was taken of the discovery
of wind parts at the Foundling Hospital, for the benefit of which institution
Handel directed a performance of the work every year in the chapel from 1750 to
1758. A further cleansing of the score was undertaken by Sir Frederick Bridge,
who has directed several performances by the Royal Choral Society in which
Handel's accompaniments are left intact, even Mozart's additions being dispensed
with. His minute investigation of the whole matter was made public in his
Gresham Lectures of February, 1899. Sir W. G. Cusins's *Handel's Messiah*
(Augener and Co., 1874) was one of the first attempts to set the true state of
the case before the public.

the Old Testament, and thence to the salvation of mankind through the efficacy of the great Sacrifice. It is difficult to credit Mr. Charles Jennens, the conceited Leicestershire squire whose efforts at Shakespearean criticism made him the laughing-stock of his literary contemporaries [1], with a conception of so grand an order, and Handel's admirers would fain gather a shred of evidence that the composer had a hand in it; but unfortunately, there is at present no reason to believe that any one but Jennens had anything to do with the words of the *The Messiah*. The librettist has long enjoyed the unique position of the solo objector to the way in which Handel set his words. In a letter quoted by Rockstro [2] and by many others Jennens remarks, 'He has made a fine entertainment of it, though not near so good as he might and ought to have done. I have with great difficulty made him correct some of the grossest faults in the composition, but he retained his Overture obstinately, in which there are some passages far unworthy of Handel, but much more unworthy of *The Messiah*.' The rest of mankind has considered, and considered rightly, that *The Messiah* is the supreme monument to Handel's genius, even if it be not, what many have claimed for it, the most splendid achievement of the musical art up to its own day. The choruses are far less complicated than those of *Israel in Egypt*, and with all their grand simplicity they are deeply expressive. The airs, in spite of the possibility of assigning each to one of the conventional classes of aria forms with which we shall have to deal more fully in a later chapter, speak to the heart of every hearer, and, in regard to their melodic value, they reach a point of spontaneity, which Handel himself never reached again, at least throughout a whole work. Separate songs in the earlier operas, or in the later oratorios, may vie with any one number from *The Messiah*, but in these other works there is nearly

[1] *Dict. of National Biography*, art. Jennens.
[2] *Life of Handel*, p. 236.

always something laboured, dull, or crudely expressed; in *The Messiah* alone is every, or almost every, number, worthy of being for ever associated with the words to which it is set. As a minor point, the originality of the work has never been impugned to any serious extent; it is true that the 'Pastoral Symphony' is based upon a tune played at Christmas time by the *pifferari* of Naples, but this is acknowledged in the autograph, by the abbreviation 'pifa' at the beginning of the number; besides, the adaptation of a theme from a traditional source has never been considered as constituting a misdemeanour. 'And with His stripes' is built upon nearly the same often-used subject as 'They loathed to drink' in *Israel*, but, as was there remarked, it has been reckoned as common property for so long that there is no proving who was the original thief. Handel's own chamber duets are laid under contribution in several of the numbers, notably 'All we like sheep' and 'For unto us,' but this cannot be alleged as a case at all parallel to the wholesale adaptations spoken of before.

Much has been said in the preceding volume of this series as to the injurious influence of public taste upon the composers before Handel's day; it is only fair that it should be recorded to the credit of the English public of his time that they were mainly responsible for the welcome change in Handel's sphere of work from the time of the success of *The Messiah* through the rest of his life. It is easy for us in the present day to realize the inferiority of Handel's operas to his oratorios, for we are not blinded by the glamour of their stage presentment, as his contemporaries were; whatever may have been the cause, the fact is beyond dispute that the patrons of music were tired of opera, and that they supported the oratorios with a surprising amount of zeal. Without this change of fashion, we may be certain that Handel would not have given up opera for oratorio, since it was entirely foreign to his nature to work on without encouragement at compositions which had no chance in their own day of finding popularity. Throughout his life he wrote what the public wanted him to write, and it is a matter of congratulation, and may well excuse a little national pride, that the artificial society of Horace Walpole's day should have given so warm a welcome as it did to works of such serious import as the Handelian oratorios, which succeeded the great masterpiece often designated simply as 'The Sacred Oratorio.'

Samson, the next oratorio of the series, was written immediately after the completion of *The Messiah*, the work being practically completed by October, 1741, although the final bravura air 'Let the bright Seraphim' was not added to the score until a year later, the work being brought out in February, 1743. The long space that elapsed between the virtual completion of the whole, and its first performance, is partly accounted for by the success of Handel's visit to Dublin, and a consequent uncertainty as to whether the new work should not be produced there instead of in London. The greater part of *Samson* reaches a high level both as regards the fitness of the music to the arrangement from Milton's *Samson Agonistes*, and in respect of unity, although here and there are lapses into something almost childish, like the echo effects in 'My faith and truth, O Samson, prove,' and the opposition of the names of Jehovah and Dagon in the famous chorus 'Fixed in His everlasting seat.' Samson's 'Total eclipse!' the splendid air 'Honour and Arms,' the whole part of Manoah, and the beautiful chorus 'Then round about the starry throne' are enough to entitle it to a place among the few Handelian oratorios that are suitable for public performance at the present day. Two fairly prominent instances of Handel's indifference to the source of his ideas must be mentioned in connexion with this work; the minuet in the overture is adapted, with some very slight alterations, from a minuet in Reinhard Keiser's *Claudius*; and in the chorus 'O first-created beam,' there is, at the words 'To

Thy dark servant light afford,' a quotation from Legrenzi's motet 'Intret in conspectu tuo[1].'

Of *Joseph*, the composition of which occupied Handel during August and September, 1743, and in which the title part was adapted successively to a contralto, lower alto, and mezzo-soprano voice, there is not much to be said; the victory of Dettingen was the occasion of the composition of the *Dettingen Te Deum* and the *Dettingen Anthem*, and from the latter work the final chorus of *Joseph* was taken.

Belshazzar contains some interesting numbers, though it is perhaps too unequal to be revived under present conditions. The bass *aria all' unisono* for Gobbias, 'Behold the monstrous human beast,' is a good example of its class, and the six-part choir has at least two fine opportunities, in 'Recall, O King,' and 'By slow degrees'; the naïve realism of the latter at the point 'precipitates the thunder down' must not blind us to its vigour and power. The treatment of the moment at which the handwriting appears upon the wall is certainly dramatic, though the arrival of the magicians, in an 'Allegro Postillions,' can hardly fail to provoke a smile.

Next come two works which, although they are not founded upon sacred subjects, belong to the class of oratorios rather than to any other branch of Handel's compositions. They are *Semele* and *Hercules*, the former of which was rather ambiguously described by Mainwaring, in his life of Handel, as 'an English Opera, but called an Oratorio, and performed as such at Covent Garden.' It was written in June, 1743, and brought out in February, 1744; with the possible exception of *Acis and Galatea*, few of the composer's larger works have a greater charm, a higher kind of unity, or a better right to be heard as a whole. The dramatic song for Juno, 'Awake, Saturnia,' offers a splendid opportunity to a mezzo-soprano, and every tenor loves 'Where'er you

---

[1] Chrysander, *Händel*, i. p. 179.

walk'; Semele's 'O Sleep' has a gentle suavity all its own, and the quartet 'Why dost thou thus untimely grieve?' is an interesting specimen of Handel's treatment of the solo voice in concerted music.

Hercules, written July and August, 1744, and produced at the King's Theatre, January, 1745, is in a more tragic vein than *Semele,* but the style of both works would be enough to show that they were not intended for real dramatic presentment; the choral treatment is not different from that which distinguishes the sacred oratorios, and indeed, in many of these, though the personages dealt with are among those whose names are mentioned in the Bible, their stories are treated without any very great degree of reverence, and the interpolated love-scenes which occur in some of the later works point unmistakably to the fact that Handel saw no reason why a certain amount of mental relaxation should not be allowed his audience.

The *Occasional Oratorio* (1746) was no doubt suggested by the quelling of the Jacobite Rebellion of the previous year; its third part is a verbal and literal repetition of many of the choruses in *Israel,* and of the rest, the Hallelujah which ends part 2 is the most important number; a good many numbers are borrowed from *Athaliah.*

July and August of this year, 1746, were occupied with *Judas Maccabaeus,* the oratorio which comes nearer than any other to the degree of public estimation bestowed on *The Messiah* and *Israel in Egypt.* The patronage of the Jews, which replenished Handel's funds after the blow of his second bankruptcy in the previous year, suggested for the next few librettos that Dr. Morell wrote for him the choice of Jewish stories, whether Biblical or otherwise. Not only has the whole plan the unity which, as we have seen, is a comparatively rare quality in the Handelian oratorios, but almost throughout there is much of the inspiration that characterizes the two great works to which Handel's position is mainly due. The choral numbers have some of the importance of those in *Israel*, while the solo parts are fairly dramatic and contain many of Handel's best and most popular numbers, such as 'Arm, arm, ye brave,' 'Sound an alarm,' and 'Father of Heaven'; the trio and chorus 'See the conquering hero comes' was incorporated into *Judas Maccabaeus* after its successful appearance in *Joshua*.

In *Alexander Balus*, written in the summer of 1747, there is a touch of oriental colouring in the introduction for two oboes and bassoon, before the chorus of Asiates; Cleopatra's air 'Convey me to some peaceful gloom' is graceful and effective, but as a whole the work is not among the permanent successes of Handel's creation.

In *Joshua* (July and August, 1747) there is an even greater number of the usual defects that pertain to a second effort in the same direction as a former success. The unity that distinguished *Judas* is sacrificed for the sake of bringing in the love-scenes of Othniel and Achsah, and matters are not much improved by the recurrent dialogues between Joshua and the Jewish host; still, such a chorus as 'Glory to God,' and such solos as 'Shall I in Mamre's fertile plain' and 'Oh, had I Jubal's lyre' should be enough to preserve it from neglect.

Solomon, written in May and June, 1748, and performed in the following year, is remarkable for the elaboration of its choral treatment, the double choir being generally accompanied on two organs; beside the lovely 'Nightingale' chorus, and the joyful 'Your harps and cymbals sound,' there are some stately choruses in five parts; and if the general design be not as purely sacred as in some of the other oratorios, certain parts of the work, as the scene of the judgement, and the air 'What though I trace' must take high rank.

Susanna, dated a little later than *Solomon*, and brought out in the lenten season of 1749, contains, in the music for Susanna herself, certain things which are as fine as any single songs of Handel; the prayer 'Bending from Thy throne of glory' has admirable sincerity and melodic flow; and 'If guiltless blood' has something which can only be called individuality. In this work Handel seems to have striven after characterization, a quality which is most rare with him and the majority of his contemporaries; the trio which is the most prominent example of this, is extremely interesting, although it must always have been a matter of difficulty to listen to it with becoming gravity, so oddly are the two elders, a languishing tenor and a bass of the most burly and defiant kind, contrasted with each other, and with Susanna's music.

By the next Lent, when *Theodora* was brought out, the popularity of the oratorios seems to have considerably abated, since the failure of the work can hardly be ascribed to any inferiority to *Susanna* or many others of the series. In Handel's own words, 'There was room enough to dance there, when that was performed'; and it was in allusion to one of the ill-attended representations of this work that Lord Chesterfield remarked that he 'thought it best to retire from the Oratorio, lest he should disturb the King in his privacy.' It is true that the story is not carried on with any great dramatic effect, but there are at least the average number of songs and single numbers which must have seemed quite as beautiful in their own day as they do now. 'Angels ever bright and fair,' for Theodora, Irene's 'Lord to Thee each night and day,' and Didimus's 'Sweet rose and lily' have remained among the most favourite strains of Handel's music in existence; and in the composer's own estimation, the chorus 'He saw the lovely youth' was to be preferred to the 'Hallelujah' chorus. He may have been right in saying that 'the Jews would not come to it, as they did to *Judas Maccabaeus*, because it was a Christian story; and the ladies would not come to it, because it was a virtuous one.' It is probably a mere coincidence, rather than a cause of the failure of the work, that even in the favourite songs from *Theodora* there should be observed a kind of inconsequence in the melodic invention which is not without parallel in Handel's other works, but which is seldom more evident than here. In Theodora's first song, the slow crotchets on which she sings the word 'Angels' have nothing to do with the more rapid phrase to 'ever bright and fair,' and at every recurrence of the theme as a whole, it falls into two sections which have no integral connexion with one another. The continuation of a subject from the germ contained in its opening notes was never a very strong point with Handel, and in 'Sweet rose and lily' we have an opportunity of comparing his methods in this respect with those of his quondam rival, Bononcini, who hit upon nearly the same melodic idea in his best-known song, 'Per la Gloria[1].'

It will strike every reader that the melodic germ of the subject, which is the figure in the second bar of each, is left by Handel quite undeveloped, while Bononcini carries it on in a delightful addition of two bars, and alludes to it again in the last bar but one, giving the whole strain a more obviously flowing character.

The composition of *Jephtha*, the last of the oratorios, was interrupted by an illness, which has been assumed to be a return of Handel's former complaint, and for which he had recourse to the waters of Cheltenham. At the same time,

[1] It is unnecessary to point out that the key and time-values in Bononcini's song have been changed in order to facilitate comparison.

the first symptoms of his approaching blindness were perceived, and the autograph score, which bears dates from January to August, 1751, shows very clearly that after his return from Cheltenham he lost some of his old certainty of intention, and fell into the habit of altering his ideas, as in the case of 'Waft her, angels.' The recitative 'Deeper and deeper still,' which is generally associated with that air, not only comes in the preceding part or act of the work, being separated from it by the chorus 'How dark, O Lord, are Thy decrees,' with its naïf treatment of the closing sentiment 'Whatever is, is right'; but the recitative was written before the visit to Cheltenham, the air afterwards. Beside the chorus mentioned there are several important choruses, such as 'No more to Ammon's lord and king,' and 'When His loud voice in thunder spoke'; and if the solo-songs are not of exceptional value apart from Jephtha's well-known air, the concerted numbers, a quartet 'Oh, spare your daughter,' a duet and quintet 'All that is in Hamor mine,' are in advance of the usual style of ensemble music. The characters are well individualized, yet without incongruity, and the general texture of the concerted writing is smooth and uniform. The quintet was only added to the score in 1757, after Handel's blindness had proved to be entirely incurable. He had been couched for cataract in May, 1752, by William Branfield, and for a time it was hoped that his sight would be spared, but it was only a temporary amendment. A passage in the amusing work of the quack oculist, the Chevalier J. Taylor [1], throws some light upon Handel's condition, although the exact period of the operation is not to be discovered :—

'I have seen a vast variety of singular animals, such as dromedaries, camels, &c., and particularly at *Leipsick*, where a celebrated master of music, who had already arrived to his 88th year, received his sight by my hands; it is with this very man that the famous Handel was first educated, and with whom

[1] *History of Travels and Adventures,* 1761, vol. i. p 25.

I once thought to have had the same success, having all circumstances in his favour, motions of the pupil, light, &c., but
upon drawing the curtain, we found the bottom defective, from
a paralytic disorder.'

The statement often made on rather slight authority, that the
same man Taylor operated upon the two most illustrious
musicians of their time, seems to rest on this passage for its
documentary proof.   Bach died at the age of 65, and was never
Handel's teacher; still, Taylor was in Prussia and Saxony in
1747 and 1748, just at the time when Bach's sight was affected,
and there is no one else whom the reference will fit among the
musicians resident at Leipzig at that time.   The closing years
of Handel's life were taken up, as far as his artistic achievements went, with remodelling certain existing works; he added
to *Judas Maccabaeus* and to *Jephtha*, and in 1757 prepared his
early Italian oratorio for a second revival in London, under
the English title of *The Triumph of Time and Truth*.   The
last work of his life was to conduct a performance of *The
Messiah* on April 6, 1759, after which he was obliged to keep
his bed.   He died on April 14[1] and was buried in Westminster
Abbey on the 20th of the same month.

There is nothing more curious than the fact of Handel's
retaining for so long a time a virtual monopoly of oratorio
writing at a period when this form of entertainment was at
the height of its vogue.   Beyond De Fesch's *Judith* (1733)
and *Joseph* (1745), Bononcini's *Giosuè*, and Arne's first essay
in oratorio, *Abel* (1755), there is no trace of any work of importance being produced during the career of Handel; and
it is needless to say that none of these is of any historical
value.

[1] For a summary of the discussion as to the date, see Rockstro's *Life of Handel*,
pp. 362-4.

CHAPTER VI

THE KEYED INSTRUMENTS

I. The Organ.

THE importance of the keyed instruments in relation to the other sound-producing agents, whether instrumental or vocal, was very great in all branches of the art, though the conditions were so different from those of the present day. The organ, both in its constitution and its functions, was more closely akin to its modern counterpart than any of the rest. Its position in the world of sacred music—and for secular it was very seldom employed—had been fixed long before the period under consideration, and has changed but comparatively little since. The time was one of the finest in regard to organ manufacture, and the balance of the various tone-qualities, like the timbre of each, was, generally speaking, as fully understood then as it is now. Then, as now, the essential feature of pure organ-playing was the association or contrast of two or three qualities of tone, by means of the various manuals or 'sets of keys' as they were more commonly called. The larger organs always had more than one key-board, and the largest number that were in practical use seems to have been four, exclusive of the pedal-board. The 'Hauptwerk' and 'Oberwerk' of the German organs of Bach's time seem to have corresponded more or less closely with our 'Great,' and to have contained the stops most usually employed when special effects were not wanted; the 'Brustwerk' had a good deal in common with the English 'Swell,' although the swell-box itself did not come into vogue until much later in Germany.

The ' Rückpositiv' is the exact equivalent of the English
' choir' or ' chair' organ, consisting of a group of pipes placed
at the player's back, often serving as a screen between him and
the congregation below him. A special effect of some of the
German organs was the so-called ' echo organ' containing
stops which reduplicated the whole, or sometimes only the
upper portion, of certain stops on the main organ, and, being
enclosed in a box by themselves, produced the effect of being
heard from a distance. It is curious to see how long it took
the organ-builders of the continent to add the apparently
simple contrivance of shutters, by which the English maker,
Abraham Jordan, about 1720, enabled the player to increase
the tone of these ' echo stops,' and so made the first ' swell.'
Handel was struck by its ingenuity and practical advantages,
and sent a description of it, written by Snetzler, to a ' particular
friend at Berlin, who wished to introduce it there[1].' Snetzler
assured Burney that if the invention had gone no further than
Berlin, he would at least find it there; but Burney repeatedly
tells us that he found no trace of it either there or anywhere
else on the continent, except in the Michaelskirche at Hamburg,
where a small and ineffectual swell is noticed; and as he gives
the particulars of many continental organs, we are bound to
accept his statement as correct. The mechanical part of the
organs of the first half of the eighteenth century was far from
perfect; Burney notices the noisy keys of the principal organs
in Paris, and the interesting report on the organ of the Univer-
sitätskirche in Leipzig, drawn up by Bach himself, may be
found in Spitta's *Life*, vol. ii. p. 288 ff. (English translation).
The disposition of the stops in classes seems to have been
more or less the same in France as elsewhere, for the organ
of St. Roch, built about 1750, had four manuals, of which ' the
great and choir communicate by a spring; the third row of
keys is for the reed stops, and the upper for the echoes[2].' The

[1] Burney, *Present State of Music in Germany*, ii. 102.
[2] *Present State of Music in France and Italy*, p. 36.

'spring of communication' between one of the manuals and another, or, as we should say, 'coupler,' is noted as if it were a new invention; the three sets of keys in St. Michael's church at Vienna could be played all together by this means[1]. Even in 1772, when Burney made his tour in Germany, the organ in Frankfort cathedral had so heavy a touch that it required the weight of the whole hand, and he notices the same defect in the Alte Kerke at Amsterdam. On this, notwithstanding, Pothoff, the organist, played 'as if it were a common harpsichord' and 'very full, seldom in less than five parts, with the manuals and pedals[2].' In another place, he compares the light touch of some recently-built English organs with those of the average continental specimens he examined; and in his Italian tour, he notices that 'the organ stile seems to be better preserved throughout Italy than it is with us; as the harpsichord is not sufficiently cultivated to encroach upon that instrument[3].' The difference of touch may have had something to do with the difference in styles, of which we receive a very definite idea if we compare any of Handel's organ concertos with some of the most characteristic of Bach's solos, such as the great fantasia in G, where the rapid passages of the opening and closing movements, and the massive grandeur of the middle one, suggest a far heavier touch than is implied in Handel's passages; these do not differ very widely from harpsichord passages, their smoothness and the exact observance of the cessation of each note which they demand, are totally unlike the bewildering rush of Bach's movement labelled 'très vitement,' in which a certain vigorous roughness is required, and which undoubtedly loses something if played with too much refinement of detail on a modern organ with a very light touch. It was the tendency of the age to discount massive contrapuntal movements in favour of the superficial

---

[1] Burney, *Present State of Music in Germany*, i. 272.
[2] Ibid. i. 74; ii. 286.
[3] Burney, *Present State of Music in France and Italy*, p. 375.

brilliance and thinness of effect which was noticed in connexion with the church music of Italy, and it is all the more
curious to read Burney's statement as to the pure organ style
being kept longer in Italy than in England. There is an
abundance of testimony concerning Bach's style of playing
the organ; his biographer, Forkel, tells us that he used combinations of stops that were so uncommon that the organ-
builders and organists of the time were frightened when they
saw him use them[1].' And again he describes how, when asked
to play apart from any service of the church, he would choose
a subject and execute it in all the various forms of organ-
composition; so that it remained the groundwork of his performance, even if he played without intermission for two hours
or more. First he used it for a prelude and fugue with all
the stops; then in a trio or quartet, then in a chorale, with
the melody intermingled with the principal subject; finally
another fugue with all the stops[2].' A little further on he says
that Bach began upon a new organ by trying all the stops
at once, ' that he might know whether the organ had good
lungs.' Quantz, in his famous treatise, *Versuch einer
Anweisung die Flöte traversière zu spielen*[3], refers to Bach
as having brought the art of organ-playing to perfection, and
looks forward with apprehension to the time when his good
traditions will be forgotten, and when the essential difference
in style required by the organ and clavicymbel respectively
shall have disappeared. Bach's pupil, J. P. Kirnberger, who
in his *Wahre Grundsätze zum Gebrauch der Harmonie*
devotes a large portion of his space to a minute analysis of the
B minor fugue at the end of the first part of the *Wohltemperirtes Clavier*, refers to his master as ' the greatest harmonist
of all times,' and in a footnote supports his opinion by reference
to the ' astonishingly skilful way in which Bach would improvise

[1] Forkel, *Life of Bach* (Eng. transl.), p. 33.
[2] Ibid. p. 36.
[3] XVII. vi. 18.

(*fantasiren*) in many parts.   He also animadverts on a foolish
criticism in the *Jenaische Zeitung* in which a famous description of Bach as an organist and a conductor in Gesner's
Quintilian is said to be equally appropriate to Vogler and
Bach.   This passage, although not confined to Bach's organ-
playing, may be quoted in this place, as it gives us a vivid and
most precious picture of the man :—

'All these, my Fabius' (Quintilian is speaking of the capacity
possessed by man of comprehending and doing several things
at once, adducing as an example a player on the lyre, who can
utter at the same time words and notes, play on his instrument
and keep time with his foot), 'you would deem very trivial
could you but rise from the dead and see Bach (whom I mention
because not long ago he was my colleague in the Thomasschule
at Leipzig) how, with both hands, and using all his fingers, he
plays either on our harpsichord, which embraces many lyres in
one, or on that instrument of instruments the organ, of which
the innumerable pipes are fed by bellows, how, with hands
going one way and hurrying feet the other, he draws forth whole
troops, so to speak, of the most diverse yet mutually agreeing
sounds : him, I say, could you only see him, how he achieves
what a number of lyre-players and six hundred flute-players
could never achieve, not as one who may sing to the lyre and
so perform his part, but by presiding over thirty or forty
musicians all at once, recalling one to time and accent by a nod,
another by a stamp of the foot, a third by a menacing finger,
giving to each performer his note, now at the top,
now at the bottom, now in the middle of the scale, this
one man, standing alone in the midst of the loud sounds,
and though his individual task is the hardest of all, can discern
at every moment if anything is wrong, and can keep all the
musicians in order, restore any waverer to certainty and
prevent him from going astray, with the rhythm in his every
limb, seizing on every harmony with his acute ear, as it were,
and singing every part within the narrow compass of his own
voice.   I am a great admirer of antiquity, but I hold that this
Bach of mine, and any one who may be like him, contains
within himself many Orpheuses and twenty Arions[1].'

[1] Gesner, *In Marcum Fabium Quinctilianum*, i. 12, 3 (p. 61 of his commentary).
The original Latin is given, with a translation into English, in Sedley Taylor's
Life of Bach, Cambridge, 1897 ; another translation, from the German, is in
Spitta's *Life of Bach* (Eng. transl.) ii. p. 259.   In the above rendering, parts
of both versions have been taken.

It is interesting to contrast with this Burney's remarks on Bach's organ-playing, as compared with Handel's; while admitting that the two were the 'most renowned in the present century,' he refers to the 'grandeur, science, and perfection' of Handel's playing, and gives, on the authority of Marpurg's treatise, *Abhandlung von der Fuge*, an extract in which Bach 'is said to be many musicians in one; profound in science, fertile in fancy, and in taste easy and natural.' He adds a note to these last words, as follows :—

'To this part of the encomium many are unwilling to assent; as this truly great man seems by his works for the organ, of which I am in possession of the chief part, to have been constantly in search of what was new and difficult, without the least attention to nature and facility. He was so fond of full harmony that, besides a constant and active use of the pedals, he is said to have put down such keys by a stick in his mouth, as neither hands nor feet could reach. He died at Leipsic, 1754 (*sic.*)[1].'

It is amply clear from this and many other passages in which the two great organists were compared, that Handel's special characteristic was 'easy and natural' playing, at least in its effect upon his hearers. Burney[2] quotes from Reichardt's *Musikalisches Kunstmagazin* an opinion that while no composer of any nation exhausted every possibility of harmony so much as Bach, yet 'if he had been possessed of the simplicity, clearness, and feeling of Handel, he would have been a greater man.' The well-known passage in Hawkins' *History* about Handel's playing[3], goes to support this, although indirectly, because the fact that 'A fine and delicate touch, a volant finger, and a ready delivery of passages the most difficult, are the praise of inferior artists,' and 'were not noticed in Handel,' may be held to show that it was a commonplace of criticism to point out that Handel possessed these in a marked degree; the rest

---

[1] Burney, *History of Music*, iv. 593
[2] Ibid. iv. 595.
[3] Hawkins, *History of Music* (ed. 1853), ii. 912.

of the quotation refers to 'his amazing command of the instrument, the fullness of his harmony, the grandeur and dignity of his style, the copiousness of his imagination, and the fertility of his invention.' It is a valuable record that 'when he gave a concerto, his method in general was to introduce it with a voluntary (i.e. an extempore movement) on the diapasons, which stole on the ear in a slow and solemn progression; the harmony close wrought, and as full as could possibly be expressed; the passages concatenated with stupendous art, the whole at the same time being perfectly intelligible, and carrying the appearance of great simplicity. This kind of prelude was succeeded by the concerto itself, which he executed with a degree of spirit and firmness that no one ever pretended to equal.'

Another famous comparison between Bach and Handel as organists occurs in Mattheson's *Critica Musica*, but its value is so clearly proved by Spitta to be of the slightest, that it may be disregarded here[1]; and Spitta's own summary of the case is well worth quoting. After pointing out that Bach 'started from the organ, and remained faithful to it all his life,' and that organ music 'was to him the basis of all creation, the vivifying soul of every form he wrought out,' while Handel's attention had been turned in various other directions, he says:—

'The accounts handed down to us are equally clear, and leave no doubt in our minds that Handel's organ-playing was not, properly speaking, characterized by style in the highest sense— was not that which is, as it were, conceived and born of the nature of the instrument. It was more touching and graceful than Bach's; but the proper function of the organ is neither to touch nor to flatter the ear. Handel adapted to the organ ideas drawn from the stores of his vast musical wealth, which included all the art of his time, just as he did to any other instrument. In this way he evolved an exoteric meaning, intelligible to all, and hence the popular effect. To him the

---

[1] Mattheson, *Critica Musica*, i. p. 326; Spitta, *Life of Bach* (Eng. transl.), ii. 25 ff.

organ was an instrument for the concert-room, not for the church. It corresponds to this conception that we have no compositions by Handel for the organ alone, while it was precisely by these that Bach's fame was to a great extent kept up till this century.'

M. A. Pirro, in his interesting monograph, *L'Orgue de Jean-Sébastien Bach* (Paris, 1895), has collected all that is to be found concerning Bach's manner of registering in connexion with the organ, and gives, but unfortunately without quoting his authorities, several details of his manner of 'registering,' such as that the opening chorus of the St. Matthew Passion contained the direction 'sesquialtera' in the organ part at the point where the chorale ' O Lamm Gottes, unschuldig' enters, and again in the chorale-chorus, ' O Mensch, bewein' dein' Sünde gross.' But we have one piece of irrefragable testimony concerning Bach's use of the stops in the chorale-arrangement for three manuals and pedals of 'Ein' feste Burg ist unser Gott[1],' where, at the beginning, the 'fagotto' is indicated for the left hand, and ' sesquialtera' for the right, there being then no pedal part going on; Spitta has a most interesting passage on this work, proving from it the date of composition, 1709, and showing from the specification of the Mühlhausen organ that the 'fagotto' was a sixteen-foot stop[2]. In the arrangement of ' Wie schön leuchtet der Morgenstern[3]' a dialogue between the 'Oberwerk' and the 'Rückpositiv' is directed, and in ' Ach Gott und Herr[4]' the chorale-tune is brought out in a highly ornamented form, on the 'Rückpositiv' supported by the calmer progress of the harmonies of the 'Oberwerk.' Something of the same kind occurs, but without the specific names of the manuals, in 'Christ lag in Todesbanden[5],' where the words 'forte' and 'piano' are used obviously to imply an alteration of manuals.

---

[1] B.-G. edition, xl. 57.   [2] *Life of Bach* (Eng. transl.), i. 394 ff.
[3] B.-G. edition, xl. 99.   [4] Ibid. p. 4.   [5] Ibid. p. 52.

One of the most suggestive of the many coincidences in
the career of the two great contemporaries, who never met
face to face, was that Bach and Handel both repaired, as
young men, to Lübeck, where Dietrich Buxtehude was organist.
Handel went thither, in the company of Mattheson, who
relates the incident in his *Ehrenpforte*, p. 93 ff. One of them
(Mattheson characteristically says it was himself) had been
invited to enter as successor to Buxtehude, but the succession
to the Lübeck organistship involved marrying the preceding
organist's eldest daughter, and as Anna Margaretha Buxtehude
was twelve years older than Mattheson, and sixteen years
older than Handel, it is no wonder that, according to Burney's
account[1], 'thinking this too great an honour, they precipi-
tately retreated to Hamburg.' The account of Bach's journey
to Lübeck is a strange contrast to this; he was drawn there
by no desire of succeeding Buxtehude, but simply in order
to hear him play, and for this purpose he had to trudge the
whole distance from Arnstadt, fifty miles. Although allowed
only four weeks of absence, he stayed away at Lübeck nearly
as many months, and had to be recalled to his own duties
by the consistory of Arnstadt[2].

II. The Harpsichord and Clavichord.

As the ordinary medium of accompaniment, and the most
usual and indeed indispensable adjunct to musical performances
of all kinds, the harpsichord held, in the eighteenth century,
a position more or less analogous to that of the pianoforte
in the present day. It shared with the organ the duty of
giving the complete harmonies from the figured bass, thorough-
bass, or *basso continuo*, in vocal and instrumental music alike,
and both in chamber and orchestral music. The question of

---

[1] Burney, *Present State of Music in Germany*, ii. 240.

[2] Many interesting details as to the manner most in favour in Germany of
arranging the stops, &c., for chorale-playing and elsewhere, will be found in
Mattheson's *Vollkommener Kapellmeister*, part III, chaps. xxiv and xxv.

its use in actual church performance has been ably discussed by Spitta, ii. 655 (English translation), but it can hardly be maintained that its employment for the accompaniment of solos, &c., even in church, was quite unknown, and the eminent author in another part of the same volume (pp. 327-8) shows that harpsichords were placed in the organ-loft of various churches in Germany. For the opera of the time it was indispensable, and in fact the usual arrangement was to have two, one placed so that the conductor would face the singers on the stage, the other placed lengthwise in the orchestra for the accompanist or maestro al cembalo, on which he might play the harmonies from the figured bass for the soloist.

As there is a lamentable confusion in the various names by which instruments of this class were called in various countries, and still more in regard to the manner of their use, it will be best to describe their action and limitations as briefly as may be. The essential principle is the plucking of strings, not by the finger, but by a plectrum of quill or leather set in motion by keys. The Spanish name 'exaquir,' and the French 'échiquier,' may possibly refer to the chequer-like effect of white and black keys; the name 'virginal,' once supposed to convey a delicate compliment to Queen Elizabeth, has been proved to be of far greater antiquity than her date, and to be derived either from the fact that the instrument was commonly used by young ladies, or from the hymns to the Virgin which may have been accompanied upon the instrument. The Italian 'spinetta' was long held to imply that thorns, or quills shaped like thorns, were used in the early examples; but the derivation from the maker's name, Spinetti, a Venetian, seems a good deal more likely to be right. These names and their various counterparts and derivatives, are more or less closely confined to the trapeze-shaped instrument with only one row of keys; the long shape, more or less like the grand piano, but narrower and often longer, is generally provided with some means of altering the quality of the tone,

even if it has only one manual. The best examples of this
instrument, to which the name harpsichord is assigned, have
two keyboards, and pedals like those of the organ seem to
have existed in some German specimens. The usual German
name for the whole class of instruments is Clavicymbel, or
Cembalo, both derived from the Italian clavicembalo; clavi-
cytherium is another name sometimes applied definitely to the
upright specimens. The Italian manicordo, gravicembalo (an
obvious corruption from clavicembalo), and clavicordo, are used
of harpsichords, not of the clavichord, though the last name
might seem to apply to that instrument. The varieties of
the tones of the harpsichord were altered by means of stops,
of which the greatest number usually employed is five. The
plectra already spoken of are jerked, by the action of the keys,
past the strings in an upward direction, and it is obvious
that if the 'jack' were unprovided with something to prevent
it, its return to the original position would be accompanied
by a repetition of the 'pluck' by which the vibrations of the
string are excited. This is got rid of by a rudimentary
'escapement' which allows the middle part of the jack, in
which is fixed the tongue of quill or leather, to bend outward
when it touches the string on its downward course, so that
the tongue passes quite silently; the small dampers which
then deaden the vibrations cause the sound to cease as soon
as the finger is raised and the jack falls. This arrangement,
with different methods of restoring the jack to position without renewing the note, is common to most of the earliest
examples; but the plan of placing the jacks in ranks movable
sideways by a lever acted on by the stops, belongs exclusively
to the harpsichord. By this means the plectra can be removed
away from the strings, so that, although the jacks must rise
whenever the keys are pressed, no sound comes from those
not required. The difference in tone between leather and quill
plectra is very marked, the former being much fuller and the
latter giving a brighter tone; besides this difference there was

introduced in the finer harpsichords a second set of jacks plucking the strings at a point nearer to their ends than the other jacks, and so producing a more nasal, reedy, quality; the 'octave' stop, setting in motion a set of shorter strings underneath the others, completes the number of different ways of exciting the vibrations of the strings, for the *jeu de bufle,* or ' buff ' stop, consists only of a piece of leather pushed against the strings as one set of jacks plucks them; it gives a sound in exact imitation of a harp, but both this, and the 'Venetian swell,' by which flaps can be opened in the lid to increase the sound, seem to be of later date than the lifetime of Handel. With a two-manualled harpsichord, provided with these stops and the contrivance for combining them, the player has at his immediate command, first, a distinctively harpsichord tone of a peculiarly sharp, brilliant quality a little like a very much improved *pizzicato* on strings; second, a more mellow tone which can be closely assimilated to the harp quality; third, the expressive timbre of an oboe or bassoon, and fourth, an octave effect, which in combination with other stops produces an impression not wholly unlike an organ. Thus opportunity is given for continual contrast and variety of tones, each quality being of invariable strength, except on the later harpsichords, where the swell gives considerable powers of gradation; and it is this more than anything else which distinguishes the instrument from the clavichord and the pianoforte, both of which in widely different degrees possess the power of gradation, and nothing else, if we except the ' soft-pedal ' effect on the modern piano, which introduces a separate quality of tone-colour.

The clavichord can produce, even in the most favourable circumstances, only a very diminutive amount of tone for its loudest effect; but between this and the softest of which it is capable there is an almost infinite series of gradations, far outnumbering, indeed, those which an ordinary pianist of moderate powers can get from the best modern instrument.

Within its exceedingly narrow limits, every shade of tone is available, and each one comes out with wonderful clearness, so that the intertwinings of a fugue, for example, can be interpreted with as much clearness as if each part were performed on a separate instrument or voice. The clavichord is the lineal descendant of the monochord with movable bridges, as it is the direct ancestor of the pianoforte. Each key has at its further end a small tangent of metal which, when raised by the depression of the key, strikes and at the same time supports one of the set of strings stretched longitudinally in a direction more or less parallel to the keyboard. The strings are far more nearly the same length than is the case with the harpsichord or spinet, as the sounding length is determined by the point at which they are struck. It is evident that if a string be stretched along a box and struck at any point of its length it will sound on each side of the tangent; and to prevent two notes sounding together on the same string, a strip of flannel is passed between the strings at one side of the instrument, so that only the part on the right of the tangent can sound. A survival of the movable bridges of the monochord was that in many of the older examples of the clavichord the same string was employed for more than one note, by two tangents striking it at different points, in a manner distantly analogous to the stopping process by which each of the four strings of the violin and kindred instruments is made to produce notes of different pitch. The general practice was to make two adjacent semitones sound on the same string, but specimens exist on which as many as four adjacent semitones have but one string among them. This renders the simultaneous sounding of any two of the four a matter of impossibility[1]. How great a drawback this was in the execution of part-music of any degree of elaboration

[1] In a clavichord belonging to the Rev. F. W. Galpin, of Hatfield Broad Oak, the F, F sharp, G, and A flat are on the same string, so that the interval of a third between the first and the last cannot be sounded.

may easily be imagined; yet the instruments possessing it—the technical term for them is 'gebunden'—are not by any means rare in Germany, while those that have a string to every note—or 'bundfrei' instruments—are not easy to procure. The fact that there is no mechanism but the single lever connecting the finger of the player with the string—there is not even so much of an 'action' as the simple jerk of the harpsichord—makes possible the beautiful effect known as the 'Bebung,' for the finger, being in virtual contact with the string during the whole time the key is kept down, can, by altering the degree of pressure, produce a slight variety in intensity, and thus a certain kind of tremolo. The power of altering the degree of pressure exerted creates also a danger of over-pressing the string, and thus of putting it out of tune for the moment, if not of actually breaking it. The far-away sound of the clavichord, the directness of power on the string, and this characteristic effect of the 'Bebung,' make the instrument an ideal medium for the interpretation of all that is most spiritual, most intimate, and most expressive in the old music. The power of emphasizing any note in a chord fits it more especially for intricate part-music, and for such fugues as those of the *Wohltemperirtes Clavier* where the parts are constantly crossing and interweaving with each other. This immortal collection, in which Bach contributed his share to the controversy about equal temperament, was intended, not for the harpsichord, but for the clavichord, and it is not difficult to decide by internal evidence the primary destination of any fugue or elaborate prelude of Bach; for in those works which were meant for the harpsichord there are nearly always traces of the transference of one part or other to a different manual, the parts for the two hands being kept almost entirely independent of each other, so as to allow the interchange of the two different qualities of tone. In the 'Italian Concerto' the directions *forte* and *piano*, and other signs engraved by Bach himself, clearly indicate a change of manuals; and in many

of the famous thirty variations dedicated to Goldberg, the
employment of two manuals is implied in the frequent crossing
of scales and arpeggios which is next to impossible on a
single keyboard. This great work gives us some insight
into Bach's practice with regard to the use of the single or
double manuals, for each variation is headed 'a 1 clav.,' or
'a 2 clav.' In those for one keyboard it is not uncommon
to find the middle parts passing from one hand to another,
in the manner made familiar in the 'Forty-Eight'; the
incongruity which would arise if these were divided between
the two manuals is evident at once. To compare either
these 'Goldberg' variations or the 'Italian concerto' with the
'Forty-Eight,' the 'Chromatic Fantasia,' or the fugue in A
minor with the short *arpeggiato* prelude, is to learn the
essential differences of the two instruments more effectually
than by any verbal explanation. Beyond the fact that it was
a clavichord which Handel smuggled into his attic when he
pursued his musical studies against the wish of his father,
there is little in his works which implies the intention of
writing for this instrument; his suites, like the 'Ordres'
of Couperin, the 'Sonatas' of Domenico Scarlatti, and the
great bulk of the 'clavier' literature of the period, were
evidently meant for the harpsichord. In Bach's estimation
the two instruments seem to have ranked equally; if we are
right in interpreting the entry in the specification of his
property given in Spitta, vol. iii. p. 351 ff. (Eng. transl.),
' 1 complete (*fournirt*) clavier, which, if possible, the family
will keep,' as referring to a clavichord in contradistinction to
the four 'clavesins' entered immediately below, it may be
taken as certain that the special value set upon the first
instrument (80 thalers, as compared with the 50 at which the
'clavesins' are valued) reflects a preference of the master's
own; but the tiresome word 'clavier' which is used indiffer-
ently in German for everything from a virginal to a grand
pianoforte, makes the evidence of this document very uncertain.

With regard to Bach's technique on the harpsichord, there is happily a good deal of authentic testimony. In Quantz's treatise already mentioned[1], after discussing the somewhat doubtful point of the difference in tone produced by different players on the harpsichord, the author directs the student to get early into the habit of bending his fingers inwards, and, in runs or scales, to let them slide off the front of the keys, instead of being lifted directly upwards, in order that quick passages may come out as clearly as possible. He concludes with these words, 'I am confirmed in this by the example of one of the greatest of all clavier-players, who taught this method and employed it himself.' The index to the book shows that J. S. Bach is here referred to. The rapid withdrawal of the finger in an inward, rather than in an upward direction, seems connected with the ornament known as the 'Prall-triller,' which C. P. E. Bach, in his *Versuch über die wahre Art Clavier zu spielen* (1753), mentions as almost impossible to transfer to the pianoforte. He says:—

'Whilst speaking of the proper execution of this kind of shake, it is worth while to state that upon the pianoforte it is almost impossible to play the Prall-triller delicately. All 'Schnellen' (jerking, rapid withdrawing of the finger) implies a certain degree of force, and upon the pianoforte increased force produces increased tone. Now the Prall-triller is impossible without 'Schnellen,' therefore the executant will be all the more at a disadvantage, since the Prall-triller often occurs alone or in connexion with the 'Doppelschlag' (turn) after an appoggiatura, and consequently, according to the rule for such things, *piano*[2].'

It is not impossible that this defect of the pianoforte, as it evidently seemed even to one who was the ardent partisan of the new instrument, may have had something to do with his father's known preference of the older instruments. But in order to explain this, it is only necessary that the extremely

[1] *Versuch einer Anweisung die Flöte traversiere zu spielen*, XVII. vi. 18.

[2] I quote from the translation given in Mr. Dannreuther's admirable treatise on *Ornamentation*, part ii. p. 29.

rudimentary state of the pianoforte in his time should be understood. The tone, far more powerful indeed than that of the clavichord, was yet nothing like what we are now accustomed to, and the quality, as compared with that of the older instruments, must have seemed very colourless and inexpressive. It was in power rather than in quality, however, that Bach felt the shortcomings of the pianoforte: when he criticized Silbermann's earlier examples, 'he found fault only with the heavy touch and the feebleness of the upper notes[1].' It is interesting to compare with this the opinion of Kuhnau, who, in a long letter to Mattheson, given in the latter's *Critica Musica*, vol. ii. p. 236—a letter to which the student of the keyed instruments and of temperament may be referred— alludes to his admiration for the 'Pantalonisches Cimbel' (writing before 1725), and calls it 'ein charmante und nächst dem Claviere vollkommenes Instrument.' In a later part of the same volume a German translation, by one König, is given from the Italian of the Marchese Scipio Maffei, where the new invention is called a 'Claveceins auf welchem den piano und forte zu haben.' A diagram is inserted which undoubtedly shows the action of the pianoforte. A 'Clavier-Gamba' and a 'Lauten-Clavier' are mentioned in an earlier part of the same book as made by Joh. Georg Gleichmann, organist of Ilmenau, and as capable of being played loud and soft. It is now only necessary to bear in mind the all-important fact that the clavichord possessed gradation without contrast, the harpsichord many kinds of contrasts with virtually no gradation whatever. This essential difference is of primary importance to those who would fully understand Bach's 'Clavier' works, and especially to those who undertake to transfer them to the modern pianoforte.

It is not easy for us to put ourselves into the attitude of the men to whom the harpsichord represented the *ne plus*

---

[1] Spitta, *Life of Bach* (Eng. transl.), ii. 46.

ultra of force in the way of instruments with keys and strings; yet that it was so regarded there is sufficient proof. Although it is commonly asserted that its tone, always *staccato*, was incapable of giving sustained effects, the truth is that the duration of its sound is at least as long as that of the average pianoforte, while it must have far exceeded the early specimens of the piano in this as in so many other respects. It was considered as a useful agent in strengthening the hands of the performers, as is proved by Burney's reference to the comparative merits of this and the clavichord in his tour[1], where he describes the performance of some of Scarlatti's sonatas by a child of eight or nine, who—

'played upon a small, and not good pianoforte. The neatness of this child's execution did not so much surprise me, though uncommon, as her expression. All the *pianos* and *fortes* were so judiciously attended to; and there was such shading off some passages, and force given to others, as nothing but the best teaching, or greatest natural feeling and sensibility could produce. I enquired . . . upon what instrument she usually practised at home, and was answered " the Clavichord." This accounts for her expression, and convinces me that children should learn upon that, or a Piano Forte, very early, and be obliged to give an expression to Lady Coventry's Minuet, or whatever is their first tune; otherwise, after long practice on a monotonous harpsichord, however useful in strengthening the hand, the case is hopeless.'

NOTE.—While these pages have been passing through the press, a valuable contribution to the literature of the harpsichord has been published by Fratelli Bocca, of Turin: Signor L. A. Villanis' *L'Arte del Clavicembalo* treats, in a scholarly and interesting way, of the development of the instrument in all countries, and discusses the music written for it and for the kindred instruments with wide sympathy and literary skill.

[1] Burney, *Present State of Music in Germany*, i. 278.

CHAPTER VII

THE ORCHESTRA

At any time before the close of the period of Bach and Handel the term 'a full orchestra,' which in the present day would convey precisely the same idea to all musicians, would, if understood at all, have been defined differently by almost every one who was asked to explain it. The modern notion of a fixed and unvarying body of instruments divided into such and such groups, and consisting of precisely such and such individual instruments, had not taken shape in the days of these giants. In looking over the scores of works by Bach, Handel, and their predecessors and contemporaries, it becomes evident that composers felt themselves under no kind of obligation to use, in any part of their works, the whole body of orchestral instruments at their disposal. As far as regards the full complement of strings, they seldom departed very far from the usage which still obtains, but disposed them in two groups of violins and one of violas, while the violoncellos and double basses were generally required to play in unison (sounding as octaves) with one another. As to the particular wind instruments to be employed, the writers clearly used their own judgement. It has sometimes been suggested that their choice was restricted by various conditions under which the works were to be heard, and the number of wind instruments available. But that this was not the case in any considerable degree is proved by the scores of the greater compositions of Bach and Handel, where the wind instruments are seen to be

employed more or less in the manner of an obbligato, their
presence being not at all indispensable in the passages for full
orchestra. The *Messiah* begins with strings alone, no wind
instrument of any kind appearing in the original score until
the entry of the trumpets at 'Glory to God'; and, in exactly
the same way, and with probably the same artistic intention of
reserving his special effects till they were wanted, Bach begins
the B minor Mass with flutes, oboes, bassoons, and strings,
adding three trumpets and drums at the 'Gloria.' But even
here he does not use the whole of the instruments required for
the work, for the corno da caccia which, with two bassoons,
supplies the accompaniment of 'Quoniam tu solus sanctus,'
appears in none of the *tutti* passages. A third oboe part in
the 'Sanctus' is an addition for this number alone. Very
much the same practice must have been in use in all parts
of the musical world; Durante's five-part Mass [1] before spoken
of is accompanied at first on two oboes, two horns, and strings,
the trumpets being added at the trio 'Domine Deus.'

Whether in symphonies or in the accompaniments of solos,
certain instruments are chosen that fit the general character
of the movement to be employed, or the expression to be
conveyed. The choice once made for each section, the wind
instrument, or whatever it may be, is continued throughout
the movement as a real part, without relief of any contrasting
quality of tone, and often without more support than that of
the figured bass. Each movement or section has its own
colour-scheme, or rather may be regarded as a picture in
monochrome, in which variety and interest could only be got
by the management of the outlines or the opposition of lights
and darks. There seems hardly a trace of any systematic use
of varying colour-schemes in the course of a single section
until we come to Gluck in his maturer style, when we feel
that the beauty of relief in tone-quality is beginning to be

---

[1] Brit. Mus. Add. MS. 31,610. See p. 64.

realized. The term 'colour' has been so long employed to express the feeling for various qualities of tone, that no excuse is needed for its use in the present day. As to the practice of Bach and Handel in this respect, and the comparison between their methods, the strange opinion was started by Mosewius[1], that in Bach the strings formed as it were the groundwork of the accompaniment, the wind instruments being used to give the colour; while in Handel the organ was the groundwork of the whole, and the various parts of the orchestra, strings and wind alike, were regarded as part of the colourist's resources. A far truer statement is that of Spitta[2], that Bach built up his groups of instruments on a background of the organ, treating 'the strings as one group, the oboes and bassoons as another, a third the cornet and trombones, and the fourth the trumpets (or horns) and drums. The flutes occupied a less independent place in Bach's orchestra, but in the seventeenth century they formed a group by themselves.' The term 'cornet' in the above refers of course to the now obsolete 'Zinke,' from which was evolved the 'serpent,' formerly in general use in English churches. In so far as either of the two great masters regarded the string quartet as the groundwork of the scheme, it was Handel who did so, but even he only to a very partial extent. To neither him nor to Bach did it appear always necessary to employ all the four groups of the strings, or indeed any at all except in so far as the figured bass may have implied the assistance of the violoncello or double-bass to support the harmonies played on the harpsichord or organ. The idea that the strings should accompany all the fuller numbers seems to have been far more an English one than a German; Burney lays it down as a principle of good orchestration that no instrument should be allowed to be long idle, and praises a work by Battista San

---

[1] Mosewius, *J. S. Bach in seinen Kirchen-Cantaten*, p. 25.
[2] Spitta, *Life of Bach* (Eng. transl.), ii. 303 ff.

Martini because 'the violins, especially, are never suffered to sleep[1].'

The history of the constitution of the string band contains a good many points of interest, and some that are not at all easy to explain. The oldest member of the group, the viola, had indeed the honour of the original form of the title, all the other instruments being named, with terminations of diminution or augmentation, from it; but in spite of this, it only won its place in the orchestra by degrees. As it existed in two sizes, the large tenor violin, and the small alto such as is in ordinary use at the present day, it may well have been that efficient performers on both kinds were rare, and that the peculiar quality of tone which is now-a-days considered so valuable in the orchestra and in chamber-music was overlooked, since it was only characteristic of the smaller variety. Early examples of its use in Italian chamber-music are quoted in Grove, *Dict.*, s. v. Tenor Violin, vol. iv. p. 89; but it seems to have fallen out of fashion as a solo instrument, for in the greater part of the seventeenth and eighteenth centuries two and sometimes three violin parts are used above the basses, in concerted chamber-music, such as the sonatas of Purcell and Corelli. In the 'concerti grossi' of the latter it is remarkable that the group of solo instruments, technically called the 'concertino,' consists always of two violins and bass, while the 'ripieno' has a viola part in the usual place between the violins and the bass. Among Bach's experiments as an inventor of musical instruments is that of the 'viola pomposa,' which appears to have been identical with the 'violoncello piccolo,' having a fifth string added above the four of the ordinary violoncello; the sixth of his solos for the violoncello was written for this instrument, and it is occasionally found as an obbligato in the church cantatas. In *Alexander's Feast* Handel uses the tenors with special purpose of arousing or

---

[1] Burney, *Present State of Music in France and Italy*, p. 95.

reflecting horror, as in 'Revenge, Timotheus cries,' 'These are Grecian ghosts,' &c., disposing them in two classes, for one of which he writes in the alto clef, for the other in the tenor, the violins being silent for the time. It seems probable that he had in his mind the two forms of the viola already referred to.

The violin, although existing in a form quite distinct from that of the viol family as long ago as the middle of the sixteenth century in Italy, replaced the older instruments in that country and in Germany during the seventeenth century, while in England and France its final victory was deferred until the eighteenth century. The excellence of the Cremonese schools of violin-makers, and the rise of violin virtuosity among the Italians, are enough to account for the precedence thus gained in Italy. Although the tone of the early violins was nothing like what we are now accustomed to hear—the improvement in this respect being partly due to the mellowing influence of time, and partly to certain alterations in the disposition of the sound-post,—they were yet far more powerful than the viols, and had many other advantages which made their triumph certain and permanent. The favour they enjoyed is illustrated throughout the *suonate da camera* of Vitali, Bassani, Purcell, Corelli, dall'Abaco, and many others, in the great majority of which two violin parts and a bass are all that are employed; occasionally, as in three sonatas of Vitali's *opera quinta*, a viola or a viola alta is used, but no such instance is to be found in either of Purcell's two sets, or in Corelli's sonatas, all of which employ only violins above the bass. The fact that the means of a fuller harmony occur in the older sets, in compositions before the middle of the seventeenth century, while the viola part seems to have dropped out of use towards the end of the century, affords a curious counterpart to the tendency noticed in the Italian church music, where we drew attention to the growing preference for the employment of two soprano voices over a vocal or instrumental bass. It is impossible to say with any certainty whether the vocal music followed the lead of the instrumental, or the instrumental that of the vocal; from documentary evidence it would seem more likely that the instrumental works started the fashion; but the actual precedence is of very small importance compared with the undoubted fact that the combination of two high parts with a bass only for support was in vogue in music of all kinds, more especially in Italy. At the same time, it must be remembered that in the earlier specimens of this arrangement the inner parts of the harmonies were not absent altogether, for they were supplied from the figured bass upon the harpsichord or organ, so that the thinness of effect would not strike the average hearer until the date of the English glee, which, being unaccompanied, presents the combination in all its unconcealed tenuity. The practice of using three violins in certain *tutti* portions, and especially in the first movements of operatic overtures, seems to have come down from Lully's time; it occurs in his *Bellerophon,* and in many other places, where the five staves of the strings in the 'full' passages are marked with the following clefs:—the G clef on the lowest line of the stave, the C clef on the same line, the C clef on the second line (these three being clearly the lines of the violins), the C clef in the usual place on the middle line, for the viola, and the F clef in the usual place for the basses on the fourth line, lowest stave. As early as his *Agrippina,* Handel adopted this arrangement, and it occurs in the act which he contributed to *Muzio Scevola,* in *Ottone, Alessandro* (beginning of act II), *Siroe* (overture), and *Orlando*; while as late as *Berenice* and *Faramondo,* written near the end of his operatic period, he had not given up a practice which must have become more or less old-fashioned by then.

England was apparently the only exception to the rule that in the opera, as elsewhere, the harmonies should be supplied on the keyed instruments, leaving the violoncello and double-

bass to the delivery of the actual notes of the bass part, and
no more. The practice of supplying the harmonies in 'unaccompanied' recitatives, &c., upon the violoncello and double-
bass—a practice which attained its most brilliant point in the
times of Lindley and Dragonetti—cannot indeed be traced
further back than the early part of the nineteenth century,
but it is difficult to say how early it may not have arisen.
In Handel's time, indeed, the harpsichord was universally
used in England as well as abroad. The position of the
stringed instruments that are plucked with the hand is a
somewhat curious one. It was much later than this period
that the harp became an acknowledged member of the regular
orchestra; it was left for Berlioz to discover its capabilities
in the body of the orchestra; yet in Burney's tour in Germany[1],
in the list of the opera performers at Berlin, a harp is included,
and in the same book (p. 166) we find Weiss mentioned as
playing the lute in the Dresden opera. A remarkable instance
of the use of the lute in a very important way occurs in
Bach's *Passion according to St. John*, where the beautiful
bass air, 'Betrachte, meine Seel' ' ('Consider, O my soul'),
is accompanied with an elaborate lute obbligato, with a running
arpeggio accompaniment over reiterated bass notes, while two
viole d'amore, with their veiled tones, carry on a quiet accompaniment above, and the *continuo* or figured bass part
sustains the harmonies, the warning 'pianissimo' appearing
over the bass line, out of consideration, no doubt, for the
weak tone of the lute. Both the harp and 'teorba' (i. e.
theorbo or arch-lute) appear in the score of Handel's *Giulio
Cesare* (1723), but it is clear that the picturesque shape of
the instruments had something to do with their introduction
into a scene of apotheosis, where Parnassus was opened,
and the instruments with their players were visible to the
audience. An orchestra of more usual design performs the

---

[1] Burney, *Present State of Music in Germany*, ii. 95.

ordinary work of accompanying in this opera, in which, for
almost the first time, we meet with anything like experiments
in scoring.

It is true that in *Rinaldo* (1711) Almirena's song 'Augelletti' is accompanied by a flauto piccolo, with quite an
elaborate obbligato part, two ordinary flutes, and strings; but
it is evident that the flutes are here used with special reference
to their bird-like character. The elegiac quality, as it may
be called, of the lower notes of the flute is finely brought
out in the 'dead march' in *Saul*, but it is clear that, for
some reason or other, the flutes were not greatly in favour,
for, although they are used freely as obbligato instruments,
they are by no means an essential part of the full orchestra.
And their comparative inferiority is proved by the curious
fact that in the Handel Commemoration of 1784, there were
only six flutes against twenty-six oboes and twenty-six bassoons.

As the oldest members of the 'wood-wind' part of the
orchestra, the oboes held the most prominent place during the
whole period of Bach and Handel. They are very commonly
used in unison with the violins, and are not seldom entrusted
with the task of carrying on a dialogue with the trumpets,
in explanation of which we must remember the enormous
numbers of oboes employed in the orchestra of Handel's day,
and also their former use as the main representative of the
higher parts in military music. They and the bassoons were
an essential part of the full orchestra; for a small band, in
the accompaniment of solos, no combination is more usual
than a single oboe part with strings; and in spite of Miss
Burney's *Evelina*, who says 'the hautbois in the open air is
heavenly,' we are met by the difficulty of understanding how
audiences in the eighteenth century could endure the strident
tone of a number of oboes, sometimes equal to that of the
violins, and constantly in use. The oboe d'amore, which was
such a favourite instrument with Bach, had a tone more like
that of the cor anglais, standing a minor third lower than

the oboe, and having a slight difference in the shape of the mouthpiece. The other variety which is frequently found in Bach and elsewhere is the oboe da caccia, well described in Grove's *Dictionary* as 'a bassoon raised a fourth,' while the cor anglais, with which it is often confounded, is 'an oboe lowered through a fifth.' Although the bassoon, curiously enough, does not appear in the score of Bach's *Passion according to St. Matthew*, he uses it frequently in the cantatas and elsewhere; in the 'Quoniam' of the B minor Mass, there are two obbligato parts, together with the corno da caccia. Before passing to the brass instruments in use, it may be well to point out that the clarinet, though apparently invented in some form or other as early as 1690, did not find an entrance into the regular orchestra till a considerable time after Bach and Handel. Only in Mozart's time was it definitely established as an important element in the full orchestra. The qualities of the oboe and flute tones are thus referred to in an interesting passage in Avison's *Essay on Musical Expression* [1].

'The *Hautboy* will best express the *Cantabile*, or singing Style, and may be used in all Movements whatever under this Denomination; especially those Movements which tend to the *Gay* and *Chearful*. In Compositions for the *German* Flute, is required the same Method of proceeding by *conjoint Degrees*, or such other natural Intervals, as, with the Nature of its Tone, will best express the languishing, or melancholy Style. With both these Instruments, the running into *extreme Keys*, the Use of the *Staccato*, or distinct Separation of Notes; and all irregular Leaps, or broken and uneven Intervals must be avoided; for which Reason alone, these Instruments ought never to be employ'd in the *Repieno Parts* of Concertos for Violins, but in such Pieces only as are composed for them; and these, perhaps, would be most agreeably introduced as principal Instruments in some intervening Movements in the Concerto, which might not only give a pleasing variety, but shew their different Expression to the greatest Advantage.'

[1] Page 95.

This extract gives a definite proof that the usage of the eighteenth century, of keeping special instruments for certain movements, was considered to provide enough variety of tone-colour, and that the idea of giving the flutes or oboes parts of their own to play in the full orchestra, of a nature more suitable to their character than the slavish following of the violin part, was more or less foreign to the musicians of the time.

Before considering the true brass instruments, it will be best to refer to the cornetto or Zinke, a family of instruments which, in Bach's time, was rapidly disappearing from use, even in Germany where they lasted longest.   Mattheson, in *Der vollkommene Capellmeister*, mentions the fact that they were becoming obsolete on account of the force of lungs required to play them.   They had enjoyed a great popularity in church performances as the treble of the trombone family, since their quality was something like that of the trombone. They were made of wood, covered with leather, and had six holes for the fingers and one for the thumb on the lower side; one member of the family, the 'serpent,' remained in use in England as long as the rustic bands in village churches had the duty of accompanying the choir.   This instrument seems to have been better known in England than in Germany, for there is a story [1] to the effect that when Handel first heard it, after his settlement in England, he asked, 'What the devil be that?' and on hearing that it was called the serpent, remarked, 'Aye, but it not be the serpent what seduced Eve.' The smaller members of the family, the cornetti, occur in a few of Bach's scores, and are mostly used to support the voices; in the curious wind-band which forms the only accompaniment of the cantata *O Jesu Christ, mein's Lebens Licht*, the cornetto appears with its usual companions, the three trombones, and two instruments marked 'lituus,' which are evidently some kind

[1] R. Rstro, *Life of Handel*, p. 294.

of trumpet, not belonging to the cornetto family, as is implied in Walther's Lexicon. (See the preface to the *Bach-Gesellschaft*, xxiv, p. xxxi.)

Turning now to the real brass instruments, we find that the solemn effect of the trombones, which modern composers have used with so much success, was realized in Bach's time; he uses four trombone parts in 'Ich hatte viel Bekümmerniss,' and in many other places where a special impression of grandeur is wanted. The special uses of certain instruments, as of horns for hunting, and of trumpets for military signals, must have suggested their employment in the orchestra at a very early date with definite allusion to these particular purposes; the trumpet obtained its entrance into the regular band much earlier than the horn, and in Bach's time became a favourite instrument for the most elaborate obbligato parts, such as those in the mass in B minor, and in many of the cantatas. These passages were considered unplayable upon the trumpet usually employed in modern music, and it was only by a happy accident that a German trumpeter, Herr Kosleck, discovered, in a curiosity shop in Berlin, the remains of an old trumpet which enabled him to restore the instrument for which Bach wrote these parts. When this rediscovered trumpet was first heard in England, at the Bach Choir Festival of 1885 at the Albert Hall, its effect was overpowering in the beauty and sweetness of its tone; in its upper notes, which reach to the high D of the soprano voice, it is of a quality almost more like a very powerful flute than that which we generally associate with the trumpet. It is not an absolute restoration, for it has keys, which the old trumpet had not; but it is something very much nearer to the old trumpet than anything previously available. The old trumpet is probably the instrument mentioned by Burney[1], as 'the long trumpet, played lately in London'; if so, it is curious that no other tradition of its use in England should remain, beyond the fact that the

---

[1] *Present State of Music in Germany,* ii. 42.

obbligato of 'The trumpet shall sound' suggests this rather than the modern trumpet. The group of the trumpets was divided into the 'clarini' and 'principale,' as in Handel's *Dettingen Te Deum* and Bach's cantata, *Denn du wirst meine Seele*; from these and similar passages it is inferred, by a writer in Grove's *Dictionary* (s.v. Trumpet), that 'the Principale was obviously a large-bored, bold-toned instrument resembling our modern Trumpet. It was apparently of eight-foot tone as now used. To the Clarino I and II of the score were allotted florid, but less fundamental passages, chiefly in the octave above those of the Principale. They were probably of smaller bore, and entirely subordinate to the "herrlich" Principale, both in subject and in dominance of tone.'

The difficulty of producing the notes between the natural harmonics on the French horn (corno da caccia) seems to have been the chief reason for its tardy recognition as part of the regular orchestra; in 1717 Lady Mary Wortley Montagu complains of the fondness of the Viennese for the instrument, which she considers 'a deafening noise.' The final chorus of Handel's *Radamisto* (1720) is a famous early instance of its use, and by the date of Bach's B minor Mass, where it is used as an obbligato to the bass solo 'Quoniam,' it seems to have lost its special 'colour' as suggesting the idea of music for the chase. Handel uses two horns in the passage referred to, and three years later, in 1723, in *Giulio Cesare*, he introduces four horns into the first chorus. From that time onwards the horns appear fairly regularly in the scores of his operas, but even then they are only used for certain special numbers.

The drums are used by both Bach and Handel not only as an essential part of any music of a military or quasi-military character, but in the ordinary full band; as in the present day, their number was usually two.

With so many kinds of instruments at their disposal, it is strange that the leading musicians of the time should have made such hesitating progress as they did towards the attainment of the quality of change and 'colour' which gives to the orchestra of the present day its infinite variety. As has been said in an earlier part of this chapter, each separate movement, song, or section of a larger work, sets out with a certain number of instruments fixed according to more or less arbitrary conventions; but once fixed, each part maintains its own steady course through the movement, possibly in unison with some other instrument throughout, or independently, being in the latter case treated as a real addition to the fabric of the counterpoint. If the oboes play in unison with the violins, they may be left out for a few bars in some specially soft passage, coming in again afterwards ; and as a rule in songs, the middle portion, before the inevitable 'da capo' brings back the repetition of the first, is more lightly accompanied than the main section. We most rarely find Bach making any further alteration than this during the course of a movement, except in two cases; where the structure is assimilated to that of the concerto, in which solo instruments are relieved against the *tutti*, or certain departments of the choir against the whole; and where the suggestions of the words require some interchange of voices and instruments, as in the triple fabric of the first chorus in the *St. Matthew Passion*, where each of the choirs has its own orchestra. In Handel, and more particularly in his opera scores, there are many more instances of the interchange of different tones for purely sensuous reasons of acoustics, apart from the obvious suggestions from the words, and from the structural peculiarities of the concerto-form. Two instances of uncommon combinations of instruments have already been quoted from *Giulio Cesare*, and it would seem that, from the date of this work, Handel grew bolder in experiments, and more confident in using special orchestral colouring for a brief space, without being compelled to keep all the instruments chosen sounding through a movement. In *Alessandro*, a concerted number, 'Fra le guerre,' shows in its alternation of two horns and two oboes above the strings, some sense of contrast, and there are plenty of examples of such dialogues scattered through the operas after this date; the dance-music of *Ariodante*, with the musette for flutes and strings opposed to the combination of horns, oboes, bassoons, and strings before, and the dialogue in the final scene between the oboes and bassoons on the stage and the rest of the orchestra; the way the flutes are used in Ruggiero's air, 'Mio bel tesoro' in *Alcina*; the interchange of different qualities in the finale of *Faramondo*; and many other examples, show that the composer was ready to enlarge his means of expression, even in a class of work where conventionality of all kinds reigned supreme. Perhaps the fact that the conventions of opera were enforced by the spoilt singers of the day may have led Handel to indulge his own instincts in orchestral experiments; but, whatever be the reason, the fact remains that there are more experiments in the direction of the modern way of treating the orchestra in the operas than in the later series of his works, the oratorios. But even when we have catalogued all the examples of the interchange of various tone-qualities in the operas—and if the average number of instances were as much as one example to each opera, this would not be a very large proportion—the amount of freedom is remarkably small as compared with that of the earliest attempts of Haydn or Mozart. By their time complete liberty in this sphere had been won, and it is possible to discern in the maturer works of Gluck, and in such a work as C. P. E. Bach's oratorio *Die Israeliter in der Wüste*, the gradual advance towards the modern manner.

It is clearly quite impossible, in the absence of any direct evidence, to explain why a certain innovation was not found out before the actual date of its discovery, but there are two things that may help us to understand why such masters as Bach and Handel, to say nothing of their contemporaries, were not more advanced than they were in what we now call the art of orchestration. In the first place, it must be remembered

that the science of free part-writing had not yet so completely
superseded that of counterpoint as it did in the latter part of
the eighteenth century. We have repeatedly seen, in different
departments of music, that the massive harmonies and the
strict counterpoint of the older masters was in many places
giving way to a simpler, clearer style of writing; but this new
style had all the weakness and crudity of youth, the laws
that were to govern it were not yet found, and its early
examples were assuredly not such as would be likely to get
the new style accepted by definitely musical people. It is
hardly necessary to point out that the whole idea of frequent
changes in the quality of orchestral tones belongs to the art
of part-writing, not to that of counterpoint.

A more cogent reason for the lack of enterprise, as it must
seem to modern students, shown by the greatest masters of
their day, lies in the entire want of balance from which the
orchestra of the early eighteenth century must have suffered.
We have a few lists of important orchestras of the time, from
which, when taken together, we may realize the general outlines
of the system on which an orchestra was arranged.   In the
valuable memorial addressed by Bach to the Leipzig Council
in regard to the music in the Thomaskirche in 1730[1], while
sixteen singers (four to each part) are recommended, the
instrumental music was as follows:—two or three first violins,
two or three seconds, two first violas, two seconds, two violoncellos and one double bass, one or two bassoons, three trumpets
and one drum (i. e. one drummer, with, no doubt, a pair of
drums).   Rockstro, in his life of Handel, quotes from the
archives of the Foundling Hospital that in 1759, the year
of Handel's death, the orchestra consisted of twelve violins,
three 'Tenners,' three violoncelli, two contrabassi, four oboes,
four bassoons, two horns, two trumpets, kettle-drums, and
organ[2].   Burney, writing in 1770, says that the performers

[1] Spitta, *Life of Bach* (Eng. transl.), ii. 248.
[2] Rockstro, *Life of Handel*, p. 259.

employed in the ordinary service of the Church of the Santo,
at Padua, numbered forty, consisting of eight violins, four
violetti or tenors, four violoncellos, four double basses, and four
wind instruments, with sixteen voices[1]. In another place he
tells us that the basses are all placed on one side of the choir,
the violins, oboes, French horns, and tenors on the other,
from which we may assume that the oboes and French horns
are the four wind instruments mentioned in the former list.
At the San Carlo Theatre at Naples a more eccentric disposition appeared, for there were eighteen first violins, eighteen
seconds, five double basses, and but two violoncellos. (Nothing
is said about violas here.) The opera orchestra at Berlin was
more reasonably constituted, but he gives us only an incomplete
list of the players, since, after saying that[2] 'the band consists of
about fifty performers,' he gives the following, which amount
to forty-two at most (the 'composers' can scarcely have been
counted among the fifty performers):—'two composers, the
concert-master, eleven violins, five violoncellos, two double
basses, two harpsichord players, one harp, four tenors, four
flutes, four hautboys, four bassoons, and two French horns.'
It happens that in the score of Handel's *Fireworks Music*
the number of players engaged upon each part has been noted,
and from this we get an idea of the proportion between the
different wind instruments, though unfortunately no strings
were employed in that piece:—the overture requires three
first trumpets, three second, and three 'principal'; three
'tympano,' which we are probably warranted in taking to
mean three pairs of drums; three first horns, three second,
and three third; twelve first oboes, eight second, and four
third; eight first bassoons, and four second. From the
disposition of the first 'monster' performance of Handel's
music, in the commemoration held in Westminster Abbey
in 1784, we can at least appreciate the notions in vogue

[1] Burney, *Present State of Music in France and Italy*, p. 129.
[2] Burney, *Present State of Music in Germany*, ii. 95.

among musicians of the day as to the proper proportional
strength of the different classes of instruments.   There are five
hundred and twenty-five performers, viz. fifty-nine sopranos,
forty-eight altos, eighty-three tenors, and eighty-four basses;
forty-eight first and forty-seven second violins, twenty-six
violas, twenty-one violoncellos, fifteen double basses, six flutes,
thirteen first oboes and thirteen second, twenty-six bassoons,
one double bassoon, twelve trumpets, twelve horns, six trombones, four drums, and the conductor.   Various interesting
details are given concerning the constitution of the band in
Burney's account of the commemoration, such as that there
was a difficulty in finding any English players on the 'Sacbuts'
or trombones, but that 'in his Majesty's military band' were
found six musicians who played the instrument in its three
varieties.   From the context it is uncertain whether or no
these musicians were found in England or Germany, but their
names, given in the complete list of the performers, have an
unmistakably German sound about them.   The double bassoon
had, according to Burney, been made 'with the approbation of
Mr. Handel' for the coronation of George II, but, owing to
some difficulty, had not been used before this commemoration.   The valuable plan of the orchestra, and the engraving
representing the west end of the Abbey as arranged for the
performance, show that the double bassoon player occupied
a very prominent position, standing in front of the conductor.
The 'four drums' in the above list mean four drummers,
whose names are given, and therefore eight drums, of which
one pair were 'double-base kettle-drums' made for the occasion,
while another pair were the famous 'Tower drums,' taken by
the Duke of Marlborough at Malplaquet in 1709.

One peculiarity appears in all the foregoing lists, and it
is borne out even more strongly in the plan of the Handel
Commemoration than anywhere else; the enormous preponderance of the oboe and bassoon quality as compared with
that of any other class of instruments must strike the most

casual observer. In the plan the oboists stand nearer the audience than the violins, to which they bear a more powerful relation than that of one oboe to four violins. The Foundling Hospital list shows a proportion of one oboe to three violins, and in both the German lists the proportion is even greater, Bach's own list giving two or three oboes to four or six violins. One other relation must be referred to in passing, viz. that between the singers and players. Though, for an orchestra of 250, we should in the present day feel justified in increasing the number of the chorus far beyond the number 274, the idea of the singers outnumbering the players at all was a new one until after this performance, and even then it remained peculiar to England for some time. Two years after the Handel Commemoration *The Messiah* was given in the Domkirche of Berlin under Johann Adam Hiller with 118 vocalists and 186 instrumentalists [1]. The odd proportions of the choir in its own subdivisions is not difficult to explain ; the fact that the trebles sat in the very front of the platform, at the most advantageous spot for the acoustic effect, and that the altos were all male voices, is enough to account for the great preponderance of number among the tenors and basses. The orchestral conditions must be confessed a mystery that is at present insoluble, except by assuming that the men of Handel's time and the next generation had no sense whatever of proportion in music. If we could find any evidence that the tone of the oboe has increased in modern times, so that what formerly required many instruments can now be brought out clearly with one, or if there were any proof that the tone of the violin had decreased in strength from what it was, the explanation might seem to lie in that direction ; but the exact reverse is true, at least of the violins, which, in the present day, are considerably more powerful than they were in Handel's time, owing to various structural improvements, the heightened

[1] Spitta, *Life of Bach* (Eng. transl.), ii. 305.

pitch, and the mellowing effect of time upon the instruments of the best make. The trumpets and oboes are so often opposed to each other in Handel's operas and elsewhere, that the necessity for a large number of oboes is clear in this particular class of work; but in the usual work of the orchestra such details would hardly be considered, beside the strange overpowering of the tone of the strings that must have taken place.

But whatever may have been the cause of the total want of balance in the Handelian orchestra, it seems clear that it had the result of delaying the time when the orchestra was to find a language of its own. If we consider how few were the mellowing influences in the old orchestra; the total lack of the clarinet tone, the comparative weakness and insignificance of the violas, and the entirely subordinate position occupied by the flutes, we shall be able to form some idea of the effect of an eighteenth-century band. The treble and the bass parts would stand out with raucous insistence, varied only by the occasional withdrawal of the oboe tone for a brief space, or the occasional addition of the trumpets; and the fact that the central harmonies were filled up on the harpsichord or organ would do but little to weld the instruments into a homogeneous whole, capable of serving as a background to individualized instruments. It speaks eloquently for the powers of the great masters of the eighteenth century that, even in days when our ears are accustomed to the luscious glow of the modern masters of orchestration, the unspoilt works of the older men should still convey to so many minds, as they undoubtedly do, their full message of emotional intensity or sublime beauty.

CHAPTER VIII

THE GROWTH OF FORM

THE establishment of the rules of musical form marks the great and salient difference between music that we must call ancient or at least old-fashioned, and the beginning of the art as it appeals most directly to ourselves. Although we must regard Bach as far in advance of his age in respect of what must be called the modern element in his style, the fact remains that the gradual development of structural design in instrumental music means nothing less than the creation of a barrier between all that went before and all that followed after. It may seem strange to deny the presence of structural design to the music of a period when the elaborate and detailed conventions of the fugue on the one hand, and the prim formalities of the various suite-movements, on the other, represented the main ideals of the instrumental composer's aim. Putting aside for the moment the extraordinary achievements of the great masters within the arbitrary limitations imposed on them by these forms, it is hardly too much to say that the contrast between these and the perfected symphonic movements of a later generation is analogous to that between a set of stiff geometrical figures and a perfectly drawn outline of the human frame. In the same way, in vocal music, the single voice was seldom used except in the one settled form of the *da capo* aria. (The vocal recitatives of the oratorio and opera-writers, like the preludes of many suites by Handel and others, are intentionally formless and inorganic, serving to introduce and throw into strong relief the set pieces in which the more definite musical idea was to be presented.)   If we went through the music of the early part of the eighteenth century, and set aside all compositions that conformed to one or other of the conventional types, such as the fugue, the variation, including the chaconne and passacaglia, the *da capo* aria, and the dance-measures of the suite or partita, we should find ourselves left with a great body of choral movements on the one hand, and on the other a fairly small number of perfectly vague instrumental pieces called 'fantasias' or 'capriccios,' consisting of little beside flourishes and passages of display unconnected in any organic manner.   Two more forms exhaust the structural possibilities of the age, each allied to a definite purpose; the overture, with its distinctly preludial function, and the concerto, with its scarcely less definite object of exhibiting technical skill.   It will be necessary to show the share which each of the established forms had in the development of what was ultimately accepted as the 'sonata-form,' that pattern upon which many of the greatest creations of the art have been built.   In the single detail of the length of musical compositions we again find, on the one hand, the dance-measures with their strictly-defined pattern of a certain number of bars, the fugue limited by the impossibility of combining its elements in more than a certain number of ways, the arias with their conventional *da capo* regulating their extent more or less exactly, and the choral movements for which the exigencies of the text would provide limits that could not be transgressed; and on the other hand the wayward, arbitrary design, or rather absence of design, in the caprices and fantasias which were evidently meant as a relief from the formalities of the recognized structures.

The term 'sonata,' which was to have such a vast importance in after years, was ambiguous in its use in the earlier times.   At first meaning something sounded on instruments, as distinguished from the 'cantata'—something sung—it was

employed by the Italian composers of the seventeenth century
for solo and concerted music for strings, divided into several
movements; and, at the same time, the great mass of Domenico
Scarlatti's works for harpsichord, consisting in all cases of a single
movement, are styled sonatas.   The discrepancy between these
two uses of the same word, it may be noticed in passing, has
left traces down to the present day, since, while the word itself
is strictly confined to the first of the two meanings given
above, we are accustomed to speak of sonata-form in regard
to the structure illustrated in one only of the movements in
a sonata consisting of several.

It is a long way from the rudimentary sonatas of this period,
whether in one movement or more, to the finished form as we
have it in Mozart and Beethoven; and the perfected structure
was not derived from any one of the forms in vogue in the
early eighteenth century, but from several of them, each giving
some element of beauty, or opening out some new method of
artistic development.   It is beyond the limits of the present
volume to trace the course of the sonata after it took ultimate
shape, but a consideration of its possibilities must be of use
in obtaining some insight into the aims and opportunities of
the composers before its time.   The principle of alternately
stating two contrasting themes, which found its ultimate
expression in the successive presentation of first and second
subjects, had been familiar to the musical world as long as
minuets and trios, gavottes, musettes, and the like, had been in
vogue, but the process by which the two subjects are allowed
to be interwoven with each other, or to generate, as it were,
new material having its origin in something that has gone
before, opened out a world of fresh possibilities to the
composers of the later times, and gave them opportunities
which had been altogether withheld from Bach and his
contemporaries.   The development of a single melodic germ
is carried to its finest and fullest extent in many of the
preludes of the *Wohltemperirtes Clavier*; and in many of

Bach's concertos we seem to see him on the very brink
of the discovery of the principle of duality, but he never
quite reaches it.   It is a curious fact that in the course
of the history of form, neither Bach nor Handel should
have taken a prominent part in trying new methods of
giving their instrumental works the special kind of unity in
variety which was destined to such high uses in after years;
but the reason is probably that Bach's wealth of invention
made the task of developing a long movement from a single
germ especially fascinating to him, leading him to a complacent
attitude towards forms as they were, while Handel's time was
fully occupied in preparing operas or oratorios for his English
patrons, or in compiling suites and concertos more or less
definitely intended as vehicles of display.   Beside the dialogue
of the contrasting subjects, the sonata-form made it easier
than it had ever been before to ensure a perfect proportion
in regard to length.   The exposition of the themes with the
compulsory repetition, the development or 'working-out'
section, and the recapitulation, formed a natural plan of
division which could be easily followed, and within whose
limitations even the tyro could not go very far astray, while
the greatest genius might find abundant scope for his most
original ideas, and the most individual manifestation of his
technical skill.

The sonata as we know it derives something from almost
if not quite every form in vogue in the time of Bach and
Handel; and it will be useful to pass these forms successively
in review, in order to obtain a clear idea of the materials
out of which the sonata-form was evolved.

THE FUGUE.

It need hardly be pointed out that the supremely important
form in the time of Bach was that of the Fugue; if evidence
were needed of the fact, it would be forthcoming from a mere

superficial glance at the compositions of the time, in whatever mould they were ostensibly cast, for, apart from actual fugues so called, there occur so many types of imitation in almost every possible guise, that it is hardly too much to say that it would be difficult to find any composition of the time of considerable extent in which such points do not occur, or where the *fugato* style is unused from beginning to end. The actual machinery of the fugue, and the great majority of the devices in which the fugue-writers exhibited their skill, had been reduced to a system by the Italians of the older generation, who, as Naumann has well said (*History of Music*, Eng. Transl. i. 626), 'transmitted the form to Bach in a state so perfect that he had but to put the finishing touch to it, whilst in certain features he had nothing to improve or add.' What was the 'finishing touch' which Bach gave to the fugue-form, and in virtue of which his name is for ever connected with the idea of the perfected fugue? It was certainly not in the direction of the orthodox methods, by any strict observance of the laws laid down by the older men, for he transgresses these laws at so many points that more than one eminent writer on fugue has found himself face to face with the necessity either of saying that Bach was wrong, or of adopting the difficult position that all the theorists were mistaken, and of building a new system or the practice of Bach himself. But the truly scientific way to look at such a case as this is surely to acknowledge that it is not without parallel in the history of the arts that the man who, of all others, has identified himself with a particular form of art, should be the very one who has most often broken its rules. The position of Beethoven as the creator of the noblest things ever written in sonata-form is on all hands acknowledged; yet no sonatas of the great period depart so far as his from the stereotyped pattern which only the less gifted men employed in all its strictness. Bach, like Beethoven, had earned the right to be a law to himself,

and we need not assume his fugues to have been written
solely as illustrations to a text-book. It is true that a whole
set of very fine fugues of his was so intended, but it is the
student of fugal structure rather than the musician of average
education who will uphold *The Art of Fugue* as one of Bach's
greatest works. He could not, it is true, make anything he
wrote seem academic or dull, but in the whole collection we
may trace an absence of the quality which must endear the
Wohltemperirtes Clavier fugues to all who have ordinary
musical susceptibilities.

The fact that this collection is a mere exhibition of
contrapuntal skill, and of variety in the treatment of the
same subject throughout the work, may have something to
do with the undeniable fact that it has never won the place
in musicians' esteem which is granted to the earlier collection
already mentioned. Yet *The Art of Fugue* was the last work of
Bach's lifetime, and was published by Emanuel Bach in 1752,
together with a number of fragments and sketches, some of
which have nothing to do with the plan of the work. It
has been stoutly maintained by Spitta[1] that the great fugue
on three subjects, only about three-quarters of which were
finished (the point of development reached at the 239th bar,
the last that remains, is such that another quarter of the
fugue is wanted to complete it) has nothing to do with the
scheme of the whole book, and that its subjects have no
connexion with that on which all the rest of the fugues are
built. But it is surely not a great stretch of imagination
to regard the first subject,

as an alteration of the theme of the whole, first announced
thus:

[1] *Life of Bach* (Eng. transl.), iii. 197 ff. 204, 5.

the second subject,

is indeed independent, while the third is on the notes whose names make up the name 'Bach.'

Such tasks as the composer set himself here, of writing numbers of fugues on the same subject, or on a theme arbitrarily chosen, like the subject given him by Frederic II on his celebrated visit to Potsdam in 1747, seem to have appealed strongly to Bach more particularly in his later life. The *Musikalisches Opfer* was the outcome of that visit, since Bach was anxious to prove to the king what he could do with the 'thema regium,' beyond and above what he had been able to do at the extempore performance at Potsdam. The two fugues entitled 'Ricercare' may be said to touch the extreme height of difficulty, as their name implies; but the difficulty of the second, in six parts, is rather for the player than the composer, and no doubt had its origin in the king's request for a six-part fugue played extempore.

But it was not in these mighty intellectual efforts that Bach put the finishing touch to the fugue form of his day; it is by the emotional quality and the expressive power of his fugues that he stands far above all composers of any age who have attempted fugal writing. This emotional quality appears most distinctly in the famous *Forty-Eight Preludes and Fugues*, the two series of which were compiled in 1722 and 1744 respectively, though not published in Bach's lifetime. In spite of the twenty-two years which intervened between the two books, it is convenient to discuss them as one collection in this place; and there is little trace of any difference in style to be found between the two sets. Each book is arranged on the same plan, that of giving one prelude and fugue in each of the twenty-four keys, major and minor, with the idea, implied in the title *Das wohltemperirte Clavier*, of encouraging the adoption of equal temperament by the clavichord-tuners of the time; but neither this, nor the strictly educational style of the full title [1], gives one any idea of the poetical value of the collection, which, after all, is the quality that has preserved it in full activity of life and influence. To take the fugues by themselves, the first four give us in some sort a foretaste of what we are to hear afterwards; the exquisitely simple, straightforward design of the first, the plaintive innocence of the second, the tender grace and charm of the third, and the magnificent intricacy and varied character of the fourth, each is but one example of a large class. The note of pathos, so gently suggested in the second fugue, is increasingly evident in Nos. 8, 12, 16, 18, 20, and 22, until in the last fugue of the first book, it speaks with irresistible power in a fugue which may almost be called a tragedy in itself. Nos. 2, 8, and 22 in the second book are almost the only minor fugues that have the same poignancy of expression, although many of the major fugues of the second book are deeply emotional, as, for example, the ninth, so aptly called by Sebastian Wesley 'The Saints in Glory,' the seventeenth, and the twenty-third. It almost seems that the possibility of expressing sadness in the major mode was only discovered in the second book,

---

[1] 'Das wohl temperirte Clavier, oder *Praeludia* und *Fugen* durch alle *Töne* und *Semitonia* sowohl *tertiam majorem* oder *Ut Re Mi* anlangend, als auch *tertiam minorem* oder *Re Mi Fa* betreffend. Zum Nutzeu und Gebrauch der Lehrbegierigen *Musical-isch* Jugend als auch derer in diesem *Studio* schon *habil* seyenden besondern Zeit Vertreib aufgesetzt und verfertiget von *Johann Sebastian Bach, p. t.* Hochfürstl. Anhalt-Cöthenischen *Capell*-Meistern und *Directore* derer Cammer-*Musiquen.* Anno 1722.' ('The well-tempered Clavier, or preludes and fugues in all the tones and semitones, both with the major third, or Ut, Re, Mi, and with the minor third, or Re, Mi, Fa. For the use and practice of young musicians who desire to learn, as well as for those who are already skilled in this study, by way of amusement; made and composed by Johann Sebastian Bach, for the time being Capellmeister to the Grand Duke of Anhalt-Cöthen, and Director of his Chamber-Music. In the year 1722.')

and in the same way several of the fugues which correspond
in mood to the gayer numbers of the first book, such as
Nos. 7, 9, 11, 13, 15, and 21, are in the minor in the second
book, such as Nos. 6, 10, 12, and 24, while the more jovial
fugues in the major, such as Nos. 11, 15, and 17, are
comparatively few.   Apart from the pathetic or inspiriting
effect of the fugues upon the hearer, they are marvels of
skill, but of skill subordinated to the emotional message they
convey.   The play of the subject and the two important
counter-subjects in the fourth fugue of the first book, in
C sharp minor, have all the strongly-marked individuality
of persons in a drama; and in places too numerous to mention
some technical device carries with it the peculiar conviction
of fitness, of inevitability, which is an important element in
what we call inspiration.   It is the association of the perfect
and easy skill of counterpoint with the unfettered power of
direct expression, which makes the 'Forty-Eight' as eloquent
in the present day as they were to the few worthy students
for whose benefit they were originally written.   Perhaps no
better example can be adduced than two passages in the
fugue in E major, in the second book, No. 9, already
mentioned, on this subject :—

where the theme is brought in in diminution, with the
astonishing effect of an entirely new subject :—

and again, where the close stretto between the lower parts
is joined to the diminished inversion of the theme in the
top part :—

At both these points the hearer, whether he be acquainted with the technical structure of the fugue or not, can hardly fail to receive the kind of thrill which belongs to the supreme things in all the arts.

The consideration of the preludes which belong to these immortal fugues must be left to a later part of this chapter, but this may be the best place to refer to the question of their inner or thematic connexion with the fugues. This connexion, it must be admitted, cannot be very obvious, since it has been hotly denied by many great authorities, and upheld by others not less keenly. A careful examination of the whole collection shows that while in ten cases of the first set and eight of the second no connexion can be traced, in fourteen of the first set and sixteen of the second it is possible to establish some kind of interdependence between prelude and fugue, even though it be no nearer than in the case of the second of the first set, where the germ of the fugal theme clearly provides the figure on which the prelude is built. In No. 3 the pairs of notes which appear first in the bass of the prelude seem to be alluded to in the second bar of the fugal theme; in No. 19 the similarity only becomes apparent in the twenty-seventh bar of the fugue, where the figure of the second bar of the prelude appears. The resemblance in the wonderful twenty-second prelude and fugue is mainly due to intensification of the climax in both, but there is also in the counter-subject of the fugue a reference to the figure of the prelude. The twenty-third pair have the same notes at the beginning of their themes; and in the thirteenth of the second book the fugue is built on the last notes of the prelude in a way which cannot be mistaken.

When we consider the wealth, not only of invention, but of emotional variety which is contained in the collection, it is curious to see what a large proportion of the themes of the minor fugues have the same harmonic foundation. Every theme, whether of a popular song or of a fugue, implies a certain sequence of harmonies; as compared with the possible combinations of implied harmonies it is surprising to discover throughout the eighteenth century the large use that is made of the alternation of the tonic with that diminished seventh which has its unheard root at the dominant. The implied harmonies may be thus expressed :—

Out of the twenty-four minor fugues in the two parts of the *Wohltemperirtes Clavier*, there are no fewer than thirteen which conform to this pattern in the implied harmonies of their themes. Thus they outnumber representatives of all other combinations of minor harmonies put together; and over and over again we find the composers of the time choosing to work on subjects of this particular pattern with evident love. The theme which Frederick II gave Bach, and on which the *Musikalisches Opfer* is founded, is

and some examples may be taken to illustrate the frequency with which the sequence of harmonies was used in the ' Forty-Eight [1].'

No. 16. Book I.

No. 20. Book I.

---

[1] There is nothing peculiar to Bach in this implied harmonic progression, which occurs throughout the music of the eighteenth century : an instance of its almost incessant use is Caldara's *Suonate a tre*, Amsterdam, 1700.

The last of the themes given is a subject which became recognized as common property in the eighteenth century; prominent instances of its use are 'And with His stripes' in *The Messiah*, and 'Cum sanctis tuis' in Mozart's *Requiem*. Two more clavier fugues must be shortly referred to, as among the supreme things in the kind, one the great fugue in A minor with the *arpeggiato* prelude, and the other the fairy-like little fugue in the same key, which is written with evident consideration of harpsichord effects on this subject:—

The preludes to the organ fugues have a more evident connexion with the fugues themselves than was to be traced in the *Wohltemperirtes Clavier*. The great fugue in three distinct sections, known as 'Saint Anne's' in England because of the familiar hymn-tune with the same opening notes (see chapter xiv) has no prelude, but the solemn introductions to such fugues as the D minor—

prepare the hearers' minds for what is to come as effectually as the brilliant pieces which usher in the G minor—

or the A minor—

while the intimate connexion of sentiment between the short
prelude and fugue in E minor—

cannot be mistaken for a moment. Notwithstanding the fact
that the fugue had little or no direct influence in the constitution of the sonata form, it is worth mentioning that the two
were amalgamated ultimately in Mozart's overture to *Die
Zauberflöte*, while Dr. Riemann and Professor Prout acknowledge that in the 'Forty-Eight' there are examples which
show a close affinity to the sonata structure in their return
to a recapitulation section after an episodical excursion to
more or less remote keys.

This simple plan of a statement of a theme, an episode,
and a recapitulation of the original statement, is easily to
be traced in the majority of the dance-movements which
make up the suites, and which had their own effect on the
sonata form, in virtue of the principle of the association of
a number of separate movements into one artistic and organic
whole. Not that the suites themselves were organic in the strict
sense, for it is nearly always possible to omit single numbers
even from the most beautiful suites without creating the sort
of disturbance which would result from the omission of a
sonata-movement. It is curious to find that a kind of arbitrary
arrangement lasted in the suite far later than in any other
branch of music, *viz.* the identity of key in all the sections.
The origin of this is undoubtedly to be found in the books
of songs to be accompanied on the lute, and its reason was
in order to avoid retuning the open bass strings of the lute
between one song and the next; but it is strange to find
the practice enduring as far down as the time of Bach, long
after it had been recognized that a change of key was desirable

in long compositions, and when the principle of key-sequence
seems to have been perfectly understood in operas and oratorios.
The alternation of fast movements with slow was the ruling
principle of the suite, and this seems to have had its origin
in the practice of the early writers who joined the dignified
'pavan' to the sprightly 'galliard' in such collections as are
preserved in the *Fitzwilliam Virginal Book* and many others.
In those times the place of the 'alman' and 'corranto' were
not recognized in any kind of association, but these two
became, with the 'saraband,' the essential parts of the suite.

In the great majority of suites the 'allemande' was followed
immediately by the 'courante,' the two making an effective
contrast both of rhythm and style. The former is, with hardly
an exception, a highly ornate melody of semiquavers in common
time, the melody being almost entirely confined to a single
part; the latter is in triple time and polyphonic in style, and
its quick, lively character distinguishes it from the graver,
more earnest triple measure of the 'sarabande' which follows
it. Three different kinds of courante are referred to in Grove's
Dictionary, but the third or hybrid kind seems of such rare
occurrence outside the works of Handel that it may be disregarded. The regular divisions of the class are two, the French
courante, the form generally used in Bach's suites, which has
the peculiarity that the last bar of each section is in $\frac{6}{4}$ time,
in contradiction of the time-signature, $\frac{3}{2}$. This gives a very
individual swing to the measure, and suggests that some
feature of the dance corresponded to the change of metre.
The Italian form of the courante, or corrento, is illustrated
in the fifth of Bach's partitas, the fifth of Handel's first set
of lessons, and the fifth and sixth of Bach's French suites.
It is more rapid and homophonic than the French courante.
An interesting comparison between the two forms of the same
dance will be found in Mattheson's suites, No. 4, where two
courantes appear side by side, with the title 'courante françoise'
over the second.

As the allemande is the first of the regular component
parts of the suite, the gigue is its regular close; Bach
departed from this rule in regard to the gigue only once,
in the second partita, where a 'caprice' in $\frac{2}{4}$ time takes its
place, but out of Handel's sixteen suites, five do not end
with the gigue; and out of Mattheson's twelve, a gigue ends
no more than four. Still these are but the exceptions which
prove the rule; and the place of the gigue is almost as
universally recognized as that of the allemande, courante, or
sarabande. In Bach, and occasionally elsewhere, are distinguished two classes of gigue. The first and simpler has
a continuous movement of quaver triplets, as in the second
of the English suites, and the first of the partitas; the second,
illustrated in the third and fifth of the English suites and the
fifth partita, as well as in many other places in Bach, consists,
in the first part, of a regular fugal exposition[1], and in the
second part, of a freer but still fugal treatment of the subject
inverted. In both the instances mentioned from the English
suites, it is curious to notice that the entries in the second
part follow precisely the same plan; the first note of each
is the supertonic of the key, but with this exception the
phrase is an exact inversion of the opening; the second
voice has a 'real' answer, and not till the entry of the third
does the inverted phrase come in in its strict way beginning
on the tonic of the key. This modification of the first note
of the inverted phrase was evidently due to a desire to
maintain the impression of the dominant harmony at the
start of the second section, after the dominant close of the
first section.

The opening of the suite was far less a matter of strict
conformity to precedent. Only three out of Mattheson's
twelve suites begin with the allemande; in the rest the
allemande is preceded by an introductory movement, called,

---

[1] Ebenezer Prout, *Applied Forms*, p. 33, &c.

not merely by such obvious names as 'prelude' or 'overture,' but by such titles as 'fantaisie,' 'boutade,' and 'symphonie,' to say nothing of a very broken-backed 'fugue,' which opens the eleventh suite. All six of Muffat's *Componimenti Musicali* begin with preludes or overtures, and the eight suites of Handel's first set have introductory movements, each of the second set beginning with the allemande. In much the same way Bach, in his French suites, begins each with the allemande, preserving complete uniformity of arrangement until after the sarabande, and ending always with a gigue. In the English suites he has an elaborate prelude, so called in all cases; and in the partitas he must needs have a new name for each of the six introductory movements, and calls them successively prélude, sinfonia, fantaisie, ouverture, préambule, and toccata. The partitas for violin without accompaniment are much freer in arrangement than the six suites for viol-da-gamba, all of which conform to the strictest pattern of the suite.

Between the sarabande and the gigue was the usual place for the insertion of the short movements of lesser consequence, such as the minuets, passepieds, bourrées, gavottes, or what not, that might fall into the general scheme of the suite. The French and English suites of Bach conform to this without exception, each of them having one or more of these movements in exactly this part of the work. In two of the partitas there is an 'air' between the courante and the sarabande, and Handel divides his allemande from his courante in the fourteenth suite by an allegro. But whatever variety in number, arrangement, names, or rhythms of the measures, the structure of all except the prelude was very much the same. They conform to what is known as the 'binary' structure, in which the composition falls into two sections, the first leading as a rule from tonic to dominant, and the second, by a rather longer way, from the dominant back to the original key. In many gigues, the theme of the second part is the inversion of the opening. In the case of the smaller measures just mentioned, it was very common to couple two specimens of the same dance together, so that the second minuet or bourrée would be played between two repetitions of the first, thus carrying out the *da capo* form which survives in the scherzos or minuets of the modern sonata. The smaller and the larger dance-measures alike were apt to be accommodated with 'doubles' or variations, generally consisting of one ornamented version of the original, sometimes headed 'Les agrémens de la même sarabande' or the like.

The longer sets of variations were generally placed at the end of the suite, as in two well-known instances in Handel, the first of which, that in D minor, presents a curious instance of quite modern practice in regard to using the same theme in more than one movement. The 'presto' which succeeds the last of the 'doubles' is quite clearly not to be regarded as a variation on the theme; its time is changed from common time to $\frac{3}{8}$, and yet its opening phrase is evidently derived from the theme of the variations. A specially interesting case where something of the same kind occurs is in two of Pergolesi's 'sonatas,' published in London between 1771 and 1777, in the fourth of which the giga is a variation upon the subject of the gavotta, and in the sixth of which the whole suite, with the single exception of the prelude, is a set of variations and a suite at the same time. The allegro (allemanda) has two variations in its own rhythm, like Handel's doubles just mentioned, and after that a vivace in Siciliano time is marked 'var. 3,' and a minuet 'var. 4.' The so-called 'Harmonious Blacksmith' variations of Handel, and the Gavotte with variations in A minor by Rameau, are good typical instances of the occurrence of this form in the suite. A very special kind of variation was the form, or pair of allied forms, of the 'Chaconne' and 'Passecaille,' or ciacona and passacaglia.

So contradictory are the definitions of these two forms given
in the various dictionaries, &c., in the time of their most
extensive use, that it is best to regard them as practically
identical. The strict rule of both was that they must be in
triple time[1], and that the central motive of the composition
should be the continual reiteration of the bass, so that the
'ground-bass' of Purcell's time, and the 'ground' of the
composers before him, are closely allied to the chaconne.
The convention in vogue at one time that every opera should
end with a chaconne is one of the few that remained down
to the time of Gluck's *Orfeo*; so that the form, in one guise
or another, had a remarkably long term of life, and its
resuscitation in the finale of Brahms's E minor symphony
was enough to prove that its possibilities were not exhausted
by the eighteenth century masters. As its length was limited
only when the composer's invention ran short, it was evidently
a convenient thing to put the chaconne or passacaglia at the
end of the suites in which it appears; and accordingly all the
most celebrated instances of its use as part of the suite occur
at the end, as in the case of Handel's G minor passecaille, an
exception to the rule of triple time. Bach's D minor suite for
violin alone ends with the most wonderful chaconne the world
has ever seen, built upon five themes, each of them made,
as it were, to deliver up its whole wealth of musical suggestion;
whether separately or in marvellously skilful combination, the
work is not only an exhibition of the highest kind of technical
dexterity, but a monument of emotional beauty such as is
hardly to be found elsewhere. The older generation had
used the form freely; Buxtehude wrote several *ciacone* for
organ, in which we may see the model of Bach's own organ
passacaglia; in Johann Pachelbel's collected clavier works are
six *ciacone*, Georg Muffat's 'Apparatus musico-organisticus'

[1] Rousseau's Dictionary refers to some older chaconnes in duple time, and
that of Couperin, called 'La Favorite,' was possibly the latest exception to
the usual rule.

contains some interesting specimens, and his son, August Gottlieb (Theophilus), finishes up his collection of suites, already
mentioned under the title of *Componimenti musicali*, with a
somewhat conventional ciacona of thirty-eight variations.

The famous set of thirty variations which Bach dedicated to
a celebrated harpsichord player named Goldberg is one of his
most characteristic works; the principle of the ' basso ostinato '
may be discerned underlying the great majority of the variations,
though it is never obtrusively prominent; yet it is this, rather
than the theme of the superimposed sarabande, which is the
groundwork of the whole. The plan is that of a series of
canons successively on every interval from the second to the
tenth, divided from one another by variations of which the
more obvious purpose is to give relief to the contrapuntal
numbers, whether in a display of the technical skill of the
performer, or in movements of a tenderly emotional cast. The
technical difficulties are mainly such as are only possible upon
a harpsichord with two manuals, on which the constant crossing
of the parts can be clearly brought out; and some of the later
variations, especially one in which alternate chords are taken
by the two hands each on its own keyboard, are almost
prophecies of some of Liszt's favourite devices. For the close
of the wonderful series, a ' Quodlibet ' on two popular songs
of Bach's day is placed over the bass, the result being a
triumphant instance of the happy concealment of consummate
art in a little piece which would only strike the average hearer
as a peculiarly jovial ending to the variations.

Before discussing the work of the great French master of
the suite, or ' Ordre ' as he preferred to call it, it is necessary
to look back at one example of the passacaglia or ' ground-
bass ' which foreshadowed, in a remarkable way, one of the
most prominent works of the French composer. In Purcell's
plaintive little ' Ground ' in C minor [1], there is a very inter-

---

[1] Purcell Society's publications, vol. vi. p. 51.

esting variety of the form; the theme, in common time, is
three and a half bars long, so that at every alternate repetition the accent comes on what was the unaccented part of the
bar, thus changing the aspect of the theme each time. But
more than this; after each occurrence of the bass theme with
a different superstructure it is repeated exactly as it began,
with its original melody. This pattern is evidently closely
allied to the rondo form, which consists of the more or less
literal repetition of the main theme, with freely invented
episodes between each repetition; the remarkably beautiful
and expressive piece which comes just before the end of
Couperin's eighth 'Ordre' is headed both 'Passacaille' and
'Rondeau'; after each of its 'couplets' the impressive theme
is brought back without any alteration, and the feeling of the
whole piece may be compared to some of the 'Dances of
Death' in old German art, in which the figure of Death is
shown as ready to seize representatives of every class and
age of life in succession.

The work of Couperin stands so far apart from that of the
masters who wrote by preference suites of more stereotyped
form, that it has been left to be discussed by itself.   François
Couperin (1668–1733) had a great influence in the development
of what we call 'form' through Bach, whose suites are full
of numbers evidently modelled on the patterns used with so
much success by the Frenchman. Of the twenty-seven 'Ordres'
which compose his best-known work, only a very few make any
attempt to follow the usual sequence of dances; but some of
the earlier suites begin with an allemande, one or two courantes,
a sarabande, and a gigue, after which occur a number of
pieces with fancy names, nearly all of them in rondeau form,
whether so called or not. The later 'ordres' of the series
consist for the most part of nothing but these early specimens
of 'programme-music.' Two kinds of structure were much in
favour with Couperin; the simple binary form in two sections
with the addition of a little coda after the repetition of the

second; and the rondeau, in which every episode is followed by a literal repetition of the main theme. It is also worth notice that he is far less strictly bound to a single tonality than his German contemporaries. With the sonatas of the succeeding generation before us, it is difficult to imagine how a man like Couperin, with so complete a command as he had of these two forms, should have failed to hit upon the plan of combining them into one, which, with certain modifications, is the plan of the sonata properly so called.

The great difference between the sonata form and anything yet considered is that the sonata-movement has not one but two main themes, and that of its various episodes not one has the structural importance which the place, the entry, and the key of the 'second subject' give it at once. All that has hitherto passed before our notice is constructed on one principal subject, whether in the form of a simple *da capo* air, the almost equally rudimentary dance forms of the suite, or the rondo form, which, as we have seen, is so closely allied to the passacaglia, and through that to the variation-structure: it remains to speak of yet another species of construction in which the single theme is used almost to the exclusion of all else. The 'prelude' of Bach and Handel's time might be a simple series of harmonies such as a player might extemporize before beginning the suite or the fugue; instances of this elementary type are to be found in several of Handel's suites, and in the *arpeggiato* prelude to Bach's great clavichord fugue in A minor. Or, its theme might be treated in a continuous, consistently homogeneous movement unrestricted as to length, but never losing sight of the subject whether in a simple or a developed form; figures or phrases might be generated from the theme, but it, and no other succession of notes would be the parent, so to speak, of every musical idea that occurred through the movement. On this pattern the six splendid preludes to Bach's 'English Suites' are formed, as well as the two-part 'Inventions' and the three-part

'Symphonies,' and the great majority of the preludes in the *Wohltemperirtes Clavier*. The form of 'Overture' used in some of the series differed from this mainly in the fact that it generally had a slow introduction in more or less dotted rhythm, followed by an allegro movement of fugal character; still there is no trace throughout of anything that can justly be dignified with the name of a second subject.

One of the most remarkable collections of pieces in the simple binary form, i. e. with one main theme, but divided into two sections, the latter as a rule longer than the first, and returning to the key of the first after an excursion into some key not far remote from that of the opening, was the set of thirty *Esercizi per Gravicembalo*, published by Domenico Scarlatti, the son of Alessandro, some time before 1746, when the Prince of the Asturias, in whose service Scarlatti held office at the time of publication, ascended the throne of Spain. Each of the thirty pieces is headed 'Sonata,' even the last of them, which is the famous 'Cat's Fugue,' on a theme supposed to have been suggested by a cat walking over the keys of the harpsichord. The form of the great majority of the pieces by Scarlatti which remain is identical; in some instances, those who look back upon the works from the point of view of the thoroughly developed sonata are able to trace the rudiments of a real second subject, but even where the presence of such an innovation seems most clearly marked, it is certain that the possible functions to be performed by the second subject were not fully grasped by the composer. It simply happened that one of the episodes held a more prominent place than the others, or that its relation to the principal theme was less evident than usual. As an instance of typographical humility, the text of the heading of the dedicatory letter may be given :— 'ALLA SACRA REAL MAESTÀ DI GIOVANI V. IL GIUSTO RE DI PORTUGALLO, D'ALGARVE, DEL BRASILE, &c., &c., &c., *l'umilissimo servo domenico scarlatti.*' This volume is far from including the whole of Domenico's work for the harpsichord; 349 sonatas are said to have been in the possession of the Abbé Santini, and the statement, which has hitherto been received with some incredulity, is more than confirmed by a close comparison of the sonatas gathered from all sources which have been published in modern times, with the contents of fifteen important MS. volumes in the library of the Ducal Palace at Venice, which brings the number of known compositions in this form to 550. Czerny's edition of 200, reprinted in a more correct form by Mme. Farrenc in the *Trésor des Pianistes,* is the largest collection now available. The astonishing mastery of the keyboard shown in them, the knowledge of effect and contrast, the sparkling brilliance of many, the quaintly artificial melancholy of a few, and the musical value of nearly all, have endeared a large number of these sonatas to pianoforte players and the public, and given them a vogue which only the very greatest works of Scarlatti's contemporaries enjoy.

There remains to be discussed one more form which had a large influence on the sonata that was to be,—the Concerto. The curious fact that every nation but our own uses the same word for the two things that we call ' Concert' and ' Concerto,' is an unconscious tribute to the fact that at the time the latter form of composition became popular, England was the only country where public ' concerts' existed. The idea which is at the root of the word, whatever its form, is that of gathering together to make music, and the same idea recurs in our expression ' concerted music.' The notion of personal display, which is now almost inseparable from the word concerto, was slow in being accepted; and the ' Concerti grossi' of Bach and Handel are in reality the precursors rather of the symphony than of the modern concerto. In their employment of a group of instruments against the full band, they are the lineal descendants of the works of Torelli and Corelli so named, but differ mainly from these in that the group of soloists is always the same with the Italians, while the two German masters vary theirs as occasion may arise. Torelli's set, published in 1709, is for two violins and orchestra; Corelli's 'Concertino' and that of Handel's twelve 'Grand Concertos,' as the group of solo instruments was called in contra-distinction to the 'ripieno' or 'concerto grosso' of the rest of the orchestra, always consists of two violins and a violoncello, against the usual complement of strings (including violas); while in Bach's 'Brandenburg' concertos some have no obvious division into solo and accompanying instruments, and in those which have a definite 'concertino' the instruments forming it vary; thus in the finale of the first, in F, a 'violino piccolo' or 'Quart-geige' is used with or without the first horn in passages of a solo kind; in the second, a trumpet, flute, oboe, and violin are accompanied by the string quartet; the fourth, in G, is a violin concerto with two flutes added to the string accompaniment; the fifth employs, as a group of solo instruments, the harpsichord, flute, and violin, and the third of the set is for strings in nine parts. The concertos which are more closely assimilated to the pattern now recognized are the various works for violin, two violins, one, two, or three claviers, and other combinations of instruments; besides which Bach adapted no fewer than sixteen concertos by Vivaldi, thus testifying to his interest in experiments of the kind.

But it is not the disposition of the concerto so much as its construction that is important in the history of musical form; whether one instrument or many appear as the chief factor in the music, the rule, in all but the most orchestrally-conceived concertos, is that the solo instrument or instruments should have theme to discuss apart from the main theme, which is given out by them and the accompanying instruments together. The alternation of these solo passages with the 'tutti' portions is a device obviously very similar to that of the rondo, but here is the essential difference between the two; in the rondo, every

recurrence of the theme is cut and dried, and divided off from
the episodical matter with unmistakable distinctness; in the
concerto, the texture, so to speak, of the movement is much
closer, and the interplay between the tutti and the solo parts
much less stiff, thus approaching the sonata form of the future
in a manner which suggests, in some cases, that the movement
is just on the point of becoming a fully developed sonata-
movement. Perhaps the most remarkable instance of the
closeness of Bach's approach to the sonata as we now understand it is in the 'Italian Concerto' for harpsichord, in which
the absence of all passages written for mere display makes the
features of the structure easier to point out. There is of
course no accompaniment, and it is at once evident that the
work is nothing more than an imitation of the concerto style
in the matter of form, and of form alone. There are clearly-
marked 'tutti' phrases both in the first movement and in the
finale; but the arrangement of the episodical material shows
that the 'second subject' is far from being recognized as such.
It first appears in the same key as the opening phrase, the
second strain of which is in the dominant; and after modulation to the dominant, the first subject is brought back in that
key, with its second phrase in the tonic, thus corresponding
to the rule in regard to the answer of a tonal fugue; but with
the briefest restatement of the main subject new episodical
matter comes in, leading to D minor, the relative minor, in
which key a second important episode enters, leading up to
a short allusion to the main theme in the sub-dominant;
something like a recapitulation appears shortly afterwards,
over a running bass, and the second episode, formerly introduced in the relative minor, now appears in the dominant
major, after which a literal repetition of the first thirty bars
is heard by way of ending the movement. The exquisite
pathos of the slow movement, a highly ornamented minor air
over a persistent bass, and the gaiety of the finale, a more or
less free rondo, are qualities which make the work a favourite

with all intelligent players and listeners; nor does the fact
that the structure of its first movement stops just short of
the happy state of development reached after Bach's death
by his son, Carl Philipp Emanuel, take away from its musical
value or emotional beauty. On the whole, as regards general
effect, it is the nearest thing we have to the orthodox sonata
before the moment when the elevation of the second subject
into an all-important factor gave limitless opportunity for the
exhibition of the highest originality and variety. It must not
be forgotten that others besides Domenico Scarlatti used the
word 'sonata' at a date when its present meaning could not
in the nature of things be applied to the word; from Purcell's
sonatas of three and of four parts, which were short successions of movements mainly in a more or less imitative or
canonic style, through Johann Kuhnau, whose 'Biblical Sonatas'
endeavour to follow the stories chosen, and sometimes manage
to do so with exceedingly quaint results, the word had been
applied more or less constantly to a composition in many
movements. Bach's own use of it seems to have been as
applied to a particular kind of suite, in which the prelude
and fugue at the opening usurped the greatest share of
importance; these were followed by one or more of the
usual suite-movements. The same or a similar plan was
employed by him in the six overtures for orchestra, in which,
beginning with movements of some severity, the composer
adds to them a number of dance-measures of the simplest
kind.

We have traced the influence of the various kinds of instrumental music in the work of generating the sonata that was to
come; and have seen how the prelude with its single theme,
the rondo with its well-defined episodes, the concerto with its
episodes more closely welded in with the main theme to form
a continuous whole, went to suggest different elements in the
first movement form; how the *da capo* air was developed,
without any very great alteration, into the typical slow move-

ment; and how the rondo and variation forms combined to suggest the shape of the last movement. The influence of the fugue-form upon the sonata is a good deal less direct and evident, but the dance-movements which formed the most popular elements in the suite found their place in the sonata, and, as minuets or scherzos, have held it with very little modification ever since.

CHAPTER IX

THE RISE OF VIRTUOSITY

No feature of the musical history of the period under consideration is more remarkable, and few more important in influence and effect, than the prominence gradually gained by executive skill, manifested in vocal or instrumental music. Looking away from the giant forms of Bach and Handel, the world of their contemporaries seems to have been given up to the admiration of virtuosity pure and simple, that is to say, of technical ability acquired and practised for its own sake, not for the sake of interpreting the nobler thoughts of the great composers. Many causes combined to bring about this state of things; in the first place, solo performances were a comparatively new invention in music of an artistic or cultivated kind, and as a matter of course they gave a splendid opportunity for the growth of that spirit of emulation which is inherent in humanity; in the second place, the virtual non-existence of concerts, using the word in its modern sense of an entertainment open to all who can afford to pay for admission, had the result of limiting the enjoyment of the more elaborate kinds of musical performances to the nobility, and at the same time of giving enormous importance to the preferences of individual amateurs, most of whom were but half-educated in musical matters. Until about the middle of the seventeenth century there are few, if any, traces of that cleavage between the professional and the amateur musicians which in later days has crippled the influence of both classes alike. The performance of madrigals, of concerted instrumental music, such as the early *sonate da camera*, are difficult to associate with the payment of a fee by those who listened; the opera in its early stages of development was distinctly an amateur invention; and it was by ecclesiastical rather than by mercantile restrictions that the singers of church music were separated from the rest of the world. The most prominent instances of professional standing were the members of the various bands maintained at every court in Europe, and by many noblemen; and in the case of such salaried officials as these, it would have been out of the question to regard them as being paid at so much for every performance. It was when the standard of execution was so high that it could only be attained by devoting the greater part of the performer's life to practice, that the custom became necessary of receiving payment for the exhibition of the skill thus painfully acquired; and as no amateurs could hope to vie with the executants who sacrificed everything to this side of their art, the only way in which the amateur could make himself felt was by setting up for a judge on the merits of rival performers. The delight of this occupation was greatly increased when the mere fact of having been present at some performance by a renowned virtuoso was enough to stamp the amateur as a member of the aristocracy, and we need not be surprised at the amount of interest excited by the frequent contests of skill between pairs of eminent musicians, or by the fact that Burney, both in his 'tours,' and in his history itself, devotes far more space to the details of the execution of the music he hears than to the character or the merits of the music itself. It is most fortunate for us that Burney and the men of his time were so much more busied about the performance of music than about the compositions themselves, for in the great majority of cases the works they heard are accessible in the present day; it is only the manner of their execution that has passed out of reach.

While fully recognizing that the virtuoso element in music

is very far from being the highest, it is necessary that we should bear in mind the artistic result of this wave of admiration for the powers of the great executants. Without it, it is unlikely that the concerto would have reached exactly the stage of development at which it exerted, as we saw in the last chapter, so strong an influence upon the sonata form of the future; without it, such *arie di bravura* as 'Rejoice!' from *The Messiah*, 'Let the bright Seraphim,' from *Samson*, or 'Sweet bird,' from *L'Allegro*, could hardly have been written, since the skill they require in the singer would not have been gained; and without it, Bach's 'Chaconne' for violin alone, the harpsichord sonatas of Domenico Scarlatti, and the 'Trillo del Diavolo' of Tartini must have been widely different from what they are. Again, the rage for technical skill had an important result upon the next generation, since it brought about a wider recognition of the legitimate resources of all the instruments at the composer's disposal, and thus had a good deal to do with the settlement of the orchestra into a regular and acknowledged entity.

It would be difficult if not impossible to trace a continuous history of virtuosity, and it would be untrue to represent it as steadily advancing from the unaffected simplicity of the earlier days through successive stages of regular development to a condition where it monopolized public attention to the exclusion of all else. It is rather like an epidemic bursting out for no apparent cause in different countries and periods, and dying down again without any obvious reason. Its earliest appearance would seem to have been in the virginal music of the time of Queen Elizabeth; such a collection as the *Fitzwilliam Virginal Book* contains abundant instances of pure virtuosity, in variations, &c., of which the technical difficulty is the only attraction; but in the better specimens of the kind, it is curious to notice how the passages of purely technical interest are subordinated to those for which musical value may be claimed, so that after the utmost speed possible upon the instruments of the time has been attained, it is usual

to find a concluding variation of massive structure, depending
entirely upon harmonic sonority for its effect. But after the
date of the completion of this collection, about 1625, there
occurs, for many years, no further attempt to write difficult
harpsichord music for the sake of its difficulty; and the suites
of Purcell are as wholly free from· the typical virtuoso style
of writing as are his sonatas of three and four parts, or that
for violin solo, recently published. In the same way, although
J. J. Walther (b. 1650) had apparently learnt in Italy the art
which found expression in many compositions for the violin,
of small musical interest but considerable technical difficulty,
going up to the sixth position, and abounding in arpeggios and
difficult double-stoppings, &c., there is no trace of the virtuoso
influence upon Corelli, who was his near contemporary. With
him, as with Purcell, it may have been a conscious abandonment of difficulty for its own sake, in favour of the higher
beauties of purely musical ideas; but on the other hand, it
may have been partly from other considerations. From various
stories current about Corelli, it would appear that he lacked the
temperament of the typical virtuoso altogether; in his own
compositions he never goes beyond the third position, and
their solid style is enough to show that passages of mere
display must have been repugnant to his nature. It is difficult
to imagine what can have been the passage in Handel's overture
to *Il Trionfo del Tempo* which so disconcerted Corelli in
Rome[1]; but the unusual height of some of the passages agrees
oddly with the fact of Corelli's own limitations in this direction
as exhibited in his own works. Another story represents
Corelli as being compelled to endure a reproof from Alessandro
Scarlatti caused by a persistent mistake he made in a work of
that master's; and the humiliation of this, coupled with the
extreme favour bestowed in Rome upon a younger violinist
named Valentini, is said to have shortened Corelli's life. But,

[1] See p. 80.

whatever his position in regard to technical display, it is certain
that as a violinist he 'laid a firm foundation for all future
development of technique and of a pure style of playing,' and
that ' by rigidly excluding everything that appeared to him
contrary to the nature of the instrument, he not only hindered
a threatened development in the wrong direction, but also
gave to this branch of art a sound and solid basis, which his
successors could and did build upon successfully[1].'   Corelli's
solo parts do not differ in any essential feature from those
he gives to the orchestral violins.   In Vivaldi's concertos we
find a more complete independence, and a distinct feeling
for solo effects as we understand them.   This composer
(c. 1675–1743) has a special importance in consequence of
the fact that Bach arranged a number of the violin concertos
for harpsichord; and his influence was no doubt strong on
Bach's treatment of the solo violin.   Francesco Maria Veracini (c. 1685–1750) is credited with the manifestation of
a strong individuality, both in his playing and compositions;
his passionate nature exposed him to the charge of eccentricity,
and he has strong claims on our esteem, not only for the
sake of his compositions, but on account of the influence
he had on Tartini, a far greater man.   We get a clearer idea
of Veracini's impulsive temperament from the various stories
concerning his oddities that are given in Burney's history than
from his own compositions, which, as Burney says, were ' too
wild and flighty for the taste of the English at that time.'   His
boldness in modulation seems to have been the chief drawback
to the popularity of his works in the England of his day.
Although such a passage as the coda of the first movement
of his sonata in E minor is easily understood in the present
day, and the sequence of harmonies is accepted almost as
a commonplace by every ear accustomed to music, it must
have sounded very eccentric at the time it was written :—

[1] Herr Paul David, in Grove's *Dictionary of Music and Musicians.*

Were it not for the testimony of the dates, it would not be difficult to persuade oneself that Giuseppe Tartini (1692–1770) was a leader of the modern romantic movement in music, whose passionate ideas, by his own choice, were thrown into the concise forms of an older day. The circumstances of his life were as romantic as his musical ideas, and matched them with a rare exactness. Born at Pirano in Istria, he was intended for the priesthood, and his musical studies were only taken up in earnest after he had devoted himself successively to the science of law and the art of fencing, and had moreover contracted a secret marriage with a niece of the Archbishop of Padua. The consequences of this last exploit drove him to seek the seclusion of the monastery at Assisi, where for two years he studied music, being taught composition by the organist, Czernohorsky, called 'il Padre Boemo,' whose nationality may perhaps support the theory of those who love to trace all musical influence to eastern Europe as its source. It is hardly astonishing to find Burney referring to the uncertain temper of Tartini's wife; for no sooner was her offended uncle pacified, and the couple re-united, than Tartini, happening to hear Veracini at Venice, determined to prosecute his violin studies to more purpose than before (he had hitherto been, apparently, his own teacher), and despatching her to his relations at Pirano, he betook himself to Ancona, where, about 1714, he lit upon the discovery of the 'third' or combination-tone, which results from the association of two notes in perfect intonation.   From 1721 onwards he lived in Padua, with the exception of a three years' stay at Prague as chamber-musician to Count Kinsky. His position at Padua was that of solo violinist and conductor of the orchestra at the church of San Antonio. His salary was 400 ducats a year, and his services were only required on great festivals; yet, says Burney, who went to Padua only a few months after Tartini's death, 'so strong was his zeal for the service of his patron saint, that he seldom let a week pass without regaling him to the utmost power of his palsied nerves.' That a change came over his character about the time of his residence at Assisi, changing his impulsive nature to one in which modesty and patience were the most remarkable traits; and that in after years he altered his style to some extent ('from extreme difficult to graceful and expressive,' says Burney, who gives the date 1744 as that of the change in his playing), seems admitted on all hands. It seems to have been at Ancona that he acquired the wonderful mastery over the bow, in regard to which it may be mentioned that he used a longer and more elastic bow than had hitherto been in favour. A glance at the table in Grove's *Dictionary*, Art. Bow, will show that Tartini's bow approaches more nearly to the perfect Tourte proportions than to those of Corelli's time. It is logical, seeing how powerful an agent the bow is in regulating the quality of tone, to connect these improvements with the emotional character of Tartini's own compositions, even if many of his followers failed to realize as he had done the possibilities thus opened out. His command of double stops, and the ease with which he accomplished shakes and double shakes, is brought home in the present day to every hearer of his famous 'Trillo del Diavolo'; and his 'Arte dell' Arco' gives the student as good an idea as possible of the point to which his technique had come. His 'divine adagio' may have been the main feature of his later playing; but the fact that his Op. 1, which apparently was published about 1734, contains the passionate sonata in G minor, makes it hard to accept Burney's date for the change in his style. This work, more than any other of its date outside the compositions of Bach, contains in its three short movements a wealth, eloquence, and sincerity of expression that have hardly been surpassed in modern times; and not the least surprising part of it is that the stiff conventional forms in which it is cast seem not to hamper the directness or intensity of its emotional power in the least. Besides the 'Trillo,' issued after his death, forty-eight sonatas for violin and bass were published, as well as twelve concertos and twelve sonatas for two violins and bass. There is some confusion in the opus numbers, as 'Op. 1' appears on the title-page of the first six concertos, as well as on that of the first twelve sonatas. An enormous number of sonatas, &c., are reported to have existed, Gerber giving 200 as the total of unpublished violin concertos, while Fétis' estimate of forty-eight unpublished sonatas coincides so exactly with the number known to have been published in his lifetime that it may be disregarded [1].

In yet another way Tartini was a romanticist long before the time when that word was first used. He would connect his music with suggestions from the outside, such as sonnets of Petrarch, and would write the words of favourite poems underneath his violin-parts; with the evident susceptibility to impressions from many quarters, we need not be

---

[1] The theoretical works of Tartini will come under consideration in the next volume of the series.

surprised to find the melancholy of Assisi reflected in some
of his movements, or the emotional import of some of
Petrarch's sonnets revealed in others. The story of his
dreaming that the devil played him an exquisitely beautiful
violin sonata, of which the 'Trillo del Diavolo' was but the
faint remembrance, is of a piece with his romantic temperament, and we need not care whether the vision was
actually seen in a dream or not. In spite of the formidable
difficulties of many of Tartini's works, he was scarcely more
of the typical virtuoso than Corelli. He must have been
looked upon as something of a reactionary, for all induce-
ments to leave his beloved church for the brilliant career of
a public performer in England were in vain.

One of the first of the typical Italian virtuosi of
the period was Tartini's senior by twelve years. Francesco
Geminiani (1680–1761) studied with Corelli, and is said to
have been Alessandro Scarlatti's pupil for composition,
England near the beginning of the eighteenth century had
become an ideal soil for the fostering of virtuosity; and
Veracini and Geminiani, who arrived here in the same year,
Veracini preceding Geminiani by a few months only, divided
the favour of the amateurs who were privileged to hear
them in the private houses where their talents were chiefly
exhibited. Like his rival, Geminiani was an eccentric, but
in spite of his free employment of the shift and his ease
in double-stopping, his chief period of success was after
the departure of Veracini to Dresden in 1720. He had his
revenge, for when Veracini returned in 1735 to London, his
success was materially impaired by Geminiani's established
fame.

Many of the symptoms of the ordinary virtuoso are to be
traced in Geminiani's history; he refused to play at a court
concert in London unless Handel accompanied him, and a
foolish passion for dealing in pictures, of which he had no
special knowledge, landed him in money difficulties; his pupil,

Lord Essex, had to free him from gaol, and afterwards procured him, it is said, the appointment of the leader of the Viceroy's band in Dublin. Horace Walpole is said to have objected to the appointment on the ground of Geminiani's religion; and the place was given to Dubourg, his pupil. Geminiani was in Paris from 1748 till 1755, and his death took place while on a visit to Dubourg in Dublin. Geminiani's compositions, which consist of thirty-six solo sonatas for violin, and twenty-four concertos (concerti grossi), besides arrangements of works of his own and of Corelli for different combinations of instruments, and a book of harpsichord lessons, have considerable boldness of design, but cannot compare either with Corelli's simple, austere beauty, or with Tartini's passionate emotion. The work by which Geminiani's name deserves to live is his famous instruction book on *The Art of Playing on the Violin*. The question of the date of this work is a difficult one[1], but, in the shape in which it is acknowledged as Geminiani's, we shall not be far wrong in attributing it to the middle of the century. Herr David, in Grove's *Dictionary*, says of its contents: 'It has the great merit of handing down to posterity the principles of the art of playing the violin, as they were finally established by Corelli. The rules which Geminiani gives for holding the violin and bow, the manage-

---

[1] The date given in Grove's *Dictionary*, 1740, is not impossibly a printer's error for 1748, the date given by Burney; in Mr. E. Heron-Allen's *De Fidiculis Bibliographia*, part v., section 2, it is noted that the contents of this, and of the companion tutors, *Compleat Instructions for the Violin*, &c., by 'Geminiania,' are virtually identical with those of some books published anonymously considerably before this date, viz., 'The Art of Playing on the Violin with a New Scale showing how to stop every Note, Flat or Sharp, exactly in Tune, and where the shifts of the Hand should be made,' a treatise which was included in Prelleur's *Modern Musick-Master*, dated 1731. The book in its original form is dated conjecturally by Mr. Heron-Allen 1720, but the names and addresses of its two publishers give evidence, according to Mr. Frank Kidson's valuable *British Music-Publishers*, that it cannot have been issued before 1734. This work, however it first appeared, is indisputably the first violin tutor ever published, preceding Leopold Mozart's *Violin-Schule* by at least twenty-two years; and the similarity of contents leaves little doubt that it is the first form of the treatise afterwards acknowledged by Geminiani.

ment of the left hand and the right arm, are the same as are recognized in our days. In one particular point he even appears to have been in advance of his time, since he recommends the holding of the violin on the left-hand side of the tail-piece, a practice now universally accepted and indispensable for a higher development of the technique—but, strange as it seems, not adopted either by Leopold Mozart or by the masters of the German school until the beginning of the present century.' The other literary efforts of Geminiani, including treatises on 'Memory,' 'Good Taste,' 'The Guitar,' and 'Accompaniment,' are of less value than his instruction book for his own instrument.

With Pietro Locatelli (1693-1764) Italian violin virtuosity reached almost its extreme point, and he seems, in some particulars, to have been only exceeded by Paganini in astonishing feats of skill not always very well applied. He employed the device called 'scordatura' or mistuning, by which, for certain special effects, an unusual method of tuning was employed; an example of his excursions into regions of then unheard-of height is given in Grove's *Dictionary*, from a work called *Caprices énigmatiques*; and in his compositions there is but little musical importance, although some of his more moderate sonatas have been played with effect in recent times. He was born at Bergamo and died at Amsterdam, where he had settled and established concerts for some years before his death.

Giovanni Battista Somis, the more famous of two brother violinists (c. 1676-1763), is of greater importance as a link between his master, Corelli, and his pupils, Giardini and Pugnani, than on his own account; for the latter was the master of Viotti, and thus carried down the tradition of Italian violin-playing to modern times; a third pupil, Jean Marie Léclair (1697-1764) may be said to have revolutionized violin-playing in France. Before him the best were J.-B. Senaillé (1687-1730) whose compositions have a distinct charm of their own; and J. B. Loeillet (d. 1728), a native of Belgium who settled in England.

Felice de Giardini (1716–1796) seems to have been led by popular applause into the worst habits of exaggeration, and of interpolating ornaments into the violin accompaniments of the songs in operas, &c. At Naples, during an opera of Jommelli's, the composer came into the orchestra and sat down close to Giardini. The young virtuoso took the opportunity of showing off his powers, and added a brilliant cadenza into the accompaniment of one song, at the end of which Jommelli gave him a sound box on the ear. Handel's famous rebuke to Dubourg, the violinist, on some occasion of the same kind, was in the words, ' Welcome home, Mr. Dubourg'; and the two stories show that the fashion of exaggerated ornament was not in much favour with the best composers.

Tartini's favourite pupil, Pietro Nardini (1722–1793) was solo violinist at the court at Stuttgart from 1753 to 1767, and after that devoted himself to the care of his master until Tartini's death; from him he inherited the tenderness of expression which, rather than any great technical skill, is associated with his name. Another pupil of Tartini, Johann Gottlieb Graun (c. 1698–1771), the brother of the better-known composer, was also a pupil of J. G. Pisendel of Dresden (1687–1755), who had learnt his art from Torelli and Vivaldi, and who paid a good deal of attention to Bach's newly-invented instrument, the *viola pomposa*. The other most prominent name among German violinists of the time is that of Franz Benda (1709–1786) the founder of the head of a large family of musical brothers and nephews of Bohemian origin. His compositions, to judge from the few specimens that are accessible, have decided musical value, and almost his only touch of virtuosity is in a particularly lavish use of grace notes, a characteristic which will be discussed later.

In the technique of the keyboard, mere speed of finger seems to have counted comparatively little, except in England, where William Babell (c. 1690–1723) makes a link between the virginal composers of the past and the fashioners of operatic potpourris of a later day. He was a good harpsichordist and violinist, and was organist of All Hallows, Bread Street. He found his opportunity in the popularity of Handel's operas, and set the 'favourite airs' with all kinds of meaningless ornamentation for the harpsichord. Not speed alone, but accurate judgement in distant intervals, and a perfect command of the various difficulties that arise from crossing the hands, are the chief requirements in Domenico Scarlatti's sonatas, discussed in the last chapter. In the composer's later days, it is said that he became so fat that he could no longer execute the passages which required crossing of the hands, but the continuance of the device throughout his works makes us accept the statement with reserve.

To Couperin the most important part of virtuosity was the ornamentation of his themes in accordance with the stereotyped abbreviations with which the music was so liberally supplied; by far the greater part of his excellent instruction-book, *L'Art de toucher le Clavecin*, 1717, is taken up with the explanation of the proper interpretation of these ornaments, such as the 'pincé' or mordent, the 'tremblement' or shake, and the 'port-de-voix,' a combination of an appoggiatura with a mordent. Mr. Dannreuther, in his treatise on *Musical Ornamentation*, vol. i. p. 100, points out that 'while Couperin is treating of graces, he also treats of matters which would, now-a-days, come under the head of phrasing, or style, or expression'; but the ornaments are actually connected in the closest way with the expressive side of the music of the time.

The grace notes, which are scattered with so lavish a hand over much of the music of the eighteenth century, no doubt had their origin in the compositions for the keyboard instruments, since none of these, with the exception of the clavichord with its attenuated tone, was capable of varying the power of the different notes, or of emphasizing special points in the musical phrases. It was almost certainly in order to provide some means of suggesting an accent that the important note of a phrase was so often supplied with a little shake or turn, and the actual ornaments invented were probably intended as imitations of different effects that were characteristic of other sound-producing agencies. Thus, the appoggiatura, and the various means by which an imitation of a *portamento* was attempted, were suggested, no doubt, by the art of the singer; and the arpeggio, as its name implies, was an effect at first peculiar to the harp. The 'pralltriller' and 'mordent' seem to have been the special property of the keyboard, for they appear in the music for the virginals almost as frequently as in that for the harpsichord, at a date when there is little or no trace of them elsewhere. Be this as it may, the execution of ornaments, whether written out, abbreviated, or merely understood and handed down by tradition, formed a most important branch of musical education in the eighteenth century; and it seems to have been very generally held that in them lay what we should now call the 'soul' of music. A strange passage may be quoted from Couperin's book, the gist of which is sufficiently clear, although some of the terms are employed in an unusual sense:—

'Je trouve que nous confondons la Mesure avec ce qu'on nomme Cadence, ou Mouvement. Mesure, définit la quantité, et L'égalité des tems: et Cadence, est proprement l'esprit, et l'âme qu'il y faut joindre. Les Sonades des Italiens ne sont gueres susceptibles de cette Cadence. Mais, tous nos airs de violons, nos Pièces de Clavecin, de violes, &c. désignent, et semblent vouloir exprimer quelque sentiment. Ainsi, n'ayant point imaginés de signes, ou caractères pour communiquer nos idées particulières, nous tâchons d'y remédier en marquant au commencement de nos pièces par quelques mots, comme, Tendrement, Vivement, &c., à-peu-près, ce que nous voudrions faire entendre. Je souhaite que quelqu'un se donne la peine de nous traduire, pour l'utilité des étrangers : Et puisse leur procurer les moyens de juger de l'exeèlence de notre Musique instrumentale.'

The passing allusion to the Italian musicians, both here and
in the passage which precedes this extract, where Couperin
complacently tells his readers that his countrymen play the
music of foreigners far better than the foreigners play French
music, are not to be taken as matters of fact; but they are
interesting, as bearing upon the opposition of the styles that
were characteristic of the two countries, of which opposition so
much was made, although the difference between the French
and the Italian styles is not one that can be said to be at all
obvious to students in the present day.   As time went on,
it is clear that the habit of 'gracing' a melody, as the term
was, increased; Burney[1] implies that, in 1732 or thereabouts,
it was an innovation in Germany; in his account of Quantz's
violin-playing, he says 'His music is simple and natural; his
taste is that of forty years ago' (Burney is writing in 1772);
'but though this may have been an excellent period for composition, yet I cannot entirely subscribe to the opinion of those
who think musicians have discovered no refinements worth
adopting since that time.   Without giving into tricks and
caprice, and even allowing composition to have arrived at its
acme of perfection forty years ago, yet a simple melody may
surely be embellished by the modern manner of taking
appoggiaturas, of preparing and returning shakes, of gradually
enforcing and diminishing whole passes, as well as single notes,
and, above all, by the variety of expression arising from the
superiority in the use of the bow, which the violin players
of this age possess over those of any other period since its
invention.'   But this branch of virtuosity was by no means
so modern as Burney thought, although it reached a pitch of
extravagance in his time; the air in Handel's suite in D minor
is adorned with such a profusion of grace notes that its outline
can hardly be perceived until it is presented in a simpler
form in the variations which follow; and although this is an

---

[1] *Present State of Music in Germany*, ii. p. 156.

exception among his works for harpsichord, yet it is enough
to show how early the taste for riotous ornamentation began
to be formed. As a rule, Handel stands further than Bach
from this kind of virtuosity in instrumental music; there
are instances scattered up and down the works of the latter
which prove him to have been quite cognizant of the fashion
for ornamentation, although with him, even in the cases where
it occurs, it is never allowed to overpower the groundwork of
the composition. The air of the thirty 'Goldberg' variations is
at first presented in a very ornate form, and this whole work
is one of the very few of Bach's in which the skill of a virtuoso
seems to have been thought of. In the dialogue between the
two keyboards of the harpsichord, which is kept up with so
much effect in many of the non-canonic variations of that set,
are some passages which appeal mainly and primarily to
technical skill, and in the last two variations before the final
'Quodlibet' the figures almost seem to anticipate Liszt. In
the particular point of ornamentation we may surely trace the
desire to expose the absurdity of a fashionable craze in that
section of the 'Capriccio on the departure of a Brother' in
which the traveller's friends are represented as using every
means to dissuade him from the perilous journey he is about
to undertake. Here the multitude of mordents and turns are
no less masterly in their grotesque picturing of the dangers of
the way and the wheedling accents of the timid friends, than
are the chromatic scales in a later movement, of their voluble
weeping. This work is among the few which can be dated
with absolute accuracy; Spitta[1] shows that 1704 must have
been the year of its composition, nine years before the
appearance of Couperin's first book of 'Ordres' was published.
There are in Bach, too, a small number of pieces in which the
influence of Domenico Scarlatti's peculiar kind of technical
speciality is apparent. The gigue at the end of the first

---

[1] *Life of Bach* (Eng. transl.), i. 235.

partita, and the exquisite little Fantasia in C minor have quite a Scarlatti air in the way the crossing of the hands is managed. And, in the Chaconne for violin alone, the master must have had in his mind some ideal virtuoso, whose skill would be equal to the technical difficulties, while his musical powers would enable him to decipher its contrapuntal intricacies and to present them to an audience. That this ideal was ever realized before the days of Joachim, it is impossible to believe.

Bach was brought into contact with virtuosity in one of its most characteristic manifestations, in the celebrated Marchand incident. Jean Louis Marchand (1669–1732), the private organist to the King of France, seems to have been a brilliant performer both on the harpsichord and organ; falling out of the French king's favour he was banished, and while he was on a visit to the court of Dresden, the King of Saxony, Friedrich August I, arranged for a competition to take place between him and Bach. According to one account, they had one improvised contest, Bach repeating all the variations that Marchand had just played, and adding twelve new ones of his own; but it seems more probable that the celebrated occasion in 1717 when Marchand failed to keep the appointment would have been the only regular contest. That Marchand had heard Bach play, and dreaded the encounter, is certain; his compositions, however, are better than the story would imply, and Spitta goes so far as to place them on a level with Couperin's.

Another celebrated meeting of great virtuosi had taken place in Rome some years before this, when Cardinal Ottoboni arranged a similar contest between Handel and Domenico Scarlatti in 1709. The two were declared equal on the harpsichord, but Handel, as might be expected, was pronounced the better organist. The famous *combat à outrance* between Faustina and Cuzzoni must be related in a subsequent chapter; but all these contests and the many others of which accounts have been given by contemporary historians, go to show how much importance attached to the execution of difficult music in the mind of the average aristocratic amateur. It is quite a relief to find that, at the date of Burney's visit to Berlin, a protest had been uttered against the excess of ornamentation by no less powerful a person than the autocratic King of Prussia, who would allow no operas to be performed there except those of Graun, Agricola, and Hasse. 'And in the opera house, as in the field, his majesty is such a rigid disciplinarian, that if a mistake is made in a single movement or evolution, he immediately marks, and rebukes the offender; and if any of his Italian troops dare to deviate from strict discipline, by adding, altering, or diminishing a single passage in the parts they have to perform, an order is sent, *de par le Roi,* for them to adhere strictly to the notes written by the composer, at their peril. This, when compositions are good, and a singer is licentious, may be an excellent method; but certainly shuts out all taste and refinement.' That taste and refinement depended upon the alterations of the composer's directions was a theory which the great majority of amateurs held, as well as Dr. Burney; and the technical skill of the vocalists of the t' ne was almost entirely directed to such alterations, whether made spontaneously or prepared beforehand with the aid of the singing master.

Neither in singing nor in playing, does the art of gradating tone, or as we call it, of light and shade, seem to have held an important place. Even the terms *forte* and *piano* are quite the exception in Bach, though they do occur, as in the Italian concerto, and a few other places; yet Burney notes that at the end of the oratorio, *Maria Vergine addolorata,* by Francesco Antonio Pistocchi (1659–c. 1717), 'all the degrees of the diminution of sound are used; as *piano, più piano, pianissimo,* equivalent to the *diminuendo, calando,* and *smorzando,* of the present times.'

He notices also the curious fact that in Berlin the art of musical shading was even less fully practised than elsewhere.

'The musicians of many parts of Europe,' he says[1], 'have discovered and adopted certain refinements, in the manner of executing even the old music, which are not yet received in the Berlin school, where *pianos* and *fortes* are but little attended to, and where each performer seems trying to surpass his neighbour in nothing so much as *loudness* . . . . If I may depend on my own sensations, I should imagine that the musical performances of this country want *contrast*; and there seems to be not only too many notes in them, but those notes are expressed with too little attention to the *degree* of force that the instruments, for which they are made, are capable of . . . . When a piece is executed with such unremitting fury, as I have sometimes heard, it ceases to be music; and instead of a part, the whole deserves no other appellation than that of *noise*.'

No doubt, as musical 'shading' was in such a very rudimentary condition, individuality in the performer could only be shown in alterations of the text; it is clear that it must have been so regarded, from the various passages quoted from Burney and elsewhere.   But nowhere was the practice of making these alterations carried to more absurd lengths than among the opera-singers, with whom the cadenzas were not the soul of music, as was the case with Couperin's 'Cadence,' but the breath of their own life.

The extraordinary outburst of popularity with which foreign singers were received in England, the detailed accounts of their qualifications given by Burney and others, make it clear that at the time when Italian opera was first introduced under Handel, the singers were supreme in the mind of the ordinary amateur of the day. The details of the education of many of the most famous singers have come down to us, as in the case of no other class of musicians, and we are able to gauge pretty accurately the relative importance of the different

---

[1] *Present State of Music in Germany*, ii. 202.

branches of their training. The voices of the adult males were not in great favour, and even the parts of the most virile heroes in operas were given to artificial sopranos, who had been prepared for their profession by a brutal operation at the outset of their training, whereby the higher range of the voice was preserved in perpetuity. A peculiarly soft and full quality of tone seems to have been the general characteristic of these *evirati,* who, as a class, disappeared from the operatic stage with Velluti, who retired about 1829, and died as late as 1861, but the barbarous practice remained in vogue in connexion with the Papal Choir until far more recent days; the sopranos of the Roman churches in the present day are men who sing in falsetto, but possess the usual male voice below. Among the greatest teachers of singing in Italy, where alone, in the time of Handel, the art was methodically taught, were Pistocchi and Porpora, the first of whom seems to have aimed at a comparatively pure style, since his famous pupil, Bernacchi (c. 1690–1756) only adopted the practice of excessive ornamentation after he had sung in Handel's *Rinaldo* in London in 1717; of the vocal teaching of Niccolò Porpora (1686–1767) we hear such stories as that of his keeping Caffarelli for five years to one page of exercises, and then dismissing him with the assurance that he was the greatest singer in Europe; and the various examples of roulades, etc., from his operas given in Grove's *Dictionary* (vol. iii. p. 505, where an interesting criticism on the Caffarelli story may be read) show the direction in which excellence was aimed at. It was from the teaching of Bernacchi that Porpora's other distinguished pupil, Farinelli, learnt to perfect himself in the art of vocal ornamentation. He had learnt from Porpora some wonderful feats, such as holding and swelling a note of extraordinary length, purity, and volume, so as to be able to surpass a certain famous trumpeter for whom Porpora had written a special obbligato part for the occasion[1]. But yet he

[1] Grove, *Dictionary of Music and Musicians,* i. 504.

had to acknowledge himself conquered when he was pitted, after the fashion of the time, against Bernacchi, who repeated every roulade of Farinelli's in such perfection that the latter entreated his conqueror to give him lessons. Farinelli, whose career as a performer belongs to a later chapter, had evidently the art of inventing new and more or less interesting embellishments rather than meaningless ornaments, for he was a man of high culture, good taste, and rare generosity and power. That Nicolini, who was considerably older than Farinelli, had ' a few antiquated tricks in his cadences' is recorded in a book which gives us the best ideas of the vocal art of its time.   In 1723, Pier Francesco Tosi published his *Opinioni de' Cantori antichi e moderni, o sieno osservazioni sopra il Canto figurato* at Bologna; and in the following year it was translated into English by J. E. Galliard, as *Observations on the Florid Song; or, Sentiments of Ancient and Modern Singers*. A good epitome of the contents is given in Dannreuther's treatise on Ornamentation, already quoted; a special interest attached to the English notes on the text of Tosi, since they show that the taste for excessive ornamentation had already begun to decline a little. One of Tosi's special aims is to explain the intervals at which the appoggiatura can be taken; and incidentally he gives information of considerable practical value as to the intervals in just intonation, before the system of equal temperament was adopted elsewhere than on keyed instruments. He shows his contempt for the composers who think it necessary to mark the appoggiaturas, but it is not to be supposed that he is referring to Bach, the most conspicuous instance of the practice of marking them; and Galliard, in one of his notes, points out that the reference is to the modern Italian writers. Tosi says:—

'If the Scholar be well instructed in this, the Appoggiaturas will become so familiar to him by continual Practice, that by the Time he is come out of his first Lessones, he will laugh at those Composers that mark them, with a Design

either to be thought Modern, or to shew that they understand the Art of Singing better than the Singers. If they
have this Superiority over them, why do they not write
down even the Graces, which are more difficult, and more
essential than the Appoggiaturas? But if they mark them,
that they may acquire the glorious Name of a *Virtuoso alla
Moda*, or a Composer in the new Stile, they ought at least
to know, that the Addition of one Note costs little trouble,
and less Study. Poor *Italy!* pray tell me; do not the Singers
now-a-days know where the *Appoggiaturas* are to be made,
unless they are pointed at with a Finger? In my Time their
own knowledge shewed it them. Eternal shame to him who
first introduced these foreign Puerilities into our Nation! . . . .'

On this passage Galliard remarks:—'In all the Modern
Italian Compositions the Appoggiaturas are mark'd supposing
the Singers to be ignorant where to place them. The *French*
use them for their lessons on the *Harpsichord*, &c., but seldom
for the Voice.'

The directions concerning the all-important subject of the
shake are mainly of the same kind as those which refer to
the appoggiatura, that is, it is unlawful to use the semitone
in certain parts of the scale, &c. There are several amusing
touches which give the reader a certain insight into the
practice of the men of Tosi's and Galliard's time in regard
to the performance both of vocal and instrumental music.

'The Defects of the *Shake* are many. The long holding
out *Shake* triumph'd formerly, and very improperly, as now
the Divisions do; but when the Art grew refined, it was
left to the Trumpets, or to those Singers that waited for the
Eruption of an *E Viva!* or *Bravo!* from the Populace. That
Shake which is too often heard, be it ever so fine, cannot
please. That which is beat with an uneven Motion disgusts;
that like the quivering of a goat makes one laugh; and that
in the Throat is the worst; That which is produced by a
Tone and its third is disagreeable; the Slow is tiresome;
and that which is out of Tune is hideous. . . . .' Galliard
adds 'The using so often *Beats*, *Shakes*, and *Prepares* is
owing to Lessons on the Lute, Harpsichord, and other Instruments whose Sounds discontinue, and therefore have Need of
this Help.'

The 'Divisions' mentioned above are the groups of rapid semiquavers, such as abound in Handel's 'Rejoice'; the 'Beat' is a kind of mordent, and the 'Prepare' a kind of appoggiatura. In his chapter on 'Airs,' ch. vii, we are let into the recognized manner of performing the conventional *Da Capo* song :—

'Among the Things worthy of consideration, the first to be taken Notice of, is the Manner in which all *Airs* divided into three parts are to be sung. In the first Part they require nothing but the simplest Ornaments, of a good Taste and few, that the Composition may remain simple, plain, and pure; in the second, they except that to this Purity some artful Graces be added, by which the judicious may hear, that the Ability of the Singer is greater; and, in repeating the *Air*, he that does not vary it for the better, is no great Master.

'Let a Student, therefore, accustom himself to repeat them always differently, for, if I mistake not, one that abounds in Invention, though a moderate Singer, deserves much more esteem, than a better who is barren of it; for this last pleases the connoisseurs but for once, whereas the other, if he does not surprise by the Rareness of his Productions, will at least gratify your Attention with Variety.

'Without varying the *Airs* the knowledge of the Singers could never be discovered; but from the Nature and Quality of the Variations, it will be easily discerned in two of the greatest Singers which is the best.'

The way in which the opinion of the 'judicious' or the 'connoisseur' is mentioned shows the attitude of the virtuoso in brief; the point of view of a conscientious interpreter, anxious only to set forth the ideas of one greater than himself, would have been completely foreign to all but a very few people in the eighteenth century. The only consideration is of course what will please the hearers and enhance the singer's fame; and almost the only word against the excess of ornamentation gets its support from the likelihood of tiring the audience, not from the danger of misrepresenting the composer. So, in the chapter on Cadences :—

'Every *Air* has (at least) three *Cadences*, that are all

three final. Generally speaking, the Study of the Singers of the present Times consists in terminating the *Cadence* of the first Part with an overflowing of *Passages* and *Divisions* at Pleasure, and the *Orchestre* waits; in that of the second the Dose is encreased, and the *Orchestre* grows tired; but on the last *Cadence*, the Throat is set a going, like a Weathercock in a Whirlwind, and the *Orchestre* yawns.'

Such deterrents as were urged by Tosi or Galliard, and Burney's rather half-hearted condemnation of excessive orna-ment, do not seem to have had much influence in stopping the admiration of the 'connoisseurs' for marvellous feats of virtuosity; but as time went on, the influence of the operatic reforms of Gluck, and other causes, brought about a better state of things. There is an interesting link between the worst degradation of violin virtuosity and the dawn of what is sometimes called the 'Classical' era, in Antonio Lolli, an empty-headed violin player, who, born at Bergamo in 1730, lived to bungle sadly over a quartet of Haydn in London, and died in 1802. His skill in all the virtuoso's usual repertory of double-stopping, harmonics, etc., seems to have reached a point beyond which no progress in that direction was possible.

CHAPTER X

THE PROGRESS OF OPERATIC CONVENTION

To pass from the consideration of virtuosity in general to the study of the causes which led up to the reforms of Gluck, is to make but the slightest change in the point of view, and to regard one special manifestation of virtuosity in surroundings the most congenial to its growth. Almost ever since the invention of Opera, a ceaseless struggle has gone on between those who regard it as an ideal means of stirring human emotion by the dramatic representation of great deeds or tragic motives, and those who look upon it as an expensive amusement, a vehicle for personal display, or a means of ostentation of one sort or another. On the one side were the best of the composers, the men who felt that the vivid realization of dramatic situations was the main object of the musical stage as it has always been of the non-musical; with these were from time to time associated the higher class of librettists, and a minority of the patrons of opera. On the other side were ranged the great body of singers, and of the persons who frequented the representations. So overwhelming has always been the preponderance of the latter class and the strength of its influence, that the only wonder is that the other class should ever have got opportunities of realizing the true ideal of opera, an ideal which at all dates has been far more unanimously agreed upon than might be supposed. Often as the ideal of dramatic realization has been denounced as impracticable or ridiculed as dull, it has from time to time come to be accepted as a practical possibility if only as a relief from the fatiguing repetitions of conventionalized opera.

The beginnings of opera have already been dealt with in the preceding volume of this history, and by the time of Bach and Handel the opera had become more or less firmly established in all the civilized countries of Europe. In England, where the wonderful truth and pathos of Purcell's *Dido and Aeneas* seem to have gone almost unnoticed by the public, opera had degenerated to such a degree that the time was ripe for the successful introduction of Italian opera under Handel; in France, the imitators of Lully carried on his traditions, furnishing the music for rich pageants, and undoubtedly preparing the way for a truly national opera; in Italy, the vocal melodies which were the national inheritance of the composers were gradually bringing on the day when the dramatic aspect of the opera was almost lost sight of; and in Germany the foundations were being laid of the greatest national opera the world has yet seen, in the work of Reinhard Keiser and the men of his time, such as Brenner, Krieger, Graupner and Grünewald, all of whom wrote for the opera at Hamburg, where Theile's *Adam and Eve*, 1678, was, according to Mattheson [1], the first opera sung in German on the German stage.

Hamburg remained the centre of operatic activity for a considerable time, and it was not until 1740 that German opera ceased to be given there. Of the men just mentioned, Keiser was by far the most important, and he seems to have been a rare instance of a man who both deserved and received the hearty approbation of his contemporaries. Born at Weissenfels in 1674, he was educated at the Thomasschule of Leipzig and the university; he wrote his first opera, *Ismene*, for Wolfenbüttel in 1692, and from the date of his *Basilius*, Hamburg, 1694 (on a subject taken from Sidney's *Arcadia*), hardly a year

---

[1] *Der Musikalische Patriot*, 1728, contains a full list of the operas performed at Hamburg down to the date of publication.

passed until 1717 without his writing three, four, or even five
operas for the Hamburg stage. He was of a self-indulgent
and extravagant habit, and was involved in the financial troubles
of his partner in the management of the theatre, a man named
Drüsicke; he disappeared from view in 1708, but as he produced eight new operas in the following year, he was fully
reinstated in public opinion. In 1722 he was appointed
Capellmeister to the King of Denmark, and wrote *Ulysses*
for the Copenhagen opera; he succeeded Mattheson as Cantor
and Canon of the Cathedral at Hamburg in 1728, and wrote
the last of his 116 operas, *Circe*, in 1734, dying at Hamburg,
1739.

With all his luxury and extravagance, Keiser seems to have
resisted the growing faults of his time, although as the manager
of the opera, he might easily have been led into the particular
kind of conventionality that was the bane of so many of his
contemporaries. It is only, of course, the minority of his
works that are now extant, but those which are still in MS.
in Berlin have been carefully analysed by E. O. Lindner, in
his *Erste stehende deutsche Oper*, the appendix to which
contains a good many examples of his work. From these,
and such books as the collected airs from *La Forza della
Virtù*, published at Hamburg 1701, and 'Erlesene Sätze aus
der Opera (*sic*) L'Inganno Fedele' it is possible to see that
Keiser had a distinct gift of originality, not merely in the
actual manufacture of melodies that could be called fresh,
but in adapting them to the sentiment he wished to reflect.
In the former of these two works, the third of the operas
written for Hamburg, he tried various experiments in the
way of writing obbligato parts in rather unusual combinations;
unfortunately, we can only guess at their actual character,
for the airs are published with voice-part and bass alone,
and it is only from the headings that we can tell what the
accompaniments were. An exception to this rule is a soprano
air which begins as follows:—

There is a bass air, 'Kann von Ketten ich nicht retten,'
headed 'Con flauti senza cembalo,' so that the voice is the
bass part of the harmony. We find, further on, a soprano
air with oboe alone, and a duet accompanied by flutes alone;
while one air is headed 'senza unico accompagnamento.'
In *Claudius*, 1703, there are various concerted pieces; but
the work has maintained its celebrity by the fact that the
minuet in the overture to Handel's *Samson* is taken, nearly
note for note, from a minuet in this opera. In *Orpheus*,
one of the eight operas dating from 1709 and 1710, there is
a movement with five flutes. In *Croesus*, 1710, and again in
Jodelet, 1726, appears an instrument called a 'Zuffolo,' which
seems to have been a kind of shrill oboe. Lindner notices
that from 1712, the date of *Diana*, hardly an air is to be

found that is not accompanied with at least a violin beside
the bass, so that a decided advance in richness of orchestral
treatment is made as Keiser grows older. The published
airs from *L'Inganno Fedele*, the words of which were in
German despite its Italian title, have few if any indications
of more accompaniment than the bass; although it is noted
in the preface addressed to 'Musik-Liebender' that the airs
are printed with the bass alone. It is also stated to be
Keiser's sixty-second opera. Occasionally Italian songs
are introduced, but the bulk of the libretto is in German,
by König. The first of the two examples taken from this
work shows Keiser in his most sincere vein; not Bach himself
could have written a farewell song of greater simplicity or
expressiveness. It is perhaps worth while to notice that
what has been called the 'Scarlatti' pattern of commencement is adopted here, but only in part, for after the delivery
of the first words and the usual break between them and
their resumption of the complete first line, they are set to a
different melodic pattern.

The second example from *L'Inganno Fedele* has a special interest for students of Bach's music, for in this duet we may see quite unmistakably the germ which Bach so often used

* D in the original.

in the church cantatas, most prominently, perhaps, in *Wachet auf* (see p. 25), where the dialogue of two lovers is turned into the spiritual intercourse between Christ and the soul. The date of Keiser's work is 1714, while Bach's cantata is ascribed by Spitta to the year 1731 ; not that there is any question of actual plagiarism, for the form of the poetry would suggest the same treatment in each case, without assuming that Bach knew this particular work of Keiser's. The two long notes at the end of the first phrase are of quite common occurrence in Keiser's work, and more particularly in this opera.

The insertion of yet another example of Keiser, in a lighter
mood, may perhaps be pardoned, since it shows his possession
of the precious quality of humour, and of humour that can be
expressed in musical notes.   In *Circe*, his last opera, written
in 1734, there occurs a tenor song, which, little as it may have
to do with the story of Circe as generally accepted, is as
eloquent an expression of a certain kind of burlesque fear as
if it were written in the present day.   We must seek in
Bach's *Capriccio on the departure of a Brother* for a parallel
to the picture.   Keiser seems to have employed the directions
forte and *piano* more freely throughout his works than was
at all common in his time in Germany, and the contrasts of
tone here indicated by him in the first four bars are, no doubt
rightly, continued by Herr Lindner, from whose appendix
before mentioned the song is taken.   As he gives the original
scoring, for strings, the editor's own additions can be checked ;
at the first occurrence of the word ' schrein ' he puts in a chord
of the ⁶₄, which takes off the blunt effect of the A as it stands
in the original.   His directions as to force are enclosed in
brackets :—

The sudden changes of force at the beginning, as though
the singer's voice were collapsing with his terror, the funny
little 'wobble' which is turned to such good account in bars
9 and 10, and the final discord, as if the singer could not quite
get up to the high A, are all conspicuous touches of musical
humour; and the fact that such an ending could be allowed
to come into existence at a date when the opera in almost
all countries of Europe had become conventionalized, gives
us an important clue to the attitude of the German public in
the last days of Keiser.

It would be tedious and useless to review in detail the
works of all the operatic writers of the early eighteenth
century; but Keiser is important, not only on account of
his own powers, but on account of his undoubted influence
upon Handel. As the point of departure from which so
much of the conventionalization of opera proceeded, and as
a standard of comparison, his works have a great value.
Before passing to the consideration of Handel's operas, it
may be well to point out some of the causes of the operatic
decadence which gradually made dramatic music a dead letter
until the time of Gluck.   In the first place, every observant
student of operatic history must recognize that only those
schools of opera have risen to a position of real and lasting
influence which have employed the language of the country
in which the operas were presented.   As long as the Hamburg
opera was performed in German—there are cases of the
introduction of Italian songs into German operas in the earlier
works of Keiser, but only by way of exception—so long was
it a living thing, not merely famous among the men of the
time, but exercising a wide influence on music at large apart
from the stage.   The history of the Hamburg opera after 1740,
when it became Italianized, is of no importance whatever;
and the city of Hamburg affords us a striking example in
little of what was happening more slowly all over Europe.   In
the first instance, no doubt, opera had to be imported from

Italy, the place of its inception, into every other country; but it was the main principles of operatic treatment that were at first imported, whether into France by Lully, through Lully indirectly into England, or into Germany by Heinrich Schütz; it was not at first taken as a complete and ready-made product of a foreign country, and presented in a foreign tongue, with foreign singers and everything complete in the way of details. The non-existence of any national school of opera in England, after the one beautiful experiment in Purcell's *Dido and Aeneas,* has been already spoken of; in France, with a whole set of conventions and stiffnesses of their own, the composers after Lully had at least the advantage of employing their own and the hearers' native language. In Italy, opera from the outside has never flourished, and for the very good reason that the flowing Italian language has always seemed most perfectly fitted for dramatic music of a certain kind. Taking a rapid glance over the history of opera as a whole, it will be seen that the periods in which opera as a foreign product has been most in fashion in any country have been the periods of that country's greatest sterility in dramatic music ; not till the banishment of the Italian language from the German stage did that stage reach its culminating point of influence and world-wide celebrity; the comparatively short period in the early part of the nineteenth century, during which Italian opera was in vogue in Paris, was unmarked by any creation of importance excepting the lighter works of Auber and his contemporaries; in Russia and England, where the reign of exotic opera has been more firmly established than in any other countries, the only works that have gained a position in the history of music have been those that were given in the native language of the people. This statement is so obvious as to need no excuse in regard to modern days; but it helps to account in some measure for the surprising lack of lasting interest in the Handelian school of opera, as well as for the success which such a trifle as *The Beggar's*

Opera managed to gain in the very teeth, as it were, of the Italian fashion.

Johnson's famous denunciation of the opera as an 'exotic and irrational entertainment' indicates with remarkable insight the two causes of its real defects, in whatever country or period we regard it. The exotic nature of the fashionable opera has already been described; and the 'irrational' element in it is due to the domination of the singers for whom the operas were written. It is here that we meet the second and graver cause of operatic conventionality; airs had to be written to show off certain voices without respect to the dramatic propriety of the scene; as every one of the chief singers had a recognized position in the company, each must have exactly the number of airs appropriate to that position, not to the theatrical situation; and so, in all but a very few exceptional moments, the composer was debarred altogether from showing whether or not he could handle the sustained development of a story, or give accurate musical equivalents to a poetical motive. The result was to kill all individuality, and even as strong a nature as Handel's own could not preserve his identity of style; if we did not know that such and such airs were Handel's, it would be difficult to pick out his compositions from one of the large collections of opera songs, or to ascribe them, on internal evidence alone, to him rather than to any of the facile writers of operas, such as Jommelli, Leo, Terradellas, Porpora or Hasse. Even the general distinctions that are perceptible between Italian and German music of the period in other departments of music, are merged into one undistinguished style as soon as the composers approach the stage. Jommelli's sacred style differs as widely from Hasse's as Lotti's does from Bach's; but in their operas, the first is as conventional as the second and in precisely the same way. It is not so much that the influence of Italian art overspread the whole of Europe, in the train of the triumphant singers, as that a style of operatic writing was developed which could not be charged upon any one country; cosmopolitan in the worst sense, the style reminds us of nothing so much as of the typical courier who speaks every language imperfectly, and has the vices and shortcomings of all the nations of the world, the merits of none. Unity, whether dramatic or musical, gave place to the inevitable monotony of smooth and characterless *da capo* airs; of orchestral experiments there were surprisingly few, even in the best composers, compared with the prevalence of *obbligato* parts for a single instrument, generally intended to give the singer an opportunity for sustaining a note against a wind instrument, or for 'running divisions' with an accuracy and clearness set in rivalry with those of a skilful violinist.

Burney, a whole-hearted advocate for exotic opera, confirms the above theory as to the causes of the decadence of opera, although he is writing from exactly the opposite point of view: he says, in speaking of Gluck's reform[1]:—

'This is not the place to discuss its merit; I shall here only observe, that the simplifying dramatic music in Gluck's manner, in favour of the poet, at the expense of the composer and singer, is certainly very rational, where an opera is performed in the language of the country, and the singers have no great abilities to display, as in France; but in England, where we have frequently singers of uncommon talents, and where so small a part of an opera audience understands Italian, by abridging the symphonies, and prohibiting divisions and final cadences, in favour of an unintelligible drama, we should lose more than we should gain.'

It is merely as an important incident in Handel's career that the opera of the early eighteenth century is worth studying; the admirer of that master who should be led, by his appreciation of certain semi-dramatic works, to make researches into the operatic scores, would be grievously disappointed, from whatever point of view he approached them.

---

[1] *History of Music*, iv. 579.

He would find sequences of airs in great abundance, an astonishingly small number of which have survived the operas in which they were first heard. To attempt to revive any of the single songs that are not familiar to the public would be unsuccessful, not from the apathy of the musical world, but from the lack of inspiration in the melodies themselves. With Handel, as with all the other operatic composers of his time, the airs often begin with a short phrase which strikes the hearer as beautiful or original; but their continuation is very seldom interesting, except as a vehicle for vocal display. Of course there are exceptions in Handel, but the general level of his opera songs, as compared with those in his oratorios, is surprisingly low. The verdict of posterity has in this case been pretty just, and when such airs as 'Lascia ch' io pianga,' 'Ombra mai fù,' 'Mio caro bene,' 'Verdi prati,' 'Sorge infausta,' 'Nasce al bosco,' and a very few others, have been mentioned, the value of the Handelian school of opera has been fairly summed up. That these are masterpieces in their own way does not lessen the disappointment the student must feel in finding that there are so few of them scattered through the forty-two operas which make up his work for the stage.

The arbitrary rules of Italian opera, as summarized by W. S. Rockstro in his *Life of Handel* (pp. 62, 63)[1] give one some idea of the reasons which prevented the entertainment from claiming attention on the score of dramatic verisimilitude. There must always be six principal characters, three of each sex; the first woman was always a high soprano; the first man an artificial soprano, although he must always appear as the hero of the piece; the second man and the second woman might be either sopranos or contraltos; the third man, on rare occasions, was a tenor, and the occasional employment of a fourth man admitted a bass singer into

---

[1] Some of them first appeared in print in the amusing *Letters on the Poetry and Music of the Italian Opera*, by John Brown (an Edinburgh painter) 1789.

the company. In each act each of the principal singers must sing at least one air, and the airs were divided into five classes, though all were in the conventional *da capo* form. A most strict rule was that no two airs belonging to the same class should follow one another immediately. Some of the different classes of airs have been referred to in a former chapter; the five classes were *Aria cantabile, Aria di portamento, Aria di mezzo carattere, Aria parlante,* and *Aria di bravura.* These again were subdivided, as into *Aria d'imitazione* with an allusion to some external phenomenon, and the *Aria all'unisono* or *senza accompagnamento.* There must be a duet for the first man and woman, and at the end a so-called 'Coro' in which only the voices of all the principal singers were employed.

Handel's career as a writer of operas began in Hamburg, with *Almira*, brought out in 1705 with great success; the work shows the strong influence of Keiser throughout, and is in a mixture of German and Italian; beyond the fact that a sarabande in the third act was the origin of the beautiful 'Lascia ch' io pianga,' the music is of little importance. The scores of three subsequent operas given at Hamburg, *Nero, Daphne,* and *Florindo,* are lost,[1] and the next of the series that we possess is *Rodrigo*, given probably in Florence in 1707; the overture is a remodelled version of that to *Almira*. *Agrippina*, produced at Venice 1708, had a wonderful success, and retained its place in the repertory of the Teatro di San Giovanni Grisostomo for more than twenty years.

When Handel came to England in the end of 1710 Italian opera was not actually a new thing; in 1692 'the Italian lady' had sung in London concerts; a whole Italian 'consort' was given in 1702, 'by performers lately come from

---

[1] There is no trace of two more operas, *Oriana*, 1717, and *Zenobia*, 1721, except a record of their performance at Hamburg in Walther's Lexicon and Mattheson's *Musikalischer Patriot*: they may have been versions of other works prepared for Hamburg by Mattheson or others.

Rome'; in the following year, Margarita de l'Epine began a series of 'final appearances' which lasted till her marriage with Dr. Pepusch in 1718. Her sister appeared in the same year, and Mrs. Tofts, her constant rival, protested that it was not by her wish that a former maid-servant of hers had hissed and thrown oranges at the 'Italian gentlewoman' on the latter's first appearance at Drury Lane. Clayton's *Arsinoë*, an English version of an opera produced at Bologna in 1677, was performed in 1705 after the Italian manner, but in English, and with English singers[1]; and a version of Marcantonio Bononcini's *Camilla* was given by the English singers in 1706, and by a mixture of Italian and English performers in 1707. In the latter year Clayton's *Rosamond*, to a libretto by Addison, was given three times, and *Thomyris*, a pasticcio made up by the Count de St. Germain, from works by Alessandro Scarlatti and M. Bononcini, was given[2]. A version of Scarlatti's *Pirro e Demetrio* served to introduce the celebrated *castrato* Nicolini in 1708, when he and Valentini, Margarita de l'Epine, and 'the Baroness,' a singer only so designated[3], sang in Italian, the rest in English. One of the regular tricks of operatic management, the raising the prices of seats for special performances, was tried as early as this, for the sake of Nicolini. The famous article on this singer in the *Tatler*

---

[1] In the appendix to the anonymous English translation of Raguenet's *Parallèle*, published in 1709 as 'A Comparison between the French and Italian Music,' reference is made to the operas in England at this time in a very entertaining manner, and the book has a special value as illustrating the attitude taken towards the opera before the advent of Handel. The writer speaks of 'one Mr. Cl .... n, newly return'd out of Italy,' who 'Labour's might and main to Compose an English Opera, call'd Arsinoe; it is difficult to discover one tolerable thing in it. It ought to be call'd the Hospital of the old Decrepid Italian Operas.'

[2] The anonymous translator of Raguenet (see last note) says that *Camilla* checked various undertakings of Englishmen. 'Before this ev'ry Man that had the least smattering in Musick undertook to Compose an Opera.' *Rosamond* would not have lived to its three nights 'had not the good-natur'd Physicians supported its Spirits with a little *Aurum Potabile*.' The writer is also very bitter about *Thomyris*.

[3] Unless she were identical with a singer named Böss, with a similar title, who sang at Dresden in 1718.

will be referred to later on. Conti's *Clotilda*, another bilingual and quite unimportant production, appeared in 1709, and an anonymous opera, *Almahide* (1710), was the first opera sung throughout in Italian. Mancini's *Idaspe fedele* and Marcantonio Bononcini's *Etearco*, both given in Italian, complete the number of operas seen in England before the arrival of Handel, an event which bore its first-fruits in *Rinaldo*, brought out in 1711.

It is curious that Handel's first opera should have made so enduring a reputation as compared with the long succession of the other works he wrote for the London stage. Not merely did it make a stir among the essayists, who sneered at the flocks of sparrows let loose upon the stage in Almirena's song, ' Augelletti,' but it is agreed by all schools of later critics that its intrinsic beauties give it special claims to consideration; it is true that Burney says ' many of Handel's subsequent operas are superior to *Rinaldo*,' but after a careful analysis of all the master's dramatic works, Rockstro gives it as his opinion that ' *Rinaldo* is entitled to the first place on the list of its author's dramatic masterpieces.' From its historical as well as musical value, it would most probably be the work selected if any manager should be found enterprising enough to venture on a revival of one of Handel's operas on the modern stage. Besides Almirena's two airs, the song just spoken of and the beautiful ' Lascia ch' io pianga,' it contains, in ' Cara sposa,' the song which the composer considered the best he had ever written.

At the date of *Rinaldo*, Handel was Capellmeister to the Electoral Court of Hanover, and in the summer following its production he went to Germany to resume his duties; in the space of time that elapsed between his departure and the production of his second London opera, *Il Pastor Fido*, there were several productions, among them an attempt to set up English opera against the fashionable entertainment. Galliard's *Calypso*, to a libretto by John Hughes, was only given five times, its failure being ascribed by Burney to the fact that

the favourite singer Nicolini had no part in it. Mrs. Barbier,
who appeared in it, had made herself celebrated at her first
appearance in Valentini's part in *Almahide*, by an attack of
nervousness which drew from Addison a paper in the *Spectator*.
Addison was a staunch supporter of opera in English, and
when he drags in a reference to *Calypso* in the course of a
valedictory address to Nicolini, who was intending to leave
England about this time, Burney, who was heart and soul
in favour of the Italian opera, makes merry at his expense.
Of the overture to *Teseo*, the third of the London series of
Handel's operas, Burney says rather ingenuously, 'The last
movement has passages in it that he afterwards used in his
organ concertos and other compositions; and the divisions in
the first violin had perhaps been previously thought of by
Corelli; however the hautbois and violoncello parts, and effects
of the whole, were new and original in 1713.'

On this second visit of Handel's to London, he was for
a long time the guest of the third Earl of Burlington at
Burlington House, Piccadilly, and so beguiling was the life he
led there, in intercourse with the wits and notabilities of
the time, that he outstayed the leave of absence granted by
the Elector, until that Elector became King of England on
the death of Queen Anne in 1714. The story of how Handel
kept out of the King's way for some time, and finally pro-
pitiated him by means of the 'Water Musick' in 1715, is too
well known to be repeated at length; during these years the
only opera of Handel's brought out publicly was *Amadigi*
(1715), though an unperformed opera, *Silla*, is assigned to
this period. In the dedication of *Amadigi* to the Earl of
Burlington, the librettist, Heidegger, refers to Handel's residence at Burlington House: 'this opera . . . . . more immediately claims your lordship's protection, as it was composed
in your own family.' The next two years saw no production
of importance, and from 1717 there were no more operas in
London till the foundation of the Royal Academy of Music,

in 1720, when Handel was commissioned to engage the singers, and to act in concert with Giovanni Battista Bononcini, and Attilio Ariosti, the latter of whom had made a name for himself about four years before as a player on the viol d'amore.

The establishment of this, the nearest approach London has ever had to a permanent opera, gave Handel increased opportunities for the composition of operas; and the series of fourteen operas he wrote for it contains some of the best of his dramatic work. The first production was Giovanni Porta's *Numitor*, the second Handel's *Radamisto*, and the third Domenico Scarlatti's *Narciso*. Handel's opera had an extraordinary success, entirely due to its own merits, as neither Senesino, nor the other singers whom Handel had engaged in Dresden, appeared in London till the following autumn, when Bononcini's *Astarto* introduced Senesino and Signora Durastanti, who made so much success that, on the revival of *Radamisto*, new songs were added for them. In the second year of the Academy, the authorities endangered the success of their undertaking by commissioning their three composers to collaborate in an opera called *Muzio Scevola*, of which Attilio Ariosti wrote the first act, Bononcini the second, and Handel the third. Although as Burney says, there was no definite object of pitting the two latter composers against one another as recognized rivals, yet in this work we may be sure that the rivalry between them in the public mind had its origin. In the autumn of that year, 1721, Handel's *Floridante* made its appearance, and in the following season, in January 1723, Francesca Cuzzoni appeared for the first time in England, in Handel's *Ottone*. She made a great success, in spite of her remarkable want of beauty; Horace Walpole describes her as 'short and squat, with a doughy cross face, but fine complexion; was not a good actress; dressed ill; and was silly, and fantastical[1].' It was in a

[1] Burney, *History of Music*, iv. 299.

rehearsal of this work that, on her refusal to sing the song
'Falsa immagine' which Handel had written especially for
her, he seized her and threatened to throw her out of the
window with the words, 'Oh! Madame, je sçais bien que
Vous êtes une véritable Diablesse; mais je Vous ferai sçavoir,
moi, que je suis Beelzebub, le *Chéf* des Diables[1].' During
the three seasons in which Cuzzoni reigned supreme, the older
favourites, Mrs. Anastasia Robinson and Durastanti, were
compelled to sing secondary parts; she introduced the principal songs in the five succeeding operas by Handel, *Flavio,
Giulio Cesare, Tamerlano, Rodelinda*, and *Scipione*. The airs
in *Ottone* are stated to have been more popular than those
in any other of the series; but the only fragment of the
work still in vogue is the bass air, written for Boschi, 'Del
minacciar del vento.' From *Rodelinda*, the airs 'Dove sei
amato bene,' and 'Mio caro bene,' sung respectively by
Senesino and Cuzzoni, still survive, and the famous march
has preserved the name of *Scipio* down to the present
time.

The year 1726, which saw Handel naturalized as a British
subject, was the first year of that famous rivalry between
the two great female singers of their day, Cuzzoni and
Faustina. By a curious coincidence they had been rivals
from the first night they stepped upon the public stage; for
their début took place in Venice in 1719, in Gasparini's
Lamano. As far as can be judged by the contemporary
accounts of the two, Cuzzoni seems to have atoned for her
ugliness by a tone of remarkable sweetness, to have possessed
the power of 'conducting, sustaining, increasing, and diminishing her tones by minute degrees,' and to have acquired perfect
ease in the execution of divisions; Faustina Bordoni was
incontestably the better-looking woman, and had every kind
of skill in the execution of rapid passages, and it is recorded

[1] Mainwaring, *Anecdotes of Handel*, p. 110.

that she could invent passages of embellishment with great
success. She sang here in only two seasons, but they were
seasons of great excitement, since the ladies of the town
became partisans for one or the other of the rivals, and their
enthusiasm carried them to extraordinary lengths, so that the
admirers of one would not hesitate to hiss and make a noise
during the performance of the other; it was the fashion to
pit them against each other in the same operas, and the first
which Handel wrote after Faustina's arrival, *Alessandro*, contained parts for the two in exact equality, culminating in a
duet where the two voices continually crossed over each other.
One of the airs allotted to Faustina is the still popular
'Lusinghe più care,' the only number of the opera that is
still in fashion. In the next of his dramatic works, *Admeto*,
the story of Alcestis was entirely spoilt owing to the
necessity of providing equally important parts for the two
ladies, which brought about the invention of a counterplot.
Faustina had the part of Alcestis, Cuzzoni that of the heroine
of the counterplot; the music contains nothing that has kept
its vogue. A number of entertaining details about the two
singers and the behaviour of their friends are given by
Burney, in vol. iv. of his History; among other things, it is
related that Lady Walpole, the mother of Horace Walpole,
contrived to get both to sing at her house, by the device of
luring each away in turn to look at some china while the
other sang, so that neither was in the room during the other's
performance. The quarrel between them, or rather between their
respective partisans, reached its height at the last performance
of an opera by Bononcini, *Astyanax*, in which Cuzzoni sang the
part of Andromache to the Hermione of Faustina. The
account in *The London Journal* of June 10, 1727, quoted by
Burney [1], states that 'The contention at first was only carried
on by hissing on one side, and clapping on the other; but

---

[1] *History of Music*, iv. 325.

proceeded, at length, to the melodious use of cat-calls, and other accompaniments, which manifested the zeal and politeness of that illustrious assembly.'

From that night, the fortunes of the Royal Academy of Music began to decline; people of taste left off going to the opera, and Handel's three next operas, *Riccardo Primo* (1727), *Siroe* and *Tolomeo* (1728), were the last brought out by the organization which had begun with such high hopes, and which had actually achieved so much. In the narrative of the opera, as given by Burney, we are continually confronted by the statement that another call was made upon the subscribers, and the outlay of capital must have been out of all proportion to the receipts, although the King's Theatre was constantly full, and at prices relatively far higher than those in fashion in the present day.

Neither the severe lesson conveyed by the failure of the Academy, nor the phenomenal success of *The Beggar's Opera*, the music of which had been selected by Dr. Pepusch from old English melodies, set to Gay's words and brought out at the Lincoln's Inn Fields Theatre in the former winter, could make Handel see, as yet, that the way to secure the permanent allegiance of the English nation was to give them something the people could understand; in 1729 he went off to Italy to engage a new set of singers, and opened the King's Theatre in December of that year—himself and Heidegger being partners in management—with his opera of *Lotario*, followed by *Partenope* in 1730. To the new singers—Bernacchi, the famous *castrato*; Signora Strada; Signora Merighi; a tenor, Annibale Pio Fabri; and Riemschneider, a Hamburg baritone — there was added in the following season Senesino, the only one of the earlier company to reappear in London. He sang first in a revival of *Scipio*; and his first new part was in *Poro*, brought out in 1731. *Ezio* and *Sosarme* (1732) complete the list of Handelian operas composed before that important change of plans which gave us the great series of oratorios.   In the former, Montagnana, another new arrival, had the splendid song 'Nasce al bosco,' but beyond this and the celebrated ' Rend' il sereno al ciglio ' from *Sosarme,* neither work is of great importance.

It is a curious coincidence that, although no one seems to have thought it worth while to steal Handel's operas, the year 1732 saw two successful attempts to appropriate his first works written to English words in oratorio or cantata form. *Esther,* as we have seen, was presented first to the London public in an unauthorized way, so that Handel was compelled to give it as soon as possible after the pirated performance ; and an exactly similar thing happened in the case of *Acis and Galatea,* the serenata or pastoral drama, originally performed in private at Cannons, at an entertainment given by Handel's patron, the Duke of Chandos.   The pirate in this instance was no other than the father of the composer, Arne, the musical upholsterer of King's Street, Covent Garden, whose daughter, afterwards Mrs. Cibber, took the part of Galatea ; Burney says that 'young Arne,' as well as J. C. Smith, J. F. Lampe, and Henry Carey, were adventurers in this undertaking, and that not only Miss Arne, but Miss Cecilia Young, afterwards Mrs. Arne, was a principal female singer. Handel's own revival of his work, suggested and indeed necessitated by this performance, took place on the 10th of June, at the Haymarket, the Arnes' having been given on the 17th of May.   It was no doubt from the desire of giving the public something which they could not get at the other house, that Handel added to the English work a considerable portion of his old Italian composition on the same subject. The disposition of the different portions has been restored by W. S. Rockstro[1] with as much certainty as is now possible.   It was not till 1739 that the English work was presented once more in its purity.   The advertisement of the

[1] *Life of Handel,* p. 178.

1732 performance ran as follows: 'June the 10th, will be performed *Acis and Galatea*, a serenata, revised with several additions, at the opera-house, by a great number of the best voices and instruments. There will be *no action* on the stage, but the scene will represent, in a picturesque manner, a rural prospect, with rocks, groves, fountains, and grottos, among which will be disposed a chorus of nymphs and shepherds, the habits and every other decoration suited to the subject.' From this it will be seen that the performance of the serenata differed remarkably little from that of the operas, since it is at least probable that the amount of action usually employed in these was of the slightest, according to our modern notions. The character of the music must have more than made up for what the entertainment lacked in gesture ; for to examine *Acis and Galatea* after the series of tedious operas, with their successions of unmeaning airs, is to discern all that is meant by unity and real dramatic characterization. It is quite true that the airs and songs of the serenata are among the best and most familiar of Handel's productions in this way ; but it is not the fact of their importance or their great amount of musical value that makes the work what it is; throughout the four characters are well individualized, and in its dramatic continuity it stands higher than any of the master's works, except the two or three most famous oratorios. The fact that in the five-part choruses Handel had opportunities which the whole series of operas could not give him, may have had something to do with the great success of the work, which was performed at Oxford in the following year, as before, with Italian additions.

For one reason or other, however, he did not venture for some time to offer the public entertainments without action, but went on with his series of operas, from *Orlando*, 1733, to *Deidamia*, 1741, keeping them going, as it were, side by side with the series of oratorios, which, from 1732, were presented annually or even more frequently, as we have seen. In this later period of Handel's dramatic career he had a new difficulty to face, for Senesino, his most important singer, went off and joined the 'Opera of the Nobility,' an enterprise started apparently by the friends of Bononcini, at the theatre in Lincoln's Inn Fields. In looking at the list of works presented by Handel since the break-down of the Royal Academy of Music, it is impossible to disguise the fact that the repertory consisted far too exclusively of his own works; the occasional introduction of a pasticcio built in the main upon some other composer's operas, was obviously only due to the well-known managerial trick of putting in some stopgap until the new production is ready. Bononcini's patrons may well have felt that there was room for another opera at which the works of other composers should be heard. Bononcini had entered into distinct rivalry at the time of *Acis and Galatea*, by taking Handel's own theatre for the performance of another serenata, an incident which suggested the famous epigram of Byrom. Not only Senesino, but Montagnana and others of Handel's best singers, joined the new scheme, and in its second year Cuzzoni was engaged; Porpora came over as conductor. Later on, the illustrious Farinelli sang for the Opera of the Nobility, as a set-off to Carestini, the male contralto who made his first appearance under Handel's management, in a pasticcio, *Cajo Fabrizio* in December, 1733. The violent letter of Paolo Rolli, the librettist of the rival opera, which appeared first in *The Craftsman* of April 7, 1733, and is reprinted in Rockstro's *Life of Handel*[1], throws some light on the feelings with which Handel was regarded by the malcontents, although of course it is necessary to read it with all due allowance for prejudice and intemperate language. The struggle between the two operas began in earnest in the winter of 1733-4, when each house produced an opera on the subject of *Ariadne*. Porpora's came out on December 29, and

[1] p. 184.

Handel's on January 26. The latter work is chiefly remembered by its famous minuet, played as an accompaniment to an impressive ceremony on the stage; it had a wonderful success for many years afterwards, and it remained in fashion for nearly forty years at least, for it is mentioned, with Arne's 'Water parted from the sea,' as 'one of the genteelest of tunes' in *She stoops to conquer*. Besides this, there is a remarkably fine air, 'Qual leon,' sung by Durastanti, who joined Handel's new company in this year; in the accompaniment, which contains parts for two horns, two oboes, bassoons and strings, there is a more distinct feeling for orchestral colouring as we know it now, than in the majority of Handel's scores.

Misfortunes came thick on Handel just at this time; his agreement with Heidegger came to an end in July 1734, and his rivals took the King's Theatre, compelling him to take the Lincoln's Inn Fields Theatre, where he remained only till the next winter, bringing out no new opera there. For Covent Garden Theatre he wrote six operas in the next three years, *Ariodante*, *Alcina*, *Atalanta*, *Arminio*, *Giustino*, and *Berenice*; Signora Strada was still faithful to Handel; so was Carestini, for whom 'Verdi prati' was especially written in *Alcina*; besides the German, Waltz, a bass who had been Handel's cook, and whose name is remembered on account of Handel's criticism of Gluck, 'He knows no more counterpoint than Waltz, mein cook.' Mr. Beard and Miss Cecilia Young appeared as members of Handel's company, but his singers as a whole were inferior to those of his rivals, and for this reason, Burney says that he wisely rested his fame and fortune on his oratorios. Beside the actual oratorios, Handel brought forward at this house a setting of Dryden's Ode on St. Cecilia's Day, under the title of *Alexander's Feast*, and revived *Parnasso in Festa*, an adaptation from *Athalia*, prepared for the marriage festivities of the Prince of Orange, and produced at the King's Theatre in Handel's last season there; he gave also *Il Trionfo del Tempo,* a re-modelled version of his old Italian oratorio. *Alexander's Feast* has the rare quality of unity, and there are plenty of stirring choruses as well as solos. Like *Acis,* it has never lost its place in public estimation, and is one of the few of Handel's greater works that has been universally admired in Germany. During his tenure of Covent Garden, Handel tried to form the sopranist Conti (Gioacchino Gizziello), into a successful rival to Farinelli, and many of the best songs in the operas above enumerated were composed for him.   But neither he, nor the rest of Handel's company could vie in popularity with the other troupe, and the effort of keeping his enterprise going until just after the Opera of the Nobility had been obliged to shut its doors cost Handel a very severe illness, in which it was whispered that his reason was affected.   He went to Aix-la-Chapelle in the summer of 1737, and returned in the November of the same year, almost completely restored.

A brief account must be given of the doings of the Opera of the Nobility during the five seasons from 1733 to 1737. In going over the list of operas produced, or in reading Burney's detailed history of the rival schemes, one cannot but be struck by the amount of anonymous operas, or works of uncertain authorship, which seem to have been produced; this is but another sign of the importance of the singers above the composers in the days of Farinelli and the rest of them. In the first season, we hear of a second opera by Porpora, *Ferdinando,* and of a revival of Bononcini's *Astarto*; in the second season Farinelli made his bow to the London public for the first time, in Hasse's *Artaserse,* singing 'Per questo dolce amplesso,' and 'Son qual nave,' the latter being composed by his brother, Riccardo Broschi. Besides being acknowledged on all hands as the finest singer of his time, he must have been a man of uncommon ability, discretion, and taste. The story of his life, of his early and continuous

successes, of his residence at the court of Madrid, of the extraordinary influence he obtained over two successive kings of
Spain, the melancholy Philip V. and Ferdinand VI, of his
enforced retirement to Italy, of his long and most interesting
correspondence with Metastasio, and his death in 1782, at the
age of eighty, may be read in the utmost detail, not only
in Burney's History and in his *Present State of Music in
France and Italy*, but in the three volumes of his translation
of Metastasio's letters, the last a book that throws much
light on the operatic affairs of the time a little subsequent
to this. The singer's influence over Philip V. bore fruit in
the establishment of an opera at his palace of Buen Retiro,
where Francesco Corselli's *Alessandro nell' Indie* was given
on May 9, 1738. This was not the actual beginning of Italian
opera in Spain, for earlier in the same year a company got
together by the Marchese Scotti, who arrived from Italy
on a diplomatic mission, had started a season in the new
theatre ' Teatro de los Canos del Peral,' with Hasse's
Demetrio, the singers of which were also employed at Buen
Retiro[1].

Farinelli gesticulated much less than his predecessors, but
his vocal skill was of so surpassing an order of excellence, that
his habit of standing ' motionless as a statue ' was not felt
as a drawback. The *messa di voce* seems to have been the
quality in which he surpassed all other singers, and some of
his hearers ' imagined him to have had the latent help of some
instrument by which the tone was continued, while he renewed
his powers by respiration[2].'

In the season of 1735 Porpora's opera of *Polifemo* was
brought out, and, by way of a more direct attack upon Handel,
the composer produced an oratorio, *David*, which, as Burney
delightedly records, was performed only three times. The

[1] Don Luis Carmena y Millan, *Crónica de la Opera Italiana en Madrid*.
[2] Burney, *History of Music*, iv. 380.

royal wedding which inspired Handel's *Atalanta* drew from
Porpora a *Feast of Hymen*, of which four representations were
given, while *Atalanta* was 'continued in run till the end of
the season.' In 1736 the *Siroe* of Hasse was apparently
the only new work given at the King's Theatre, and a couple
of months after its production the custom of playing a comic
intermezzo between its acts was begun; these *intermezzi* had
such an influence on the future state of the opera, that the
first appearance of one in London is an event of some importance. It was from the side of comedy rather than from that
of tragedy that dramatic music gained a wider freedom, and
indeed a new lease of life. In Rolli's *Sabrina*, 1737, Farinelli
appeared for the last time in England; and the undertaking
of the nobility came to an end. It is clear from Burney's
account, which is supported by a reference to Colley Cibber's
Apology, that Farinelli's vogue with the London public had
passed away in the three years he had sung here. 'The
English appetite for Italian *friandises*,' says Burney, 'was
certainly palled by plenitude.'

Handel's first season at the King's Theatre after his return
from the continent was interrupted by the death of Queen
Caroline, and his new opera, *Faramondo*, was therefore not
brought out till January, 1738. The principal new singers
were the famous sopranist, Caffarelli (Gaetano Majorano) and
two ladies who went by the names of the Francesina and the
Marchesini respectively; and Montagnana came back to
Handel's company. Handel seems to have learnt that an
opera season could not be carried on with his own works
alone, for he brought out works by Pescetti and Veracini,
as well as a pasticcio made up partly from works of his own,
before the production of his own *Serse*, one air in which, the
exquisite 'Ombra mai fù,' has remained in vogue ever since
Caffarelli sang it. In 1739, while Handel was occupied in
bringing out oratorios and other pieces without action, the
'little theatre in the Haymarket' carried on operas in a very

humble way, with Carestini's support, and with no composer
of higher rank than Pescetti to provide the music. Handel's
Imeneo, a short and unsuccessful work, was brought out
in 1740, and in the following year he closed the list of his
dramatic works with *Deidamia*, an opera hardly worthy
of his hand, and certainly not worthy of the hand which
was to produce *The Messiah* later on in that year. The
first air of Ulysses in *Deidamia* has a curious resemblance,
which Burney was the first to point out, to an air by
Pergolesi, which Monticelli performed in *Meraspe* in the
following season. This air, 'Tremende, oscure, atroci,' seems
to have had a wonderful vogue ; it occurs in many of
Walsh's collections, and is so good an example of the style
most in favour with the patrons of the opera that it seems
worth while to give it in full. The similarity with Handel's
air must have been accidental, since it was not known in
England till 1742, and as Pergolesi died in 1737 it is not
possible that he should have copied it from Handel. The
dialogue carried on between the two orchestras, and the
astounding difficulties of the voice-part, with its passages of
reiterated notes, may have accounted in some measure for
its success. The difficulties of 'Son qual nave,' written for
the special purpose of showing off Farinelli's powers, are as
nothing compared with Pergolesi's (or perhaps, more correctly,
Monticelli's[1]) ornaments.

[1] Compare the example of Monticelli's reiterated notes in Burney, iv. 461.

'Tremende oscure atroci' (Meraspe)   PERGOLESI.

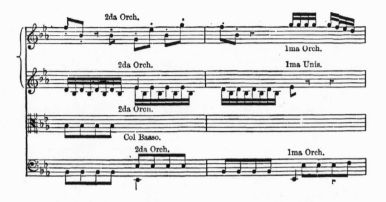

* The misplaced accent at this repetition of the theme illustrates Burney's complaint against both Pergolesi and Hasse that 'neither had yet found out the secret of exact phraseology. A subject begun in the symphony upon the first part of a bar, is by both frequently commenced, in the song, at the second' (*History*, iv. 457).

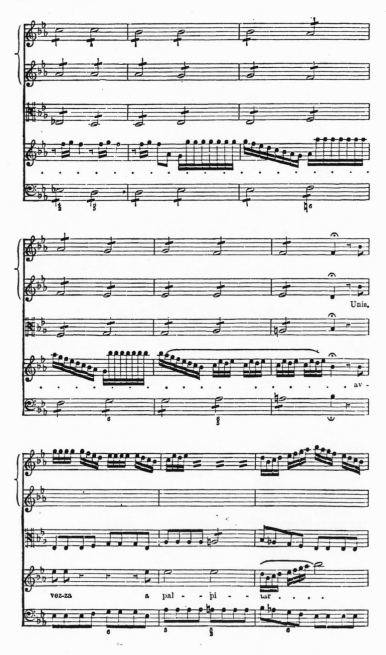

From a date considerably anterior to that at which Handel
left off writing operas, the public taste for them had been on
the wane, and it seemed as if at length the absurdity of the
conventions which had reigned so long, and at which so many
wise men in different countries had pointed their sarcasms in
vain, was beginning to be recognized.   From 1737 onwards,
pasticcios were more in fashion than ever, and the entertainment must have been simply a concert with action, the component parts of which were joined together as deftly as might
be, by the poet of the theatre at which it was presented.
Hasse, Leonardo Vinci, Domenico Scarlatti, Leo and Galuppi,
were the composers most drawn upon, and more rarely Rinaldo
di Capua and Terradellas.   Monticelli retained his popularity,

and Amorevoli, an admirable tenor, according to Burney; among
the ladies, a fat high soprano called Visconti, and Mmes. Galli
and Frasi, were the chief attractions of the London opera.
Most of the opera called *Meraspe,* from which Monticelli's air
quoted above is taken, was by Pergolesi, whose serious works
had not before been heard in England ; but there were additional
numbers by Domenico Scarlatti, Leo, and Lampugnani. This
last composer, who had been employed at Milan for many years
to put together the pasticcios, had a special aptitude for comic
music, for which Burney is continually reproaching him. The
only true dramatic music produced during these next years was
Handel's *Semele* given as an oratorio in 1744 at Covent Garden.
As in the other works of this semi-dramatic class, it has far
more unity and characterization than the operas strictly so-
called; and the beautiful choruses, such as ' Now Love, that
everlasting boy' form a most impressive background to the
splendidly vigorous scene in which Juno awakes Somnus, the
exquisite invocation to sleep, and Jupiter's love-song ' Where'er
you walk.' *Hercules,* produced under similar conditions in the
following year, has even more powerful scenes, and a remarkable
amount of dramatic unity. In the following season, Gluck
made his first appearance in England, having been invited by
Lord Middlesex, the director of the London opera, to produce
a new work here. This, his ninth dramatic work, was *La
Caduta dei Giganti,* which came out at a most unfortunate time,
as the Scottish rebellion had only just been quelled, and the
public was not in a condition to take much interest in operatic
affairs. There were many orchestral effects in it that were
new to English ears, and accordingly the epithet ' tedesco '
was freely applied to the composer as a term of reproach. In
his *Artamene,* produced two months afterwards, occurs the air
made so popular by Monticelli, ' Rasserena il mesto ciglio,'
but Burney is right when he says that no other air ' furnished
a single portent of the great genius this composer afterwards
manifested.' In his *Present State of Music in Germany,*

Burney declares that the reform in Gluck's style was due
to his want of success in England; but this was sixteen
years before *Orfeo,* the firstfruits of that reform, saw the light,
and Mr. Ernest Newman is probably right in attributing
Gluck's remark that 'he owed everything to England,' to
a wish to flatter Burney's native country[1].

In 1749 serious opera had tired out its patrons, and a first
attempt was made to present some typical examples of the
comic opera, or *opera buffa,* which had been growing in
popularity in Italy for a good many years. A manager named
Croza, who decamped a year or two afterwards, started with a
company brought from Italy, among whom were Signora Frasi,
two excellent buffos, Pertici and Laschi, with their wives, and
Latilla, Natale Resta and Ciampi, as composers. Burney's
carelessness in noticing the details of music which to him was
entirely unimportant deprives us of the only direct evidence
that we might have looked for concerning the authorship of
a certain song, a composition by which the majority of English
amateurs at the present day know the name of Pergolesi,
though he most certainly was not its author. In an opera
buffa called *Gli tre Cicisbei ridicoli,* there occurs 'Tre giorni son
che Nina,' which has for many years been constantly sung as
the serious, even tragic utterance of a lover driven mad by his
lady's death. That it was sung by Laschi is all the evidence of
its source that we now possess; and for the minute discussion
of the whole question of the song's origin, the reader may be
referred to the *Musical Times* for 1899, where at pp. 241–3
Mr. W. Barclay Squire comes to the conclusion that the song
is by Ciampi, as Signor Piatti possessed a copy of Walsh's
edition of it in which Mrs. Arne wrote the name of Ciampi
opposite this song. As its original form is not generally
known, it is worth while to give it exactly as it stands in Walsh,
with the additional verse which makes it only too certain that
the character of the song is very far from being tragic.

[1] Ernest Newman, *Gluck and the Opera,* chapter i.

Aria, Sig. Laschi, nei 'Tre Cicisbei.'

* This mistake in the signature is in the original. Compare bar 3 et seq. with the first bar of the air.

stà . . . in let - to se ne stà . . . . e Tim-pa-ni e Pif-fe-ri e

tà . . . Sve - glia-te-la per pie - tà . . . . e Cim-ba-li, e Timpani e

Cim - ba - li

Pif-fe - ri . . Sve - glia - te-mi Ni - net - ta, Sve - glia - - - - temi Ni-

net - ta, per - chè non dor - ma più . . . per - chè non dor - ma

più, Sve-glia-te - mi Ni-net - ta, Ni - net - ta, per - chè non dor - ma

The work which did most to alter the standpoint of the public in many countries towards comic opera was Pergolesi's *Serva Padrona*, brought out in Naples 1731, in London and in Paris 1752. It is little wonder that a work at once so amusing, so sincere in treatment and expression, and so masterly in invention and design, should have obtained a European success, after the stilted, conventional successions of dull airs made up on well-recognized patterns.

To our modern ears the finale of a serious opera is such an important section that it is difficult to believe it to have been merely an adaptation from the comic operas of the time. The operas of the Handelian period concluded with a 'chorus' of the principal characters, but this was quite an unimportant ending to the work; the concerted finale is said to have been the invention of Niccolò Logroscino (c. 1700–1763) who was the first to introduce a connected series of movements into the ends of his grotesquely comic operas in the Neapolitan dialect.

The history of the opera has now been traced up to the
time when the reforms of Gluck were ready to inaugurate
a new period of dramatic activity in music.   These reforms
belong to a later section of musical history; but before leaving
this part of the subject, it may be well to examine the attitude
of the more thoughtful part of the public towards the conventions which so long reigned on the operatic stage.   The
first, and one of the most famous, of the attacks made upon
operatic conventions was in No. 4 of *The Tatler*, where Steele
says :—

'Letters from the Hay-market inform us, that, on Saturday
night last, the opera of *Pyrrhus and Demetrius* was performed with great applause.   This intelligence is not very
acceptable to us friends of the theatre ; for the stage being
an entertainment of the reason and all our faculties, this way
of being pleased with the suspense of them for three hours
together, and being given up to the shallow satisfaction of
the eyes and ears only, seems to arise rather from the de-
generacy of our understanding, than an improvement of our
diversions.   That the understanding has no part in the pleasure
is evident, from what these letters very positively assert, to
wit, that a great part of the performance was done in Italian ;
and a great critick fell into fits in the gallery, at seeing, not
only time and place, but languages and nations, confused in
the most incorrigible manner.'

Steele's remarks are perhaps not too strong for the acknowledged absurdity in regard to the mixture of languages;
but their force is a good deal weakened by the very different
tone adopted by him in No. 115 of the same journal, in
which in his celebrated eulogium of Nicolini he refers to 'the
dignity and elegance of this entertainment,' although, as Burney
points out, it was the same opera he had before condemned so
strongly.   Addison's railleries in *The Spectator* were at first
directed against the childish realism of the birds in *Rinaldo*,
and Nicolini's combat with the lion in *Hydaspes*, the latter an
incident which gave rise to an extraordinary number of
witticisms ; and when it is remembered that Addison had

been concerned in the unsuccessful attempts to establish
English opera just before the arrival of Handel, we must
share Burney's opinion that the writer's motives were not
above suspicion.   His praise of Nicolini in *The Spectator*,
No. 405, shows, however, that he was not so biassed as
Burney thinks.

In No. 18 of *The Spectator* the whole question of foreign
languages as employed in the opera is very fairly discussed,
and the drawbacks to English translations of the Italian
libretti fully explained; but Addison, it is clear, is on the
side of giving all dramatic entertainments in the language
of the country where they take place.   His remark, 'It does
not want any great measure of sense to see the ridicule of
this monstrous practice,' makes it quite plain that he was
no supporter of the Italian opera.   His criticism of the English
taste that 'at present our notions of music are so very uncertain that we do not know what it is we like; only, in
general, we are transported with any thing that is not
English; so it be of a foreign growth, let it be Italian,
French, or High Dutch, it is the same thing,' is as true to-
day as it was in 1711.   The amusing paper, No. 235, on the
'trunk-maker' shows that, even as early as this, the institution
of the *claque* was not unknown on the English stage.   In the
winter of the same year an attempt was made in *The Spectator*,
Nos. 258 and 278, to win public favour for the subscription
concerts to be given by Clayton, Dieupart, and Haym in the
concert-room at York Buildings, a house which Burney states
belonged to Steele, the real author of the two papers, though
they were signed by the three managers; their second
charge, against the pasticcios which were beginning to find
a place in the operatic scheme, is better grounded than their
first, which amounts to nothing more than a statement that,
as they had first introduced the Italian style of opera into
England, they feel aggrieved by the success of the Handelian
undertaking.   From this time the essayists left the opera

almost alone, until the famous attack by Lord Chesterfield in *The World*, No. 98 (Nov. 14, 1754). Beginning with a reference to the recent revival of interest in the opera (i. e. the introduction of the Italian *opera buffa*), he sets out to defend the innocence of the entertainment, as not only do Englishmen not understand what it means, but Italians themselves are equally at a loss. Here is a passage which throws so much light on the whole question of operatic conventions that no apology is needed for quoting it at length :—

'Should the ingenious author of the words, by mistake, put any meaning into them, he would, to a certain degree, check and cramp the genius of the composer of the music, who perhaps might think himself obliged to adapt his sounds to the sense, whereas now he is at liberty to scatter indiscriminately, among the kings, queens, heroes and heroines, his adagios, his allegros, his pathetics, his chromatics and his jiggs. It would also have been a restraint upon the actors and actresses, who might possible have attempted to form their action upon the meaning of their parts ; but as it is, if they do but seem, by turns, to be angry and sorry in the two first acts, and very merry in the last scene of the last, they are sure to meet with their deserved applause.'

In the course of his paper, in which there is a warm praise of Metastasio, the author satirizes the low intellectual level of the singers, the manner in which they were fêted by the nobility, and refers to the visit of Farinelli with much the same sort of mystery with which Burney speaks, in italics, of his '*inchantments*.' 'It is to be hoped,' says Lord Chesterfield, 'that the illustrious signor Farinelli has not yet forgot the many instances he experienced of British munificence ; for it is certain that many private families *still remember them*.' In No. 171 of the same pape, the same writer resumes the subject of operatic absurdities, and again praises Metastasio, directing his satire against the 'modish Pasticcio.'

It was not the English essayists alone who cried out against the absurdities of operatic convention ; in 1720 there appeared a most amusing little book, *Il Teatro alla moda,* the authorship of which has always been attributed to Benedetto Marcello ; as an example of the endurance of certain types of people connected with the opera, the book deserves close study, for almost everything, down to the inevitable companions of the great female singers, their mothers, lap-dogs, and singing-birds, remains unchanged in the present day, and one little hit after another comes home to all who know anything about the workings of an operatic enterprise.   Marcello holds the *castrati* in wholesome abhorrence, and it is significant that in the only dramatic work of his own which is generally accessible, the 'intreccio' of *Arianna* (brought out by the firm of Ricordi, in the edition of Dr. Chilesotti), there is no part for an artificial male voice ; he confirms the statement of the historians, that it was the fashion to ascribe the necessary operation to the effects of an accident in boyhood.   From him we gather that the second harpsichord in the opera orchestra was used for giving the singers their cues, and that the pitch of the harpsichords was a standing cause of dispute with the singers who took the 'Parti buffe' in the comic intermezzi.   There is a good deal of mock advice to those who would succeed as operatic writers, and Marcello's hatred of the convention of his time is easy to read between the lines.   The composer is to end his dedication by declaring that he 'kisses the leaps of the fleas of the paws of the dogs of his Excellence'; he is of course to close his work with the 'usual chorus in honour of the sun, of the moon, or of the impresario'; at the rehearsals he must never explain his intention to the actors, for he must remember that they will prefer to do everything their own way; and he is to be always ready to insert airs to please the actors or their patrons. There is a very interesting remark upon the curious convention, so often noticed in the earlier chapters, of allowing the vocal beginning of an air to be interrupted by a resumption of the ritornello, so that the real beginning is as it were postponed : ' The modern Maestro will be careful to divide the sentiment and meaning of the words, particularly in the airs, making the Musico sing the first line (although it may mean nothing by itself) and then introducing a long ritornello of violins, violette, etc.' With regard to the overture, or sinfonia, it is interesting to compare Marcello's words with a passage in Algarotti's *Saggio sopra l'Opera in Musica* (1763). Marcello says that the overture must consist of a ' French movement,' or *prestissimo* of semiquavers, in a major key, succeeded by the usual soft movement in the corresponding (i. e. tonic) minor key, and must close with a minuet, gavotte, or gigue in the major key again ; the composer must avoid fugues and kindred forms as antiquities little adapted to modern customs. Algarotti's account of the overtures of his day, forty years after Marcello, is :—' The symphony at the very beginning of the opera is always composed of two allegros and a *grave*, it must be as noisy as possible, and must never vary but be always on this one pattern.' Algarotti complains of many things in the operas of his time, such as the overpowering accompaniments, more particularly in the treble, the intrusion of the ballet between the acts, an entertainment entirely unconnected with the subject of the opera, and of the inaccurate scenery and inartistic lighting of the theatres. His ideal of a theatre founded by a liberal and cultivated prince, where all the arts should be combined, to delight not a tumultuous rabble, but a ' solemn audience where the Addisons, the Drydens, the Daciers, the Muratori, the Gravinas, and the Marcelli might sit,' reads like a prophecy of Bayreuth.

In 1772 Antonio Planelli wrote a treatise *Dell' Opera in Musica*, in which many of the modern ideals are suggested, such as the division of operas into three acts instead of more, which is evidently intended as a support of the theories of

Gluck, whose *Alceste* he praises warmly. He attaches great importance to pronunciation, in which he includes the art of gesture as well as that of singing; and his rules for the perfect operatic style are interesting as showing how clearly he realized the causes of the former abuses in opera:—1. Style in theatrical music requires few notes ; and the words of dramatic airs should not be repeated. 2. This style abhors equally notes too high and notes too low. 3. The theatrical style loves ' il canto parlante,' not that of mere vocalization (gorgheggio). In regard to the overtures, too, he points out that in Metastasio's *Alessandro nell' Indie*, where the scene opens with the flight of the conquered army of Porus, the symphony should contain nothing but a warlike presto ; ' an allegro on the model of those of our symphonies would be out of place, and, worse still, would be a largo or a balletto.'

The main subject of Arteaga's treatise, *Le Rivoluzioni del Teatro Musicale Italiano* (1785), lies outside the scope of the present volume, but the author refers so often to conventions of a period preceding his own, that interesting details may be gathered from his pages. Burney sneers at him as being more fond of poetry than of music, but his rules for the introduction of vocal ornaments are surpassed by none of the technical authorities. They are not admissible, he says, in recitative, whether *secco* or *obbligato*, not at the beginning of an air, not in songs expressing great passion, nor in those which deal with very simple situations such as the loves of rustics ; not when the movement is swift and changing (in its harmonic progression); and not in concerted music. They may be lawfully brought in in festal and cheerful airs; in the *aria di mezzo carattere*, where there is no rush of strong passion, and the natural melody requires to be furnished with graceful ornaments and vivacious turns. Where the character is supposed to be singing, not speaking, they are allowable, but should be used very sparingly. When the ornaments are essential to the musical idea, they must be repeated, not changed in the repetition; cadenzas are to be executed with a well graduated *messa di voce*; all cadenzas written in the bravura style, or for the display of special voices, are to be eschewed; the ornaments peculiar to certain instruments, and consequently the 'arie obbligati' where the voice must imitate instruments, are forbidden; the ornaments introduced are to be of a charming and easy invention, and Arteaga apparently disapproves of allusions in the cadenza to the principal themes of the air.   There is another very interesting testimony to the author's musical perceptivity; he divines, long before any one had tried a practical experiment, that the orchestra can paint the feelings of the characters in cases where the words are at variance with their thoughts.   It is hard to believe that he is speaking of an opera in actual existence when he says : ' Zenobia shall drive her beloved Tiridate from her presence with scorn, but in the act of pronouncing the fatal decree the instruments, with their tones breathing nought but tenderness, will make it understood how dear her severity is costing her.'

A year or two before this book appeared, in 1782, died Metastasio, a man who had wielded an immense influence on the art of his time.   His libretti are thirty-four in number, and some of them, as for example his *Artaserse*, were set by as many as forty composers.   It is clear from his letters that, although his words to a modern student seem the very essence of conventional insipidity, he did really endeavour to give the composers the best opportunities for expressing the dramatic point of the scene; the three volumes of his correspondence with Farinelli and many other musical celebrities, translated by Burney, and published in 1796, are full of amusing touches, and are indispensable to the student of eighteenth century opera.   It is doubtful whether one of his correspondents, the Abbate Pasquini, was alone in regarding

the right hand of the stage as the more honourable side;
but it is evident, from Metastasio's reply to a letter from
him, that Pasquini at least was under the impression that
this was the case. There is a delightful account of a quarrel
on the stage at Vienna between Caffarelli and the theatre-
poet who took upon himself to rebuke the singer for absenting
himself from rehearsals; and the mock-heroic manner in
which Metastasio recounts it is enough to show that he had
a very pretty wit. Metastasio's opinions on the respective
merits of the various composers of his time in regard to their
powers of setting his words, are of some value; Jommelli,
according to him, was the best, and while admitting that
Galuppi may write very well for the stringed instruments,
he calls him ' a very bad workman for poets.' Not only
do his hints to the various stage-managers of the time contain much that shows him to have been a man of taste and
discernment, but his suggestions as to the nature of the
orchestral accompaniments prove that he knew and cared
about music, if no more. Of Gluck in his earlier days, he
says ' he has surprising fire, but is mad' (in a letter dated
1751). In another place, in 1756, he refers to Gluck's
setting of his *Re Pastore*, and says that his ' spirit, noise,
and extravagance, have supplied the place of merit in many
theatres of Europe, among those whom I pity, and who do
not constitute the minority of the folks of this world.' In
speaking of the archduchesses whose passion for amateur
acting must have given Metastasio a good deal of trouble,
he says that one of his difficulties was to find subjects for
the dramas he prepared for them; 'Greek and Roman subjects
are excluded from my jurisdiction, because these nymphs are
not to exhibit their chaste limbs.' In regard to the question
raised by the Chevalier de Chastellux, in his *Essai sur l'union
de la Poésie et la Musique*, as to the respective importance
of the words and the music in opera, Metastasio is very severe
on the composers who set at nought the obvious character

of the scene, and intrude their vocal ornamentations at incongruous moments. But he was no friend to what he considered over-elaboration in the accompaniments of songs; his appeal to Jommelli, at the time when that composer changed his style from the flimsy Italian manner of his earlier life to the more solid art he had learnt from the Germans, is a curious illustration of the point of view which a certain class of amateurs will always adopt, placing the power of touching the heart in opposition to the exhibition of any musical skill whatever. As Burney says, in a note on the passage:—

'Poets are always ready to join in censuring the composers' science, and performers' execution, as equal enemies to the beauties of the poetry, and interest of the drama; but, as the Public is a many-headed animal, with ears of all sorts and sizes, it is to be feared, that some of them will expect learning and science to be displayed by the composer, and powers of execution by the singer, as well as others such artless simplicity, as would reduce an opera to a level with a ballad farce.'

But even in Burney's note it is evident that he puts the composer and the singer more or less on a level with each other, and Metastasio's view of the supremacy of the dramatic story is a perfectly correct one. Near the end of his life, Metastasio referred to his own work in connexion with the stage in a way which shows the earnest intention which had been his through life:—

'Speak not to me of theatres, either tragic or comic. The first, which (as far as my powers have enabled me) I have tried to render less absurd, conspire at present to combat common sense; and the second, in the midst of such innumerable, not only supportable, but good and excellent examples with which the French have furnished us, have not yet found a tolerable imitator in Italy.'

The incongruities of the opera were a fruitful topic for all who cared for the union of the arts on the stage; and it may have been partly as a result of all the discussion as to the possibility of getting rid of operatic conventions of various kinds, that Gluck was encouraged to try the experiments which led to so famous a reform.   This reform belongs to a later section of this history; it must suffice to have traced the growth of operatic convention up to a time when a better and more thoroughly artistic attitude was about to be generally adopted.

CHAPTER XI

THE STATE OF MUSIC IN GERMANY

THE history of the arts in any country is continually interrupted by the record of foreign wars or internal tumults; a period of artistic efflorescence reaches its appointed limit, or is brought to what seems an untimely end, in some national upheaval that forces men to think of matters far removed from the arts. This is especially the case with musical history, and no more striking example of it could be found than in Germany at the period of which the present volume treats. The beginnings of German music after the great artistic revolution of 1600, were checked, before many years had passed, by the Thirty Years' War. The devastation which was the natural result of the war put a stop to all artistic activity, and for a considerable time after peace was declared 'the German nation was sunk in profound exhaustion. It had come apparently to a deadlock, both physical and mental; and during the whole period from about 1650 to 1675, . . . we find throughout the domain of music none but old musicians in any way productive; no new or fresh growth[1].' The exhaustion as far as music was concerned, was only apparent; the artistic energy, repressed during the war, lay dormant for some years after it, and found its ultimate manifestation in the long line of German supremacy in music, which went on without interruption for over two centuries. We need

[1] Spitta, *Life of Bach* (Eng. transl.), i. 41.

not assume that the war which preceded this period of activity actually produced it; but that the energy was all the stronger for the repression that had gone before, we cannot doubt, and the fancy is surely pardonable that there may have been some connexion between the long-enduring struggle and the unparalleled length of the artistic dynasty that followed it.

The fact that Bach's is the dominating figure in the German music of his time must not lead us to imagine that his case was typical of the way in which music sprang up in Germany. That the great clan of the Bachs, almost all of whom were musicians, should have given their name to the town musicians of Erfurt is enough to prove that their inherited proficiency in the art was an exceptional thing. For the rest of mankind in Germany it was not an art native to the soil, or inherited from generations of skilful ancestors; but an exotic, imported from a distance, and only beginning to flourish in its new surroundings. The more closely we study the conditions of the musical world in Germany as apart from Bach and his family, the more surely shall we be compelled to admit that even here the influence of the foreigner was of the strongest. The sacred music of the period was indigenous, it is true, and was made to conform to types that had their source within Germany itself; but in all forms of secular music, whether in the opera, or in instrumental works, the patterns were set by the Italians, and the native musicians were bound to follow in their steps with as good a grace as they might. That they were from the first admitted to a position side by side with the foreigners speaks well for their own perseverance and strength of character, as well as for the musical ability which provided the most congenial soil for the development of the germs that came from Italy. In England, as we shall see in a later chapter, the foreign element forced the English musicians into a distinctly inferior position; but this did not happen in Germany. If nearly every court of king or noble had, as its chief purveyor of music, an Italian *maestro*, the efforts of the German musicians were duly appreciated and rewarded. Caldara, who went to Vienna as Imperial chamber-composer in 1714, was even contented with the place of assistant capellmeister under J. J. Fux; this concession on the part of the foreigner seems to have been quite exceptional, and the more usual position for the Italians who took up residence in Germany was that of the complete supremacy enjoyed by Steffani at Hanover from 1688 to 1710, by Jommelli at Stuttgart from 1754 to 1769, and by Lotti during his short tenure of the post of capellmeister. at Dresden, 1717–1719. In the short space of seven years, no fewer than twenty-six operas were composed by Antonio Bioni (b. 1698.), the manager of the Breslau theatre from 1730. It was not only the composers, but the entire companies of singers, and numbers of instrumentalists, who were thus favoured by the electors and grand dukes; and in after years, Burney, whose predilections were all for music of a socially select kind, notes that 'whoever seeks music in Germany should do so at the several courts, not in the free imperial cities, which are generally inhabited by poor, industrious people, whose genius is chilled and repressed by penury[1].' Further on (p. 202), he speaks of 'the corrupted, motley, and Italianized melody to be heard in the capitals of this extensive country.' Music, it is clear, was not yet a national possession, although much was being done in Burney's time to make it so, for it was taught, together with reading and writing, in the common schools of Germany. As a result of this, he notes on his journey, that 'it is not nature, but cultivation, which makes music so generally understood by the Germans; and it has been said by an accurate observer of human nature, who has long resided among them, that "if innate genius exists, Germany certainly is not the seat of it; though it must be allowed to be that of perseverance

[1] *Tour in Germany,* i. 116.

and application." ' In Mattheson's *Neu-eröffnetes Orchester*
there are passages which amply confirm what Burney says.
There were not, indeed, many opportunities for getting practical experience of music, for the people had no performances
to which they could go but those in the churches; public
concerts were not given regularly in Germany until a much
later date, and the operatic performances at the various courts
were as a general rule reserved for invited guests of the
grandee who paid for the entertainment. Mattheson notes
with implied surprise that, at the Vauxhall Gardens in London,
' many concerts are given for money[1].'

The fact that the church was the only place where music
could be publicly heard by the people may have stimulated
the composers of sacred music to an activity which in some
cases surpassed even that of Sebastian Bach as far as extent
of production went.   Thus Telemann owns to twelve yearly
cycles of church-cantatas, nineteen settings of the 'Passion,'
while Georg Gebel, the organist of St. Christoph in Breslau
(1685–1750), speaks of having written four dozen 'choralia,'
five dozen cantatas, a Passion oratorio in seven parts, besides
numerous instrumental pieces[2].

His son, Georg Gebel the younger (1709–1753), was even
more prolific; while Capellmeister to the Prince of Schwarz-
burg-Rudolstadt, he wrote twelve operas, two passion-settings,
two Christmas oratorios, sets of church cantatas for several
years, and many other things[3].

There is no direct record of the terms upon which admission
to the opera at Hamburg was gained, but it must have been
an exception to the general custom which prevailed at the
aristocratic centres where operas were in vogue.   Hamburg
has been rightly called the cradle of the opera in Germany,
for although performances of operas in Italian took place at

[1] *Ehrenpforte*, s. v. ' Handel '.
[2] Matteson's *Ehrenpforte*.
[3] Theo. Baker's *Biographical Dictionary of Musicians*.

Torgau (1627), Regensburg (1653), Munich (1657), and
Vienna (1665), the first production of an opera in the
German language was that of Johann Theile's *Adam und
Eva* in 1678 at Hamburg.   In the chapter devoted to the
history of the opera, a short summary was given of the most
important German operas given on the Hamburg stage during
the brilliant period between 1678 and 1740, when German
opera went out of fashion for a time.   It was not exclusively
German, though for the first ten years Theile, Nicolaus Adam
Strungk, Johann Wolfgang Franck, and a physician named
Johann Philipp Förtsch provided the operas, the first foreign
importation being, strange to say, French, not Italian, Lully's
Acis, given in 1689.   Another French work, Colasse's *Achille
et Polyxène*, came out in 1692, breaking the sequence of new
operas written by Conradi, who, in spite of his name, was
a German by birth.   Johann Siegmund Cousser (or Kusser),
(c. 1657–1727), made his first appearance in 1693, with an
opera, *Erindo*; he had been previously in Paris for five years
with Lully, and after the advent of Keiser to Hamburg in
1694–5, he became conductor of the opera at Stuttgart.   His
fame is handed down by Mattheson in many books, but mainly
in *Der vollkommene Capellmeister*, where he is described as
a pattern of all that a conductor should be.   He seems to
have been of a restless disposition, according to Walther's
Lexicon, and after the termination of his engagement at
Stuttgart (1704), he was at Wolfenbüttel, and finally became
conductor of the Viceroy's orchestra at Dublin, where he died
1727.   It was he who raised the Hamburg opera to the high
position it maintained all through the management of Keiser,
and it was he who introduced the Italian method of singing.
Reference was made in the preceding chapter to the series
of 116 operas written for Hamburg by Keiser, through which
the theatre attained its remarkable position.   In dealing with
the career of the brilliant Mattheson, the Hamburg opera
will be again referred to in some detail.

The opera at Vienna was one of the first established in Germany, as we have seen, but, from one cause or another, it attained no position of European importance till Caldara became Fux's assistant conductor in 1716. In that year Lady Mary Wortley Montagu writes from Vienna that she saw an opera on the subject of Alcina (unfortunately she gives no composer's name) performed in the gardens of the 'Favorita,' where there was a single canopy over the imperial family, and when rain came on the opera had to stop. The stage, she says, was built over a very large canal, which was used for the representation of a naval fight ; there were other 'machines and changes of the scenes' which impressed her greatly.   Francesco Bartolommeo Conti (1681–1732) was court composer ; the first of his operas, *Clotilda* (1706) was given in London four years after its production, and his *Don Chisciotte in Sierra Morena* (1719) was given in Hamburg. He and Caldara seem to have been the busiest purveyors of operatic novelties during the period; and from the date of Metastasio's arrival in Vienna, in 1730, scarcely any libretti but his were brought forward. A little piece called *Le Grazie vendicate* seems to have been the first written for the two Archduchesses, who were amateurs of the operatic stage ; Maria Teresa, afterwards Empress, her sister Marianna, and another lady of the court, sang in this piece, which was set by Caldara, and Metastasio, in a letter dated February 26, 1734, is loud in praise of the 'excellent qualities of these august Princesses.'   He tells his correspondent that 'They have acted and sung like angels, and it was truly sacrilege that the whole world was not permitted to admire them ; for the festival was extremely private, as none but the Vienna ladies of the highest rank were able to obtain admission, and even these were in masks.'

A remarkable exhibition of amateur talent had taken place ten years before this, on the birth of an archduchess in 1724, when Caldara's *Eurysteus*, set to words by Apostolo Zeno, was performed by a number of persons of high rank, among them the Emperor, who played the harpsichord 'as principal director' says Burney[1].

A more ambitious amateur, the Princess Maria Antonia Walpurga, afterwards Electress of Saxony, did much to raise the opera at Munich to a high level of artistic excellence. Writing under the initials E.T.P.A. (standing for Ermelinda Talea Pastorella Arcada) she wrote words and music of a pastoral called *Talestri*, produced at Munich, 1758. The opera in the Bavarian capital has existed from 1689, when the Duke of Bavaria, Max Emanuel, founded the office of Intendant. Pietro Torri, whose operas had been first given there in 1690, succeeded Antonio Bernabei in 1732 as Capell-meister, and died in 1737. The heavy cost of the opera was defrayed by a tax on playing-cards, for the Bavarians, like most other nations at this time, were passionately fond of gambling.

The Berlin opera was in a flourishing condition at the beginning of the eighteenth century, and the ubiquitous Bononcini brothers were in high favour there, under the patronage of the Queen, Sophia Charlotte, in the years 1703–5. It must have been at this time, when the Queen accompanied, and the performers were chiefly personages of high birth, that Telemann was smuggled into the room to see the performance[2]. The opera seems to have been stopped for a time at the Queen's death in 1705, and from 1713 to 1742 there was another period of cessation from operatic enterprise. It is not hard to understand this when we remember that operas were a form of court entertainment simply, without any national existence at all. In the time of Frederick the Great the opera was revived with great brilliance; the king himself was an autocrat in the theatre, as elsewhere; 'he performs the part of director-general here, as much as of generalissimo in the field[3].' He

---

[1] *History of Music*, iv. 578.   [2] Ibid. iv. 581.
[3] Burney, *Tour in Germany*, ii. 98.

was in the habit of standing behind the conductor, and was a great admirer of Graun and Hasse, permitting few new operas but theirs to be brought forward.

At Leipzig the vogue of Italian opera lasted from early in the century down to 1720; the German opera-house, founded by Nicolas Strungk in 1693, was only open during the fair, and its position was quite a humble one as compared with that of Hamburg; the German representations were continued down to 1729. The remarkable revival of German opera under Johann Adam Hiller belongs to a later period of musical history. Of far greater significance than even the German opera, however, was the transformation of the old-established *Collegium musicum* into the public concert. There were various musical associations, of university students and others, in a more or less flourishing condition in Leipzig, and in 1704 Telemann founded such an institution, which was afterwards under the direction of Bach himself. In 1743 a 'Grand Concert' was founded by sixteen persons, both nobles and citizens; this lasted for a year under the presidency, as it would appear, of a merchant named Zehmisch, and the conductorship of J. F. Doles. The institution flourished so much that the concert was transferred to the Three Swans, an inn in the Brühl, shortly before 1746. The Seven Years' War put a stop to the undertaking, but it was revived in 1763, under the direction of Johann Adam Hiller, and eventually became the ancestor of the famous 'Gewandhaus Concerts[1].'

The entertaining description that Burney gives in his German tour[2], of the early adventures of Quantz, the famous flute player, before he enjoyed the favour of Frederick the Great, gives us incidentally a capital picture of the state of music in Dresden in the early part of the eighteenth century. Quantz as a boy was a member of the town band of Merseburg,

---

[1] Spitta, *Life of Bach* (Eng. transl.), iii. 18 ff.

[2] ii. 166, &c.

and with his colleagues was often summoned to reinforce the duke's small private band at court performances. It was thus that he had the opportunity of hearing the famous performers of Europe, and the circumstance that Burney thought it worth while to mention this shows us how difficult, nay how impossible, it was for the German people to hear these eminent models who were reserved for the enjoyment of the nobility. When he arrived in Dresden in 1714, Quantz entered into the service of the town musician, Knoll; but was thrown out of work by the great fire, and was compelled to seek his fortune as a travelling fiddler. About two years afterwards he was given another chance of work in Dresden, as temporary assistant to one of the town musicians, and, as Burney says, ' he soon discovered that it was not sufficient for a musician to be able to execute the mere notes which a composer had set on paper; and it was now that he first began to be sensible of the existence of taste and expression.' The King of Poland, the famous Augustus the Second, had a most flourishing band at this time; Volumier, his French concert-master, had been succeeded by Pisendel, who combined the French and Italian styles with so much success that Quantz declared to Burney he had never heard a better band. Besides Pisendel, there was Veracini, who threw himself out of window in Dresden five years later, without any fatal result; the name of Pantaleone Hebenstreit, one of the most important figures in the history of the pianoforte, for whom indeed its invention is sometimes claimed, occurs next to that of Weiss, the lute player, a curious juxtaposition of the old and new in the history of instruments; and most important for Quantz, there was Buffardin, the flute player, who eventually, after Quantz had adopted the oboe in succession to the violin as his instrument, taught him the flute.

We have seen something of the condition of Dresden in referring to the celebrated contest between Bach and Marchand (see p. 182). The Italian opera seems to have been established

there in the year after Bach's visit, i. e. in 1717, though Burney
assigns a date two years later for it, and says that Lotti and
a number of celebrated Italian singers were there, and that
their operas were the first Quantz had heard ; as Handel
went in that year, 1719, to Dresden to engage singers for his
London enterprise, the earlier date seems the more likely of
the two.   At a much later date, when Burney could speak
from personal experience, the opera was not only brilliant
but the most judiciously arranged, and the best disciplined,
in Europe[1].   Bach used to go to the opera at Dresden, asking
his favourite son, ' Friedemann, shall we go to Dresden again
and hear their beautiful little songs[2]? '   Porpora, who had
visited Dresden as singing-master to the Electoral Princess,
Marie Antoinette, was appointed maestro at the opera in 1728,
and on the arrival of Hasse in 1731 he found Porpora established at Dresden.   The two were constant rivals throughout
their lives ; Hasse had given up Porpora as a teacher, for
Alessandro Scarlatti, in 1724; and the success of Faustina,
whom Hasse had married in 1729, made his position so secure
that Porpora was driven out.   The various phases of the
quarrel that ensued between Hasse and Faustina on the one
side, and Porpora and his pupil Regina Mingotti on the other,
had Dresden for their chief centre ; the chronology of the
affair is difficult to disentangle, but as Mingotti was born in
1728, the writer of the article ' Hasse' in Grove's *Dictionary*
can hardly be right in supposing her to have been one of the
causes which led to Hasse's absenting himself in 1740 from
the Saxon capital.   Burney learnt from Mingotti herself that
in 1748 Hasse, in setting *Demofoonte*, had written an adagio
with pizzicato accompaniment for the violins in order to
expose her weak points, but that she ' suspected the snare,'
and by hard study turned the song into one of her great successes.   1751 saw the ultimate withdrawal of Porpora from

---

[1] Burney, *History of Music*, iv. 580.
[2] Forkel, p. 48 ; Spitta, *Life of Bach* (Eng. transl.), ii. 337.

L l

Dresden, and from that time till the siege, Hasse reigned alone; in the siege all his music and papers were destroyed, and the husband and wife retired to Vienna in 1763.

Dresden divided with Berlin the honour of being the most flourishing musical centre in Germany, at least in Burney's opinion; he makes an amusing comparison between the various German towns in regard to the qualities of their music; thus, Mannheim, no doubt as a result of Holzbauer's care, is remarkable for neat and brilliant execution; Berlin for counterpoint; and Brunswick for taste. About Vienna he uses the remarkable and prophetic words that the Austrian capital was 'most remarkable for fire and invention.'

Of all the German contemporaries of Bach and Handel, none stands out with greater distinctness, or helps us more effectually to get a true view of the time, than Johann Mattheson, a man of many gifts and of wide general culture apart from music. He was born at Hamburg in 1681, and at the age of nine could sing, play the harpsichord, and compose; he entered the opera as a singer of female parts—he describes his own voice as 'a bright and beautiful treble of large compass'—in 1696, and wrote his first opera *Die Pleiaden* in 1699, a work in which he undertook the chief part. In connexion with the second opera for which he was solely responsible—he had collaborated with Schieferdecker and Bronner in a piece called *Victor*, 1702—occurred the famous incident of the duel with Handel, the details of which are narrated in many different ways. It seems established beyond dispute that in his opera *Cleopatra*, in which Mattheson sang the tenor part of Antony, and had to disappear from the action upon his death some time before the end of the opera, he was in the habit of playing the harpsichord through the later scenes of the work. On one occasion, which does not seem to have been the first night of the production (see Rockstro's *Handel*, p. 35) Handel, who was the regular accompanist, refused to move, and thereupon Mattheson gave

him a box on the ear, the result of which was that the two
fought a duel in front of the opera-house; Mattheson's sword
broke against a button on Handel's coat, and no harm came
to either of the combatants, who were soon made friends
again. It is curious that, within a space of five pages, Hawkins
(*History,* ii. 852–7) gives two versions of what must have
been the same incident, telling us of an attempt to assassinate
Handel, founded on a rivalry between the latter and another
harpsichord player whose name is not given; saying that it
was the score of the opera which Handel was taking home
with him, that saved his life. Though his opera *Henrico
Quarto Rè di Castiglia* was not brought out till 1717, Mattheson
made his last appearance on the Hamburg stage in Handel's
Nero, 1705; after that he became tutor to the son of the
English envoy, Sir Cyril Wich, and devoted a considerable
number of years to diplomacy. It was no doubt through his
patron, and from the fact that he married an Englishwoman,
that he became acquainted with English literature, from which
he translated *Moll Flanders* and a large number of other things
into German. On the death of Sir Cyril Wich, in 1712, he
discharged the duties of British resident for some time. In
1715 he was music-director and cantor of Hamburg Cathedral,
and in that capacity gave his support to the various innova-
tions in church music which led to the development of the
church cantata as a recognized form of sacred music (see
Der göttingische Ephorus, 1727). In 1728 deafness compelled him to resign his cathedral appointment, and he devoted
the remainder of his life mainly to musical literature. His
compositions are of very slight importance, the best being
his book of harpsichord suites published in London 1714.

His polemical and historical writings endear him to all
students of the period; they are full of personal prejudices,
although they have a certain amount of real critical value.
Mattheson had the overweening self-esteem which becomes
almost a virtue in such men as Benvenuto Cellini, and which

undoubtedly gives a raciness to their books such as nothing else could give.

His earliest book seems to have been *Das neu-eröffnete Orchester*, &c., published in 1713 with a long-winded title such as it was the fashion of the time to bestow ; in this, as elsewhere, his avowed object was to give music-lovers some ground for the faith that was in them ; and there can be no doubt that Mattheson's writings did succeed in explaining to the average reader some of the essential qualities and defects that make music good or bad of its kind. In particular, he was a strong advocate for every kind of musical progress ; there was a considerable party in Germany who recommended the restriction of the modes, against which the book was obviously directed, and it called forth a reply from Joh. Heinr. Buttstedt, a composer of some merit and a good organist (1666–1727), who upheld the old system of solmisation, in a pamphlet called *Ut, Re, Mi, Fa, Sol, La, tota Musica et Harmonia Aeterna* ; Mattheson's *Beschützte Orchester*, with the sub-title ' *zweite Eröffnung* ' (1717), and his *Forschende Orchestre oder desselben dritte Eröffnung* (1721) demolished the old-world theories of Buttstedt, and marked, once for all, the rights and privileges of modern musicians. His *Organistenprobe im Generalbass*[1] (1719) and its second and third editions, called *Grosse* and *Kleine Generalbassschule* (1731 and 1735), are valuable guides to the study of thorough bass and to the method of accompanying from figured bass that was in vogue at the time. *Critica Musica*, one of the most valuable of his books, appeared, the first volume in 1722, the second in 1725 ; it was issued as a periodical, in which were included abstracts or translations of various famous treatises ; for example, the French text of Raguenet's *Parallèle* is given side by side with a German translation, and copious and interesting annotations ; the long criticism of Handel's *Passion*

---

[1] Many of these titles are given in the shortened forms by which it is usual to refer to them. All have absurdly long titles in the original.

appears at the beginning of vol. ii, and in the same volume
(p. 368) is a severe review of Bach's *Ich hatte viel Bekümmerniss*;
the first three volumes of Marcello's Psalms are reviewed in
the same part. Part vi, *Die Lehr-reiche Meister-Schule*, is
taken up mainly with a defence of Mattheson's *Orchester*
against an anonymous critic, who is undoubtedly F. X. Mursch-
hauser, and who had died shortly before the publication of
Critica Musica. Mattheson, in the course of his earlier book,
had declared that Purcell was a Frenchman, and in this review
he crushes his opponent (who has evidently reiterated his conviction that Purcell was an Englishman) by proving from the
inscription on the tablet in Westminster Abbey that there are
so many faults of orthography and expression as to imply
a foreign origin. Unfortunately he bases his arguments upon
an exceedingly incorrect version of the epitaph, which he
quotes as ' Here lies Henry Pourcel, who . . . is gone to
that blessed place, where only his Harmonie can be exceedet.'
He then proceeds to point out that the word 'lies' can only
mean *hic mentitur, hier lüget*, and that the spelling 'here
lyes' would be the only correct one; that the spelling of the
name indicates a French origin, and that the last word shows
ignorance of the English language. Even if the difference
between ' lies ' and ' lyes ' had ever been recognized, Mattheson
would still have been wrong, for the epitaph has ' lyes,' and
spells the name ' Purcell,' as well as the word ' exceeded,'
quite correctly. The story may serve as a warning to a
certain school of German criticism that is apt to build imposing edifices upon sound reasonings from incorrect statements. In the following part Mattheson quotes a letter he
has received from Handel, supporting his contention in regard
to the modes. He says: ' Leur connoissance est sans doute
necessaire à ceux qui veulent pratiquer et executer la Musique
ancienne, qui a été composée suivant ces Modes ; mais comme
on s'est affranchi des bornes etroites de l'ancienne Musique,
je ne vois pas quelle utilité les Modes Grecs puissent être

pour la Musique moderne.' At the close of his letter, Handel
promises to supply Mattheson with the particulars of his life,
evidently for a work which the latter was projecting ; this
was the *Grundlage einer Ehrenpforte*, &c. published in 1740,
another most important work of Mattheson's, since it gives
us some idea as to the respective eminence of contemporary
musicians in his regard.   Handel did not contribute his own
memoir to this work, as most of the other musicians did ; his
refusal to do so may have been due to his having seen the
severe criticism of his early work in the *Critica Musica*, or
his excuse of being too much occupied may have been a
genuine one.   In either case, we are left to Mattheson's own
account of Handel, in the course of which he says that what he
is to relate will make Handel laugh when he reads it, 'though
outwardly he laughs but little.'   He says that in early life
Handel was addicted to the composition of 'long, long arias,'
and interminable cantatas, but that his operatic experience
did him good in that respect.   It is here that Mattheson
tells the story of the duel, and of his journey with Handel to
Lübeck, where neither of them could comply with the conditions attaching to the post of organist, viz. that of espous-
ing the old organist's daughter, who afterwards became the
wife of the less fastidious Schieferdecker, one of Mattheson's
collaborators in the opera of *Victor*.   The plan of getting each
composer to recount the events of his own career was a delight-
fully simple one ; it had all the advantages of the modern
'interview,' and no doubt gave great satisfaction to the writers
themselves, while it must have caused a good deal of amusement, even to the readers of its own time, to see the different
manner in which each composer endeavours to dissimulate
his conviction that he himself is the greatest of all musicians
of the day.   Mattheson's boundless conceit comes out most
amusingly in the autobiographical section ; and the prolific
Telemann gives a very good account of himself, telling us that
he founded his style at first on Steffani and Rosenmüller, on

Corelli and Caldara. Rather a different account is given of this change of models in the Lexicon of J. G. Walther, who says that Telemann's style was at first Polish, then French, and lastly Italian. Of such older composers as Keiser, Froberger, and Pachelbel, the 'Triumphal Arch' has much to tell us; and whatever we may think of Mattheson's personality and methods, we must be grateful to him for the information he conveys so amusingly. The most extraordinary part of his book is that the name of Sebastian Bach, mentioned with warm appreciation in *Das beschützte Orchester*, occurs only incidentally, in the course of the biographies of Francisci and Reimann ; the author's request was refused or ignored by Bach, but that Mattheson should not have supplied the place by a notice of his own seems quite incredible. We are driven to suppose that the name of Bach, though it is always mentioned with the utmost reverence by his German contemporaries, stood for a person who was supposed to keep very much to himself, and was not in the general musical movement of his day; between him and such a man as Mattheson there was indeed a great gulf, but if there had been any definite dispute between them, Mattheson would have been the last man to hide his feelings. If the omission of an article on him was an intentional slight, it is odd that he did not prevent his name being mentioned by the two composers already referred to. The relations of Bach and Mattheson are ably discussed by Spitta, *Life of Bach*, ii. 21, &c. Mattheson was not above paying off old scores in the *Ehrenpforte*, as witness his notice of Reinken, in the course of which he misquotes the title-page of Reinken's *Hortus Musicus* so as to imply that Reinken had an exaggerated opinion of his own fame[1].

Among the numerous books of his must be mentioned further *Der musikalische Patriot* (1728), in which a full list

---

[1] Spitta, *Life of Bach* (Eng. transl.), ii. 16.

is given of the operas produced at Hamburg; *Kern melodischer Wissenschaft* (1737); and the famous *Vollkommene Kapellmeister* (1739), a really comprehensive treatise on all branches of practical music. His translation of Mainwaring's *Memoirs of Handel* must not be forgotten; a full list of his published works (even now some remain in MS.) is given, with their wonderful titles, in Riemann's *Dictionary of Music*.

For a great deal of most valuable information concerning the composers and other musicians of the time, we are indebted to J. G. Walther (1684–1748), whose famous *Dictionary of Music*, the first book in which biographical and other information about music appeared side by side, was published first in a small pamphlet in 1728 as *Alte und neue musikalische Bibliothek oder musikalisches Lexikon*, appearing as a book (even then of very moderate compass) in 1732 as *Musikalisches Lexicon*. Here again, Bach is treated to a notice which appears to us in modern times very insufficient ; it has been suggested that in this case some quarrel or other had caused an estrangement between the relatives, for Bach and Walther were nearly related, the mothers of both belonging to the. family of Lämmerhirt. Bach was godfather to one of Walther's children, and the two were in closest intimacy for many years. Walther was organist of the Thomaskirche at Erfurt in 1702, town organist at Weimar in 1707, and court musician (Hofmusikus) in 1720, after Bach's departure from the court. He surpassed all except his illustrious kinsman in the composition of organ-chorales ; and in the history of the treatment of the chorales his is one of the most prominent names.

There are naturally a number of musicians whose names, though not connected prominently with any of the great movements in music, such as those that have been described in previous chapters, yet cannot be ignored by the historian: of Bach's many relations it is only necessary in this place to mention two, his eldest and most gifted son, Wilhelm

Friedemann (1710–1784) and Carl Philipp Emanuel (1714–1788). The career of the latter, and his influence in the development of the sonata form, will be treated of in detail in the next volume of this series; of the former mention has already been made in conpexion with the lost Passion-Music of Sebastian. It is not certain how much of Sebastian Bach's music shared the same fate, for his eldest son was an exception to the family tradition of upright behaviour; he was hopelessly dissipated and reckless, and though he kept the place of organist of the Sophienkirche at Dresden from 1733 to 1746, and of the Marienkirche at Halle from the latter year till 1764, he fell into extreme misery in the last years of his life. A large number of his compositions are in the Royal Library in Berlin, and those that have been printed, including a fine set of polonaises, some fugues, &c. show such powers that it should be well worth while to issue a complete collection of his works. Another son, Johann Christian Bach, much younger than these two, and a group of the younger members of the great Bach clan are numbered among the great master's pupils, such as Bernhard Bach, Samuel Anton Bach, Johann Ernst Bach, and Johann Elias Bach. No fewer than four members of the Krebs family, a father, Johann Tobias, and three of his sons, were pupils of Sebastian Bach. Of the four, the eldest, Johann Ludwig Krebs, was the most distinguished; he was born in 1713 and died in 1780, and many of his works for harpsichord, in combination with other instruments or alone, have lasting merit. He was organist in succession of Zwickau, Zeitz, and Altenburg. Heinrich Nicolaus Gerber (1702–1775), a man of great talents and greater modesty, is endeared to all admirers of the great master by the fact that for a year he could not pluck up courage to apply to Sebastian Bach for instruction. Gottfried August Homilius (1712–1785), organist of the Frauenkirche at Dresden, sub-cantor of the Kreuzschule and director of the music, wrote important church music in

a lofty style; Johann Friedrich Doles (1716–1797), cantor at
Freiberg from 1744, and successor to Bach as cantor of the
Thomasschule at Leipzig, was a pupil, but not a whole-hearted
disciple, of the great master; he wrote in a sentimental, quasi-
operatic style, and the high standard of Bach's time was lost
and lowered during his tenure of office.   He got into a dispute
with the rector of Freiberg, J. Gottlieb Biedermann, over an
occasional piece which he wrote to celebrate the centenary
of the peace of Westphalia; Bach's share in the dispute is
narrated at great length in Spitta's *Life*, iii. 255 ff.   Johann
Philipp Kirnberger (1721–1783) was only with Bach from
1739 till 1741; his famous theoretical works, like those of
F. W. Marpurg, lie outside the period of this volume, but
we may point out that they were instrumental in transmitting
the method of Sebastian Bach to a later generation.   Another
link with later times was Joh. Christian Kittel of Erfurt (1732–
1809), who was only eighteen at the time of Bach's death,
and had received instruction from him.   Joh. Christoph Altnikol,
who married Sebastian's daughter in 1749, was organist at
Naumburg from 1747, and died in 1759, was an excellent
organist and a sound writer, many good MSS. by him being
in the Royal Library at Berlin.   The short career of the
brilliant young virtuoso, Joh. Theophilus Goldberg, for whom,
at his patron's request, Bacn wrote the famous 'Thirty Variations' already discussed in detail, was for a time a pupil; and
one of the best of the great master's disciples was Joh. Friedrich
Agricola (1720–1774), who was a connexion of Handel, and
who according to Burney (*German Tour*, ii. 90) was fatter
than either Handel or Jommelli, went to Berlin in 1741, and
yielded to the fashion of the place so far as to devote himself
to the opera and to the Italian manner of singing; he translated Tosi's famous treatise, adding valuable annotations, &c.
He collaborated with Carl Philipp Emanuel Bach in the
memoir of Sebastian published in 1754 in the *Neu-eröffnete
musikalische Bibliothek*, a periodical published from 1736 to

1754 by L. C. Mizler, another pupil of Bach ; and contributed notes to the *Musica mechanica organoedi* of Jakob Adlung, published 1768.

Among German authors on music Adlung's name stands high. He was born 1699 and died 1762, and beside the book just mentioned his *Anleitung zur musikalischen Gelahrtheit* and *Musikalisches Siebengestirn* are of considerable value. On the special subject of the keyed instruments must be mentioned the treatises *Organopoeia*, by J. P. Bendeler (1690), and C. G. Schröter's *Umständliche Beschreibung*, &c., published in Marpurg's *Kritische Briefe* (1763), in which the writer claims priority in the invention of the pianoforte[1]. Many other writings of Schröter are of interest, and his compositions include no fewer than seven sets of church cantatas, five settings of passion music, and all kinds of instrumental works of very small value. He was born in 1699, was Lotti's music copyist in Dresden in 1717, and was organist successively at Minden and Nordhausen.

A writer named Joh. Adolf Scheibe (1708-1776) published a musical periodical from 1737 to 1740 called *Der critische Musikus*, which was now only remembered for a savage attack upon Bach ; the author had failed to obtain an organist's post for which Bach was one of the judges, and his attacks, first made anonymously, but afterwards confessed, may well have been due to a desire to retaliate. Though praising highly Bach's wonderful skill in playing the keyed instruments, his vocal music is reproached as lacking natural grace, for a confused style, for an extravagant display of learned art, and in short, for precisely the qualities that, from the beginning of music, have been considered blameworthy by critics of a certain kind.

In the fact of his uniting in himself the career of a most eminent contrapuntist with that of an esteemed operatic com-

---

[1] The question as to Schröter's claim is ably discussed in the article ' Pianoforte ' in Grove's *Dictionary*, ii, 711.

poser, Johann Joseph Fux (1660–1741), is a unique figure
in the Germany of his time.   From the time that history first
catches sight of him, in 1696, he never ceased to be connected
with Vienna, where he held a succession of court appointments.
His compositions reach the astounding number of 405, and
comprise eighteen operas, ten oratorios, and other secular
works, besides 290 church works, such as fifty masses, and
a great number of psalms, litanies, and motets. All these, which
are still preserved in MS. in the Imperial Library at Vienna,
are of small importance beside the famous *Missa canonica*,
containing examples of every species of canon, or the three-part
church sonatas, which are still to be heard in Vienna.   The
work of his life was his famous Latin treatise, *Gradus ad
Parnassum*, in which are embodied all the rules for the treatment of the ancient modes, and in general of the whole subject
of counterpoint; it appeared in 1725, was translated into German
by Mizler in 1742, and its fame as a practical manual of
composition lasted till the time of Haydn and Mozart; while,
even in the present day, it has not been surpassed in its
special line.

The influence of Johann Kuhnau (1660–1722) upon the
earlier developments of the sonata has been already referred
to; his Bible sonatas, a very early instance of programme-
music, have been republished recently, and are of distinct
interest and value, apart from the attempt to illustrate stories
in music[1].   He was also famous as the author of a satire, *Der
musikalische Quacksalber* (1701), directed against the prevailing Italian influences at Dresden, and as Bach's pre-
decessor in the place of cantor of the Thomasschule.   An
interesting account of him is given in *The Pianoforte Sonata*
by J. S. Shedlock, 1895.

Johann David Heinichen (1683–1729), a pupil. for a time

---

[1] His complete clavier works, with an interesting preface, have been edited by
Karl Päsler, and published as vol. iv. of *Denkmäler Deutscher Tonkunst*, Breitkopf
and Haertel (1901).

of Kuhnau at the Thomasschule, was one of the many men of the time who studied jurisprudence as well as music; he published a manual of thorough bass as *Neu-erfundene und gründliche Anweisung*, &c., in 1711, and in 1728 the second edition, called *Der Generalbass in der Composition*. He was treated by an admirer of his book to a tour in Italy, where he stayed, mostly in Venice, for some five years, and in 1718 was appointed Court Capellmeister to Augustus the Strong, conducting the opera at first, until a quarrel arose with Senesino. He was a fine contrapuntist, and many of his compositions are in the Royal Library at Dresden. His coadjutor, Johann Dismas Zelenka (1679-1745), had been a member of the royal Polish band at Dresden, had probably the advantage of instruction from Fux, and had also paid a visit to Venice in the suite of the Prince Elector; he was second conductor at Dresden in Heinichen's lifetime, and succeeded him after his death, being named Church Composer in 1735. He was a prolific composer of sacred music, and among his masses and oratorios are a number of fine ideas. Another pupil of Fux, August Gottlieb Muffat, has been already mentioned in connexion with his book of suites 'Componimenti musicali' from which Handel adopted not a few themes; he was born 1683 and died 1770 in Vienna, where he was imperial Court Organist from 1717, retiring in 1764.

Johann Ernst Eberlin (1702-1762) was another very prolific composer; he was Capellmeister to the Archbishop of Salzburg, and one of the fugues in his *IX Toccate e Fughe per l'Organo* had the honour to be taken for many years as a work of Bach; Commer's *Musica Sacra* contains some interesting examples of his work; MSS. exist at Regensburg and Berlin. Ignaz Holzbauer (1711-1783) became musical director at the Vienna court theatre in 1745, and from 1750 was Court Capellmeister at Stuttgart, where he was succeeded by Jommelli, after his departure to Mannheim in 1753. He brought the orchestra of the latter place to a high state of perfection, paid many visits to Italy, became completely deaf in his later years, and left a large number of compositions, among them 196 instrumental symphonies, and twenty-six masses.

Joseph Bonno (1710–1788) was appointed Court Composer at Vienna in 1739 and in a space of thirty years wrote twenty operas, serenades, and oratorios. Bonno's colleague in the post of Court Composer, Georg Christoph Wagenseil (1715–1777), was another pupil of Fux, and held a number of court appointments; he must have been an eclectic in matters of taste, for he modelled his church music upon Hasse and Scarlatti, his dramatic works upon Leo, and his instrumental music upon Rameau. He is a link with the next generation, for when Mozart, as a little boy of six, was playing before the court in 1762, he played a concerto of Wagenseil, and summoned him to turn over for him. Burney gives an interesting account in his *German Tour*, i. 324, of a visit to Wagenseil, when the old man, though crippled with gout, had a harpsichord wheeled to him and played several capriccios and pieces of his own composition 'in a very spirited and masterly manner.' 'He had sufficient fire and fancy left,' says Burney, 'to please and entertain, though not to surprise me very much.' It is appropriate that a survey of German music in the earlier half of the eighteenth century should stop at Vienna, which was destined to be the centre of creative music in Germany for many a year to come.

CHAPTER XII

THE STATE OF MUSIC IN ITALY

THROUGHOUT the eighteenth century the Italians were regarded by the rest of Europe as the authorized purveyors of music for the educated world. Music was their birthright, and, looking at the history of music as a whole, we must admit that although the periods of artistic efflorescence may have been more important in other countries, as for instance in Germany during the long period between the birth of Bach and the death of Brahms, yet no country has enjoyed so many periods of musical distinction as Italy. Music, transplanted thither from the Netherlands very early in the sixteenth century, took root at once, and Italy's first period of musical supremacy lasted down to the time of Luca Marenzio. During the second period, that which comes under consideration in the present volume, its supremacy was less universally admitted, and we may say that in every branch of art we have been watching the sceptre passing from the Italian to the German race ; the third period, that of the Italian operas at the beginning of the nineteenth century, was almost without influence on the real art of the day, and as far as concerns creative originality in any branch of art that is of lasting importance, Italy need not be considered from that time down to the time when the taste for real music revived once again towards the end of the nineteenth century. Meanwhile, throughout all her periods of activity or of inactivity as regards creation, she was the recognized source of musical execution ;

Italian singers may have often found successful rivals in the various countries where they have appeared, but their position, as compared with singers of other nationalities, has always been at an advantage. The singers' practice, common in Germany and England, if nowhere else, of adopting Italian names, is enough to show the superiority that Italians enjoyed in the estimation of the public; and from the number of players on stringed instruments who took Europe by storm we may form some opinion as to the reputation that Italians enjoyed. As was said in an earlier chapter, the growth of virtuosity on the violin was closely connected with the development of the violin-makers' trade, and the fame rapidly gained, and never lost, by the Cremonese school of makers. The rich amateurs who travelled in Italy made a point of bringing home some cf the music of the nation, and as the art of engraving music seems to have been lost in Italy[1], an enormous number of persons must have been employed in making MS. copies of the songs in the operas, or of the motets sung in the churches. Such copies, in their paper covers once gaudy, now faded, are very frequently to be met with in the libraries of English country houses whose former owners made 'the grand tour.' Italy was so much the provider of music that the people had apparently but little time to enjoy it themselves; the best composers were from time to time away in residence at the various courts of other countries; the successful singers were always engaged at some of the German theatres, or in London; and the instrumentalists, once finished, made their fortunes abroad, returning to their native land only in their later years. A fruitful cause of the position occupied by Italy as the centre from which the other nations were provided with music was to be found in the fact that certain portions of the peninsula were in the possession of various foreign nations; the intercourse between Venice and Austria,

[1] Burney, *Tour in France and Italy*, p. 189.

between Naples and Spain, was of the closest, and in a sense these Italian cities became centres for the dissemination of music to the nations whose property they were.

In the earlier divisions of this book, the chief works of the Italian composers have been passed in review, and whether in sacred music, in operas, or in instrumental compositions, they, or the best of them, held a foremost place in the course of development of the art; they were as it were in the main stream of musical progress. While in Germany there were many composers whose works would not come suitably under consideration in tracing the main current of musical history, and while in France and England we shall see that many meritorious compositions were produced that have no bearing on the main history of the art, in Italy everything, or almost everything, that was of real artistic importance, has been already discussed in its own place.

There are a few of the opera-writers of Italy who cannot be said to have exercised any lasting influence on art, and yet whose careers must be briefly sketched, on account of the great vogue their works seem to have enjoyed. As for style or individuality, it is at the present day impossible to detect any such thing in their works; but Burney (*History*, iv. 547) claims for Leonardo Vinci that he was the first of the Italian writers to simplify recitative and melody, and to call the attention of the audience chiefly to the voice-part, by disentangling it from fugue, complication, and laboured contrivance. Vinci was born in 1690 in Calabria, and was educated at the Conservatorio de' Poveri di Gesù Cristo at Naples, with Porpora and Pergolesi, under Gaetano Greco. Two operas by him in Neapolitan dialect were given in 1719, and a number of his dramatic works were given with great success in Venice, Rome, and Naples, where his last work, *Artaserse*, was given in 1731; his death during the run of this opera[1] is said to

---

[1] Burney, *Memoirs of Metastasio*, i. 72. A later date of death is given by Florimo in his *Cenno Storico*, i. 232.

have been due to poison. It contains the only song by which he was at all famous, ' Vò solcando '; he was received into the congregation of the Rosario at Formiello in 1728, and wrote a considerable quantity of sacred music for them. Some of his sacred works were heard by De Brosses, who describes them as 'petits opéras sacrés de Métastase'; elsewhere he describes Vinci as the Lully of Italy, and his music as ' vrai, simple, naturel, expressif, et le plus beau chant du monde, sans être récherché.' It is pretty clear from these accounts that Vinci must have been an early supporter of that move-ment which has been called the 'Zopf.' It is no doubt the simplicity of his music, so much admired by the con-noisseurs of the time, that has procured the composer that complete oblivion which he now seems so well to have deserved. See Burney's *History*, iv. 547.

Davide Perez, the son of a Spaniard, was born in Naples 1711, and educated at the Conservatorio of Santa Maria di Loreto under Gallo and Mancini. He had an opera, *Siroe*, produced at the San Carlo in 1740, and in the following year he was invited to Palermo, and remained there, as maestro di cappella, till 1748, producing four operas there. In 1749 he wrote a *Clemenza di Tito* for the San Carlo, and *Semiramide* for the Teatro alle Dame in Rome in 1750. Operas by him were given in all the important cities of Italy, and in 1752 he went to Portugal, where he had a brilliantly successful career as an operatic composer and manager. His *Ezio* was given in London with great success in 1755; and after his return to Lisbon, where he died in 1778, he wrote a considerable number of works, many of them sacred ; of these the most celebrated is the *Mattutini de' Morti*, published in London in 1774. For many years he was as it were pitted against Jommelli, but in spite of his being admired ' for the elegance and grace of his melodies, and expression of the words [1] ' he was far behind his rival.

---

[1] Burney, *History of Music*, iv. 571.

As his name suggests, Domingo Terradellas was a Spaniard by birth, but ranks as an Italian composer; the other form of his name, 'Terradeglias,' is no doubt due to the Italian way of representing the Spanish sound of the double l. He was born at Barcelona in 1711, was a pupil of Durante at the Conservatorio San Onofrio, at Naples; many operas by him were given in Italy and two in London; the failure of his *Sesostri* at Rome (1751) so affected him that he died a short time afterwards.

Of Rinaldo da Capua (born about 1720), whose operas, written for Italy and for the Paris Opéra Italien, were in fashion between 1737 and 1771, no particulars are forthcoming, and it is only the earlier part of his career that comes into the period under consideration. Burney (*Tour in Italy*, p. 285) says that he claimed to have been among the first who introduced long *ritornellos*, or symphonies, into the recitatives of strong passion and distress, which express or imitate what it would be ridiculous for the voice to attempt. The conventional airs of such composers as these are incredibly commonplace; and nothing can give a better idea of the state of public taste in the later years of the 'Zopf' period than the vogue of such things.

In the eighteenth century, no country was so much visited by foreigners as Italy; and as every one who visited it seems to have thought it necessary to publish his travels on his return, there is no lack of materials from which a picture can be drawn of the way the musical conditions of the country struck those who were used to other surroundings. As in Germany, and indeed everywhere else at the period, music, other than the popular songs and dances of peasants, was either performed in church, in the theatre, or in the private houses of the nobility; the public concert was practically unknown, but the opera in all the principal towns was on a different footing from that which has been described in Germany, in that admission could be obtained on payment.

As a rule, a company of gentlemen clubbed together to
'finance' an operatic undertaking, and the scale of admission
for the public seems to have been remarkably low. In Montesquieu's *Voyages*, published by Baron Albert de Montesquieu
in 1794, the famous French writer, who was in Italy in 1728,
gives many amusing and instructive details about music.
Like other French travellers, he finds the Italian standard of
dancing very inferior to the French, more especially in Rome,
where he remarks on the prohibition of female performers on
the stage. The young sopranists, of whom he names two,
Mariotti and Chiostra, as taking the female parts, were the
chief scandal of the Roman stage, and, if we can believe
Montesquieu's account, the picture of such a singer, drawn
by Balzac in *Sarrasine*, is not exaggerated. The President
De Brosses, who travelled in Italy in 1739 and 1740, makes
many references to musical matters in his *Lettres familières*,
first published in 1836, under the title of *L'Italie il y a cent ans*.
He becomes enthusiastic over the performances of various
young girls in the 'hospitals' or conservatorios in Venice,
the first of which, the Pietà, had for a long time the reputation
of being the best for instrumental music, while the Mendicanti
possessed the best voices; later on, under Galuppi, the In-
curabili was raised to the chief place for excellence of all
kinds, according to Burney[1]. A violinist of the fourth conservatorio, the Ospedaletto, named Anna Maria, De Brosses
professes to admire more than Tartini—perhaps the fact that
she was 'si fantasque qu'à peine joue-t-elle une fois par an'
may have had something to do with it—he compares Tartini
in an interesting way with the French Léclair, saying that
both have comparatively little brilliance, but exquisite delicacy
and purity of tone. He describes how he saw 'une jeune et
jolie religieuse en habit blanc, avec un bouquet de grenades

---

[1] Burney, *Tour in Italy*, pp. 162-3, and art. 'Venice' in the Appendix to
Grove's *Dictionary*.

sur l'oreille, conduire l'orchestre et battre la mesure avec toute la grâce et toute la précision imaginables.' From this and many other passages in similar books it appears that the Italians were in the habit of conducting church performances only; at the opera there was no conductor in the modern sense, but the duty of keeping things together apparently devolved upon the *maestro al cembalo*, or harpsichord player, an official whom Marcello, in his satire *Il Teatro alla Moda*, recommends to put out the candles on the harpsichord during the airs (when the instrument is not required), for fear of setting his wig on fire, and to light them again for the recitatives. In Rome De Brosses went every Friday evening to the 'concert exquis' given at the house of the exiled Stuarts, and he remarks that 'Prince Charles Edward was proficient upon the violoncello, while his brother, afterwards Cardinal of York, sang Italian airs in the best taste in his boy's voice.' He tells also a pretty story of his entering the room while Corelli's famous concerto, 'La Notte di Natale,' was going on; and of Charles Edward's stopping it and directing that it should be begun again, for De Brosses's special benefit.

At Naples he sees a very fine performance of Sarri's *Partenope*, in which Senesino sings in such a way as to delight the French writer with his good taste and his dramatic action, although the public complained of his 'stilo antico.' He notices that an opera, to succeed in Italy, must present not merely gorgeous spectacular effects, but must include a battle scene in which 'deux cents galopins, tant de part que de l'autre, en font la représentation.' The chief impression of his journey, in a musical sense, seems to have been made by an opera of Leo's *La Frascatana*, given in Naples; he bought the MS. to carry back with him to France, and, à propos of what was said above as to the purchase of MS. music, he notes that it is only the first copies of the airs, &c., that fetch the high prices, for, when the novelty has begun to wear off, the work is less sought after, and the ease with which other copies could be made, in the absence of any copyright laws, diminished the value of the autograph or the early MS. For the music of Pergolesi De Brosses expresses the greatest devotion, and claims the sympathy of his correspondent on the early death of the composer. On his way back from Italy he went to the opera in Milan to hear some work of Leo, but found it impossible to hear it because of the noise made by the audience.

'Ce n'est point assez que chacun y fasse la conversation en criant du plus haut de sa tête et qu'on applaudisse avec de grands hurlements non les chants, mais les chanteurs dès qu'ils paraissent et tout le temps qu'ils chantent et cela sans écouter. Messieurs de parterre ont, en outre, de longs bâtons refendus dont ils frappent tant qu'ils peuvent sur les bancs par forme d'admiration. Ils ont des correspondants dans les cinquièmes loges qui, à ce signal, lancent à millions des feuilles contenant un *sonetto* imprimé à la louange de la signora ou du virtuoso qui vient de chanter. Chacun s'élance à mi-corps des loges pour en attraper[1].'

De Brosses has preserved for us a most interesting conversation he had with Tartini at Padua, when, in connexion with the ever-recurring comparison between the Italian and French styles of composition, the great violinist said that the Italian writers gave all their attention to the airs, and put together in careless haste all that was declamatory ; he also complained of the mistake which many of the instrumental composers made, of trying to write vocal works. 'I have been asked to write for the Venetian theatres,' he said, 'but I never wished to do so, knowing well that the fingerboard of the violin is not the same thing as a throat. Vivaldi, who wanted to try both kinds of composition, has always failed in the one kind, while he has succeeded very well in the other.' We learn that the composers were very poorly paid, receiving only thirty or forty pistoles for an opera, beside

---

[1] *L'Italie il y a cent ans*, ii. 484. Compare also Burney, *Tour in Italy*, p. 66 note.

what they might get by the sale of the first copy of the MS.
He notices that the Italians accompany with an amount of
light and shade that is unknown in France ; and another
novelty to French people is remarked, that of a concerto
in which there is no solo violin part. The absence of ballet
during the progress of an opera strikes him as strange, as
well as the practice of sandwiching the acts of a comic intermezzo between those of the serious operas. He notices also
Hasse's invincible prejudice against French music.

The comparison between the French and Italian styles must
be more fully discussed in the next chapter, but there are
a few remarks in the *Histoire de Musique et de ses Effets*,
by Bonnet (1715), which may be fitly quoted here. He speaks
of the musical antipathy between the nations as existing from
the time of Charlemagne ; and, while admitting the superiority
of the Italians on the scientific side of the art, gives the palm
to the French executants for their natural good taste, and
the 'exécution tendre et noble où nous excellons, surtout
pour l'harmonie des Instruments.' His disapproval of the
basso continuo is probably to be understood of Rameau's
'Basse fondamentale,' the vague theory of which may have
been, as we say, 'in the air' for a time before the publication of the *Nouveau Système* in 1726 ; in his opinion it is a
piece of unnecessary conceit to employ a key with many
sharps in the signature. He describes a triumphal procession
of Pompey which he saw at the San Salvador theatre at Venice
as being something quite exceptional in its way.

In 1769 appeared the valuable *Voyages d'un Français en
Italie*, with no author's name, but the work of J. J. Le Français
de Lalande[1]; the eight little volumes give a wonderfully

---

[1] The system of cross-references in vogue at the British Museum is so elaborate
in the case of this book, that it seems worth while to warn the anxious searcher
who may wish to consult it that, even if he knows the exact name of the writer,
he will be directed successively from the heading ' Lalande' to those of ' Le
François ' and ' Le Français,' and finally to ' Frenchman,' under which the book
is duly catalogued, as it also is under ' De Lalande.'

detailed account of the principal cities of Italy, as they were
in 1765–6. He gives due attention to the 'spectacles,' and is
so minute in his statements, that the reader cannot but feel
that he is generally to be trusted[1]. The enormous size of
the theatre at Parma is of course noticed, as it is by Montesquieu and Addison ; it was not used for operas, which took
place generally in May and June in a smaller theatre, the
prince bearing a part of the expense. From Christmas to the
carnival 'opéras bouffons' were given. About the conditions
of the Roman theatres he is in perfect agreement with
Montesquieu, noticing that the Roman idea of dancing consisted mostly of high jumps, and that the principal dancers,
like the singers, were young men. Of the eight theatres he
describes three as intended for opera, the Argentina, the
Aliberti (or Alle Dame), and the Tordinoni ; the Capranica
was devoted to comic operas. At the first of these the
audience seems to have been remarkable for its attentiveness,
although the place was not very good acoustically. At the
Aliberti operas were given between Epiphany and Carnival
to the number of thirty performances, for which a subscription of from fifty to seventy scudi was paid for the
season for the boxes, each of which held from eight to ten
people. The places were allotted by a masked official who
took the tickets at the doors, and the concealment of whose
identity was supposed to remove all danger of favouritism. The
most popular composers at the time de Lalande wrote were
'Galoupi' and Gluck, whose name first appears as 'Gloux,
Saxon,' and, in a later volume, as 'Glonek Sanon,' a version
obviously derived from the way in which he is first mentioned.
At Rome, he says that each musician gave concerts in his
own house at the expense of those who attended them ; they
were called 'Accademia.' Of Naples we are told that it was
the great centre of music in Italy ; a list of the eminent com-

---

[1] But see Burney's *Tour in Italy*, p. 356; note.

posers is given, including Corelli, Vinci, Jommelli, Durante
(the last noted as 'plus savant qu'eux tous en harmonie'),
Leo, Pergolesi, Galuppi, Perez, Terradeglias.   He gives a
good many particulars as to the barbarous operation by which
boys were prepared for the career of sopranists, and says that
it often failed of its effect upon the voice, so that care had
to be taken that the boy showed real musical ability before
it was done, in order that he might devote himself to some
other branch of music if it failed[1].   Of the three opera-houses
at Naples, de Lalande tells us some curious things about the
San Carlo (rebuilt in 1737), where there were seventy boxes
belonging to the principal families, who are not allowed to
get rid of them without the king's permission, and are obliged
to pay the impresario a large sum each season.   The season
of operas lasted from the 5th of November, the fête-day of the
King of Spain, to September, there being four series, each
consisting of twelve to fourteen representations.   He notices
that the eminent virtuosi on the stage are in the habit of
nodding to their friends in the audience while the opera is
in progress.   The Teatro Nuovo gave *opéras bouffons*, ballets,
&c., and had its chief season during the summer when the
San Carlo was shut.   At the Teatro de' Fiorentini, *opéras
bouffons* and comedies were given from early in the century
onwards ; all three theatres were open on Saturday and
Sunday nights, and each of them had another day as well,
but no theatre was open on Friday.   Monks were allowed
to go to the performances in Naples, but nowhere else in
Italy ; only in Rome they might attend rehearsals.   He only
mentions three of the famous Neapolitan conservatorios, those
of Santa Maria di Loretto, the Pietà, and San Onofrio, because
at the time of his visit the fourth, and in some ways the most
celebrated, that of the Poveri di Gesù Cristo, had ceased to
exist as a music-school in 1744, when its pupils were divided

---

[1] But see Burney's *Tour in Italy*, pp. 301-3.

among the other three[1]. These establishments were all for the education of boys.

The opera-houses of Venice are said to be four, San Benedetto, San Samuele, San Cassiano (the oldest), and ' San Moyse.' By this time, the time of de Lalande's visit, opera had ceased to be in its former vogue in Venice; comedies were the most attractive form of theatrical amusement, and, with Goldoni's plays continually before them, there is little to surprise us in this.

Another authority gives the number of Venetian opera-houses as six, omitting San Benedetto, and mentioning San Cassiano, San Mosè, SS. Giovanni e Paolo, San Apollinare, San Salvatore, and the Cavallerizza, which last was more an Accademia (or concert-room) than a theatre. In the translation of Raguenet's *Parallèle*, it is mentioned that there were in 1709 three opera-houses in Rome, four or five in Venice, and one at each of the following: Naples, Bologna, Milan, Leghorn, Pratolino, Parma, Placentia (Piacenza), Modena, Fano, Todi, Genoa, Turin, and several other places. The same amusing work notes that ' No Women are suffered to sing on the Theatre at Rome or Dusseldorp.'

In Addison's *Remarks on various parts of Italy*, published in 1705, we find strangely little about music; his interest was chiefly in regard to librettos and the subjects of operas rather than the operas themselves. He notices the custom, which prevailed at Venice for many years after his time, ' of singing Stanzas out of *Tasso*. . . They are set to a pretty Solemn Tune, and when one begins in any part of the Poet, 'tis odds but he will be answered by some Body else that overhears him.' From the way he attributes this habit to ' the common People of this Country,' it must be supposed that the custom was not confined to the gondoliers, as it was afterwards.

We have a good picture of the place the opera occupied in

---

[1] Grove, *Dictionary*, ' Naples,' ii. 444.

Florence towards the middle of the century, in the letters from
Sir Horace Mann to Horace Walpole, printed in Doran's lively
book *'Mann' and Manners at the Court of Florence*, 1876.
We need not attach too much importance to his often repeated
criticism, 'the vilest musick that ever was heard,' for that
kind of phrase was commonly used between such correspondents at the time; of one thing so described, an opera called
Andromaca (1743), the public seem to have taken the same
view as Mann, for there were only seventeen tickets taken
for the second performance.   In this he notices that the part
of Andromache was played by a singer named Bagnolese 'in
a black velvet gown covered with bugles.'   Mann approved
of the opera more heartily in 1747, when Tesi was 'taken
from involuntary retreat to act Achilles.'   Some of the gossip
reported by Mann is sufficiently amusing, as for instance when
he tells of the rumour that 'Caffarelli swears he will make
Egiziello sing out of tune' (*sic*, but the following sentence
implies that it should be out of *time*).   'He did so by the
Astrua, and then publickly beat time to her, for which he
was sent to Prison.'   He refers, like so many other writers,
to the noise in the Italian theatres, and says that in the boxes it
was the custom to serve hot suppers, the fumes of which came
out into the theatre.   In one of his earlier letters he shows
that it was the custom to wait to begin the opera until the
arrival of the royal personages: 'The Princess went last week
to the Opera; made it wait till an hour and ½; was received
at the door by a crowd of Cavaliers; behaved stiff, and went
away before the second dance.'

Lady Mary Wortley Montagu, in her letters from Naples
in 1747, confirms the general impression that the opera at
Naples is the finest in Italy; at Verona she went to the house
of the Marchese Scipione Maffei, a fairly important figure in
the amateur world of Italian music, who set apart one day
in each week for music, vocal and instrumental, 'but no mer-
cenaries were admitted to the concert.'

Of such an 'Accademia' as this, Burney says that they were 'much upon a level with our own private concerts among gentlemen in England, the performers were sometimes in and sometimes out[1].'

Of all the books of Italian travel, none is as useful to musicians as the *Present State of Music in France and Italy* of Dr. Charles Burney, a book often quoted in this and the preceding chapters. The journey was undertaken in 1770, and the book published in 1771; it had such a success that Johnson confessedly imitated it in his *Tour to the Hebrides*. It was as a preparation for his famous *History of Music* that this and the journey to Germany were undertaken; the result of the latter was the couple of volumes on *The Present State of Music in Germany*, published 1773. The History appeared in the years 1776-1789. The Italian tour is in some ways the most interesting of Burney's works, for he was in more complete sympathy with Italian music than with any other school, except that of Handel, and could therefore convey to his readers a clearer impression of its merits. The time of his visit was considerably after the close of the period covered by this volume, and therefore his accounts of contemporary performers have not here been quoted; but his information concerning institutions, compositions, &c., of a past date is quite invaluable to the historian; and much of the material that he gathered in the course of his tour, but ultimately omitted from his history, is of a kind which gives modern readers just the enlightening idea that brings history to life.

Nothing is more curious, in reading the various accounts of which the above extracts are examples, than to see how complete was the independence of one of the great Italian cities from the others; and we can the more easily understand Mattheson's words[2] that not only do the styles of different countries differ, but that a Venetian will compose

[1] Burney, *Tour in Italy*, p. 91.
[2] *Neu-eröffnetes Orchester*, p. 203.

in a different way from a Tuscan, and differently again from a Neapolitan; while the Roman style is far graver than the Venetian.

The idea of illustrating in music the different styles in vogue in the Italian cities no doubt impelled our own William Corbett to write a set of concertos in seven parts with the collective title of *Bizzarrie Universali*. He had some right to form an opinion on these styles, for when the Opera Band in London was reconstituted for the production of Handel's *Rinaldo*, he went to Italy, and lived there from 1711 to 1740, when he returned and issued these concertos. The separate titles are: ' Alla Genoese, Alla Turinese, Alla Parmegiana, Alla Olandese, Alla Cremonese (is it accidental that in this concerto the first violin part is unusually elaborate?), Alla Ventiana (qu. Veneziana? the work ends with a Furlano, a distinctively Venetian dance), Alla Todesca, Alla Modonese, Pollonese (no doubt for Polognese), Spagniola (beginning with a saraband), Paduana, and Francesa.' The contents of the second book are ' Alla Milanese, Romana, Napolitana, Fiorentina, Bolognese, Bresciana, Ceceliana (*sic* for Siciliana, as that movement is the second in the concerto), Tirolese, Inglese, Irelandese, Scocese, Bergamasca.'

[For further information on the opera in Italy, or rather in the two most important operatic centres, Naples and Venice, the reader is referred to Signor Benedetto Croce's ' I Teatri in Napoli,' a series of articles in the *Archivio Storico per le Province Napoletane*, anno XIV, XV (1891, &c.); and to Cavaliere Taddeo Wiel's ' I Teatri Musicali Veneziani del Settecento' (published serially in the *Archivio Veneto*, 1891–1897, and in book-form in 1897). An interesting article by G. Roberti in the *Rivista Musicale Italiana* for 1900, p. 698, gives many quotations from the accounts by travellers in Italy.]

CHAPTER XIII

THE STATE OF MUSIC IN FRANCE

No student of eighteenth-century music can fail to be struck with the constant recurrence, in the many books on the subject, of a comparison between French and Italian music. A famous case is the story of Corelli's excuse for his inability to play the violin part of Handel's Overture to *Il Trionfo del Tempo e del Disinganno* (see p. 80); and there is hardly a writer of any country who does not refer to the difference between the styles of the two nations. That there should be a certain amount of international jealousy is only natural; and the feeling would not be lessened on the French side by the remembrance that the foremost French composer at the end of the seventeenth century was Lully, whose Italian origin could not be forgotten. The contrast once pointed out, it seems to have been a fashionable pursuit for the amateur who travelled on the continent, or who wrote with any reference to music, to emphasize his recognition of the difference so as to prove himself a thoroughly educated musician. When it is seriously analysed, the contrast between the music of the two nations comes to something very small, as far as it affects composition. When it has been said that the Italian overture consisted generally of a slow movement between two quick ones, while the French always began with a slow movement in more or less jerky rhythm, and had a faster movement for its main section, usually marked either 'Gay' or 'Vite,' with or without a final short section in the

original slow time, there is nothing much else to say, except
that there does seem to have been a difference in the way that
recitative was treated in the two countries. The sharp de-
marcation which was of long endurance in the Italian music,
between the dry recitative and the conventional air, was far
less strong in France, where measured vocal sections in quite
regular rhythm were often labelled ' recit.,' and where the arias
were of freer form. In no part of the eighteenth century was
it absolutely necessary in France for the first part of every air
to be repeated after the middle section. These are the essential
points of the difference of styles, and it will be readily seen
that they do not amount to very much after all. Raguenet,
in his famous *Parallèle,* has a curious passage which might
lead us to suppose that the French were timid in comparison
of the Italians; ' Les Français,' he says, ' cherchent partout
le doux, le facile, ce qui coule, ce qui se lie; tout y est sur
le même mode, ou si quelquefois on le change, on le fait avec
des préparations et des adoucissements qui rendent l'Air aussi
naturel et aussi suivi, que si l'on n'en changeait point du tout.
Les Italiens passent à tout moment du *b carre* au *b mol;*
ils hasardent les dissonances les plus irrégulières.'

In execution there were considerable differences of method
between the French and the other European nations ; in
singing, for example, they are contrasted by Mattheson [1] with
the Germans, in the words, ' The French throats may do their
work delicately, but they have not the force of the Germans.'
Many other writers on the favourite subject refer to the vocal
differences in terms which make it clear that the French
voices were less remarkable for volume than for expression,
and that they were often rather apt to get shrill; in choruses,
Burney, who had indeed no partiality for French music, found
the singers even more loud and violent than the English
choristers of his time [2]. For the French instrumentalists the

---

[1] *Neu-eröffnetes Orchester,* p. 221.
[2] *Tour in France,* pp. 18, 25, &c.

writers of other nationalities have nothing but praise.   The
orchestral players are spoken of as attaining wonderful precision ; Mattheson [1] says that their incomparable decision and
accuracy are due to extreme familiarity with their music,
which they play almost by heart, so that they would be
ashamed to be required to rehearse as diligently as the German
players are obliged to do.   The best players of the time were
not above playing in the orchestra in France, but the Italians
seldom or never did so.

On the whole, the musical characteristics of the French
nation would appear to be very much what they are now, or
were up to a short time ago, when the new school arose with
its preference for abrupt transitions, and violent contrasts of
all kinds ; their ideals were clearness, neatness, precision, and
in dramatic or semi-dramatic music, expression was quite
rightly preferred to the conventions of structure which, as
we lately saw, ruined the Italian opera of the eighteenth as it
did that of the early nineteenth century.

This permanence of the national characteristics, in which
the music of France is so different from that of all other
nations, was no doubt due in great measure to what may be
called the musical 'Chauvinism' which has always prevailed
in France.   Ever since music became an art, France has held
aloof from the general stream of its development ; with her
it has been no cosmopolitan movement in which she could
exchange ideas with other countries ; she has worked out
her own line of development for herself, and has always been
content to know little or nothing about the musical history
of the rest of the world.   France is the strongest possible
contrast to England in this respect, and it is surely the former,
rather than the latter country, which deserves the reproach
conveyed in our word 'insular.'   Self-contained and self-
satisfied, the French nation has never welcomed foreign

---

[1] *Neu-eröffnetes Orchester*, p. 221.

musicians as other countries have done; and if we mention Rossini, Chopin, Offenbach, and a few other instances where musicians of foreign birth have become .the rage in France, it may be pointed out that they have only been accepted on condition of becoming adopted Frenchmen, whether actually nai'ralized or not.   The system had the qualities of its defects, and the continuity of the French school, from the beginnings of the art of music to the present day, is no less an advantage than the hearty encouragement bestowed by the French people at large to the music of their countrymen.

The dominating influence in French music, more especially in that of the stage, at the beginning of the period covered in this volume was, as has been said, that of Lully. As he himself died when Bach and Handel were two years old, eight years before his follower, Henry Purcell, his own work, with that of his life-long rival, Marc-Antoine Charpentier (1634–1702), and that of his immediate successor, Pascal Colasse (1639–1709), do not call for detailed notice in this place; but Lully was the founder of a long line of opera-composers, and really started the tradition of French opera which has lasted to the present day.   Beside the school of dramatic music, there were the makings of a great school of church music in the motets of Lalande and Campra. Michel Richard de Lalande (b. 1657) held the post of Surintendant de la Musique under Louis XIV and XV. A chorister of St. Germain l'Auxerrois, he studied under Chaperon, and when his voice broke he applied for admission into Lully's orchestra as a violinist, but was refused, on which he determined never to touch the violin again.   Before long he became organist at four different churches in Paris, and on applying for the post of organist to the king, met with another refusal . on the score of his youth, a refusal for which Lully seems again to have been responsible.   He was appointed teacher to the princesses, and in 1683 he obtained one of the appointments to the Chapelle Royale, four *surintendants* being appointed to serve, each for

three months in the year.　These offices were subsequently
united in Lalande, but the old arrangement was restored,
at Lalande's request, in 1722, Campra being one of the
assistants named.　He married twice,.and died in 1726.　The
king published the large number of motets which he wrote
for the chapel at Versailles, and they appeared in 1729.　They
are generally said to number sixty, and to be contained in
twenty books.　As each book contains only two motets, and the
most complete collection in England—that of the Fitzwilliam
Museum at Cambridge—contains twenty-one books, bound
in seven volumes, the number of forty-two motets would
seem to represent the actual amount of his work in this set
of compositions.　A preface by the composer's widow gives
many of the details of Lalande's life.　From this preface it
appears that the division of the duties of the surintendant
into four quarters was made at Lully's suggestion, and that
the competitors for the posts were required to compose motets
on the same psalm, 'Beati quorum.'　Lully of course favoured
his pupil Colasse, but the king preferred Lalande, who was
chosen to fill the place for the first quarter of the year.　The
general impression concerning the motets seems to have been
that the later works were more *travaillés* than the earlier;　on
this account they were published in pairs, to represent the
different styles he adopted;　as no clue is given to the date
of origin of each pair, it is impossible to determine whether
the first or second of each couple is the earlier.　There
is no very strong internal evidence, but as the first of
each couple is generally the more elaborate, it is perhaps
justifiable to regard it as the later.　Mattheson's remark
about the French motets as a whole, that they were not equal
to the Italian, and that they seldom let one voice sing alone [1],
is singularly wide of the mark;　for the solo voice is used in
almost all, quite as freely as it is in English anthems, which

---

[1] *Neu-eröffnetes Orchester*, p. 221.

the motets resemble more closely than any other form of music in vogue at the time. Set solos, divided off from the rest of the work like the numbers in an oratorio or cantata, are uncommon; but the alternation of single voices, or semi-chorus, with the full choir, is constant. The great majority of the motets employ a five-part choir, including a baritone part in addition to the four usual voices. The accompaniment is usually for two violins and basso continuo, but a third violin is not very uncommon. Two or three of the motets are for eight-part or double chorus, and one, 'Deus in adiutorium,' is marked 'à deux basses.' The works as a whole have great dignity of style, and far more unity than is to be discovered in the average work of the Italians such as Caldara or even Durante; the Italian conventions, noticed in former chapters, are almost completely absent; and even the form of opening to which Scarlatti's name is attached—that in which the first part of the theme is sung as part of the instrumental intro-duction—is of rare occurrence. In a prominent instance of its use, the alto solo 'Domine, labia mea' in the *Miserere*, the number is headed 'recit.' The finest, or one of the finest, of the whole set is the 'Te Deum' at the beginning of book 6; the treatment of the orchestra shows a decided sense of colouring, and from the opening, in which trumpets and drums are used, to the close, the work is one of sustained beauty, massive structure and great effect. As a rule, the choral numbers in the motets are laid out on such extensive lines and so amply developed, that quotation within ordinary limits would give no idea of their nature; but the following short passage of the 'Te Deum' is complete in itself, and presents in two places such boldness of harmonic invention, that it may stand as typical of Lalande's best work:—

SANCTUS FROM A 'TE DEUM.'

LALANDE.
Motets, liv. vi.

The little crosses which appear above certain notes no doubt indicate some kind of trill, probably a short 'pralltriller.'

At the bar before the $\frac{3}{2}$ time begins, the D of the tenor part seems as if it must be a misprint, more especially with the figures $\frac{6}{4}$ indicated above the bass; but the way it is introduced is exactly identical with the preparation of the same cadence in the last bar but one, where the figures are the same, and, taking the two together, there is no room for doubt that the bold use of the chord of the thirteenth is quite intentional.

The motets of Nicolas Berniers (1664–1734) enjoyed a vogue which must have been due to their extremely easy, not to say superficial style. There is a story of his youth according to which, not being able to get instruction in the regular way, he engaged himself to Caldara as a servant, and so managed to get a certain amount of tuition. Of Caldara's influence there is in truth very little trace; Berniers' themes are constantly light-hearted, and the naïveté displayed in the doxology of one of the motets in his second book, published 1713, is by no means exceptional:—

Sit laus . . . . . . sit laus Pa - tri et Fi - li - o.

The first set, published ten years before, contains a number of sacred solos and duets, with three motets for three voices; the second contains only one for three voices, the rest being for one or two. In some of his movements in $\frac{3}{2}$ time, we meet with a curious system of notation, which seems to have been peculiar to France just at the moment, for the two most prominent examples appeared within a very short time of each other. It is that of writing, in $\frac{3}{2}$ time, notes of smaller value than minims as open notes, and thus eliminating the crotchets altogether. Students of Couperin's harpsichord music will remember the droll 'quatrième acte' of his eleventh ordre, with the piece called 'Les Invalides; ou gens estropiés au service de la grande M∗n∗str∗nd∗s∗' in which these empty

notes have tails like quavers or semiquavers. In Berniers'
second book of motets occurs a passage noted throughout as
follows:—

In - fun - dem a - - - - mo - rem.

The five books of motets by André Campra were published
far earlier than Lalande's; the first book reached its fourth
edition in 1710, and the date of its first appearance seems
to have been before 1699, the date given by Pongin, correcting
Fétis's date, 1706[1]: his chronological place is after Lalande,
and the early appearance of his motets was no doubt a consequence of their great popularity. He was born in 1660
at Aix in Provence; and in 1679 was appointed Maître de
Musique in the Cathedral of Toulon, finding his way to Paris
in 1694. In his sacred music the prominence given to the
solo voice is remarkable; he is also said to have been the
first composer who was allowed to use instruments other than
the organ in church music; and some slight feeling for
orchestral colouring may here and there be discerned. The
finest by far is an 'In convertendo' for six-part choir, with
strings in five parts (referred to on p. 47). It contains
a fine fugal chorus in five parts 'Tunc repletum est gaudio,'
and a most dignified chorus in six parts, 'Magnificavit
Dominum.' For the most part Campra's motets are for
smaller combinations or for a single voice.

His fame rests mainly on his dramatic music, for in his
long series of operas, beginning in 1697, and only ending
four years before his death in 1740, at the age of 80, he
filled the place formerly occupied by Lully, and preceded
Rameau in popular favour. His first work for the stage,
L'Europe galante (in which were some pieces by Destouches),
throws some light on the characteristics of the different nations

---

[1] See Grove's *Dictionary of Music and Musicians*, art. 'Campra,' in app. vol. iv.
577, note 4.

as they were understood at the time; Spain, for example, is represented by a severe and pompous sarabande; and it is rather curious that in the number representing Italy occurs, as a prelude to an air, a strain of the jerky, 'dotted' style which is associated with the 'French overture,' as well as the 'Scarlatti' form of opening.   In a later work, *Les Festes Vénitiennes* (1710), occurs a scene between the Maître de Musique and the Maître de Danse containing music borrowed from 'nos plus habiles compositeurs' and from Lully.   The earliest of Campra's dramatic works appeared first under the name of his brother Joseph Campra, a double-bass player at the opera; for the composer dreaded the loss of his ecclesiastical appointments if the fact of his writing for the stage became known.   In 1700, he definitely abandoned the church for the theatre, was made director of music to the Prince de Conti and Maître de Chapelle to the King in 1722, and died at Versailles in 1744.

Both the works just mentioned are called 'ballets,' but both, like all the so-called ballets of the time, abound in vocal numbers, and are in no way distinguishable in form from regular operas, except by the introduction of dances in each act.   The only real distinction that seems to have been recognized was that the 'ballet' was not expected to deal with the adventures of one set of characters; in each of its various acts, or 'entrées,' new personages were generally introduced, and the connecting links are often to be found only in the general title.   The ballet 'entrées' were generally four in number, while the acts of the 'tragédies en musique' or regular operas were always five; and as in each case a prologue was an indispensable part of the entertainment, the number of acts was virtually five and six respectively.

Until we come to Rameau, the line of French opera-composers is not of very high importance; but it may be convenient to give a brief summary of their names and principal works in chronological order.   Henri Desmarets (1662–1741) wrote

Didon (1693), *Circé* (1694), *Théagène et Chariclée, Les Amours
de Momus* (1695), *Vénus et Adonis* (1697), and *Les Fêtes
Galantes* (1698). As the result of a secret marriage with the
daughter of a dignitary at Senlis, Desmarets found it expedient
to go to Spain, where he obtained a musical appointment
at the court of Philip V. During his absence from Paris,
his *Iphigénie en Tauride* was produced at the Académie Royale
in 1704; it was a work he had not touched for eight years,
and the authorities, in his absence, had recourse to Campra
to make such alterations as were considered necessary. In
Act i of this work there is a very declamatory air for Iphigenia,
'Phantômes de la Nuit,' with a vigorous accompaniment for
violins; there is almost a foreshadowing of Gluck in the shape
of its phrases. Desmarets was especially skilled in his treatment of the Passecaille or Chaconne form, and the number
at the end of his *Vénus et Adonis* shows remarkable freedom
in design.

Michel Pignolet de Montéclair (1666-1737) was a distinguished teacher of the violin, the author of a valuable
'méthode' published in 1720, a double-bass player in the
orchestra of the opera, and the composer of two stage
works, as well as of a number of cantatas and chamber
music. His *Festes de l'Eté* contains in its third 'entrée'
a double chorus in which the dwellers on the right and left
banks of the Seine answer each other with excellent effect.
At one point in the work the odd direction appears, 'les
Hautbois préludent de Fantaisie en C sol ut Majeur,' a point
which would hardly have been left to the discretion of the
players if the composer had not known that he would be in
the orchestra to see that they made no mistake. In the prologue to Montéclair's *Jephté* it is surprising to see that the
personages are 'Apollon, Polhymnie, Terpsicore, Vénus, Troupe
de Divinités fabuleuses,' &c. The scene is the opera-house,
and these fabulous divinities are represented as being driven
from their usual quarters by Truth and the Virtues, who

proceed to install the Old Testament characters in their stead. In a chorus in Act i, at the words 'tout tremble devant le Seigneur,' there is a good effect of trembling, expressed partly by the wavy line which is used in Lully's *Isis* and Purcell's *King Arthur*, &c., and partly by a clever figure of demi-semiquavers. A wonderful rainbow is introduced, and a miraculous passage of the Red Sea takes place ; but the climax of the story, the meeting between father and daughter, is avoided. A ballet air from his former work is introduced. That Montéclair was not unnaturally proud of this work appears from the freedom with which he introduces examples from it in the revised edition of his *Méthode pour apprendre la Musique* (first published 1700), which appeared in 1736; it is a fairly valuable treatise on the rudiments with some clear explanations of the commoner ornaments, as well as excellent hints on the best ways of joining words to music and on declamation generally.

One of the 'mousquetaires du Roi,' André Cardinal Destouches (1672-1749), leapt into sudden fame with his first opera, *Issé* (1697); so great was its popularity that it seemed worth while to Ballard, the regular publisher of works of the kind, to put on the title-page of Campra's *L'Europe galante* the words 'semblable à la dernière édition d'Issé.' His *Télémaque et Calypso* (1714) has some quite elaborate choruses, one for demons being especially good ; an alarming dream of Calypso's is described with due effect of horror, by upward runs on the strings in unison. His other works include *Le Carnaval et la Folie*, styled a 'comédie-ballet'; *Amadis de Grèce* and *Marthésie* (1699); *Omphale* (1701); *Callirhoé* (1712) ; and a cantata 'à voix seule avec symphonies,' called *Sémélé* (1719). In *Callirhoé* there is a pretty 'air en écho' in which the violins echo the trumpets with good effect. The work by which Destouches's name was longest remembered was the ballet *Les Eléments*, in which Louis XV danced at Versailles, in 1721, obtaining from the *Gazette de France*

the gratifying testimony that ' Sa Majesté dansa avec beaucoup
de grâce.' When the work was transferred in 1725 to the
stage of the opera in Paris, the King's place was taken by
a bust to which various compliments were of course paid by
various personages, among the rest by Venus, who remarks :
' Destin, faîtes-moy voir l'Image, De ce Mortel si semblable
à mon Fils.' The fine air in the prologue in which Destiny
utters the conjuration of fire, and the pretty chorus ' Paix
adorable,' are by Lalande, but his part seems to have been
confined to these two, although he is generally accredited with
having written more of the work. In the second act, that
devoted to water, there is a chorus ' Nous périssons ' with
running violin accompaniment, which it is hard to believe
Mendelssohn did not know when he wrote ' The waters gather,
they rush along ' in *Elijah*. The work has been edited in
recent years by M. Vincent d'Indy, who maintains that the
published score contains no more than the skeleton of the
accompaniments, and has therefore amplified them very considerably. A chaconne, which the editor goes so far as to
compare with Bach, appears in a far more elaborate form in
his version than in the original. Fétis says that Destouches's
Professeur de la Folie was often given after Campra's
L'Europe galante; and of the famous *Eléments* the section
of Fire continued in vogue long after the rest had been
forgotten.

T. Bertin de Ladoüé, as he is called on his title-pages
(c. 1680-1745), was Maître de clavecin de la maison d'Orléans,
and conducted the opera in Paris from 1714 till 1734. In 1716
his *Ajax* made its appearance; it contains a surprisingly good
declamatory air for Cassandra looking at the ruins of Troy,
and another later on labelled ' en fureur prophétique,' with
very appropriate accompaniment. The catastrophe must have
made considerable demands on the mise-en-scène of the day,
even in Paris; the ship in which Ajax sails off is overtaken
by a storm and wrecked; he is seen to climb upon a rock,

and from there he sings a song 'fièrement,' which ends : 'Le cœur d'Ajax n'est point fait pour trembler.' His troubles are not over, however, for Pallas, appearing above, 'lance le foudre sur le Rocher où est Ajax et la renverse dans la mer.' The *Jugement de Paris* (1718) has a very pretty 'air de musette en rondeau' with oboes and violins, bassoons, strings, and an alto solo.

Of Jean Joseph Mouret (1682–1738), called 'le musicien des grâces,' no dramatic work remains of any value or distinction. His *Ariane* (1717), *Les Amours des Dieux* (1727), and *Les Triomphes des Sens* (1732) proceed along the familiar lines; the two latter works, according to the rule of ballets, introduce new episodes and new personages into each scene. In the fourth 'entrée' of the work last mentioned, devoted to the illustration of the triumph of hearing, the Sirens' temptation of Ulysses is defeated by the superior attractions of Orpheus, whom the traveller has very thoughtfully brought with him. In his capacity of Conductor of the Concerts Spirituels, Mouret wrote some motets for solo voice, a ' Cantate Domino' for a soprano, with violins, oboe, and flute accompaniment; and a more ambitious 'O sacrum convivium,' for two sopranos with ampler accompaniment. A book of *Cantatilles françoises* contains some pretty things.

Leaving Rameau for more detailed consideration later on, we come to François Collin de Blamont (1690–1760), whose early cantata of *Circe* pleased Lalande so much that he consented to teach him. His *Fêtes grecques et romaines* was brought out at the opera in 1723, and his *Caractères de l'Amour* in 1736. In this there are various examples of love, fickle, jealous, faithful, &c.; in the last section the chief characters are Pétrarque and Laure, the former of whom is transformed into the river Rhône with a running accompaniment for violins and bassoons over reiterated notes in the bass. Blamont is at his best in sacred music, and his most ambitious work, a *Te Deum*, published with other motets in.

1732, is modelled upon the style of his master, Lalande. A number of some interest is a 'double trio,' for two groups of alto, tenor and bass, at 'Te ergo quaesumus.' Blamont wrote an *Essai sur les goûts anciens et modernes de la musique française*, published in 1754, in which he argued in favour of the older style of dramatic art, as against the tendencies which were then beginning to manifest themselves.

The joint work of François Rebel (1701–1755) and François Francœur (1698–1787) includes ten operas, a *Ballet de la Paix* (1738), and a prologue *Le Trophée*, performed in honour of the victory of Fontenoi, in August 1745, at Versailles, as an introduction to *Zélindre, Roi des Silphes,* an opera which had been brought out at Versailles a little while before. There is more movement about their music than about that of most of their predecessors; in many passages the violin part betrays the hand of an accomplished player, and points to Francœur as its author; he was one of the famous '24 violons du Roi,' and published two books of violin sonatas. One of them, in E minor, has been edited recently in Moffat's *Meisterschule*, and is a work of remarkable beauty and sterling value. He and his bosom friend, Rebel, were joint leaders of the opera orchestra from 1733 to 1744, then inspectors of the opera, and directors in 1753-1757.

In Jean Philippe Rameau we come to one who may without exaggeration be called a master. Born at Dijon, 1683, he was mainly self-instructed in his art; his only visit to Italy in 1701 was so short as to be of very little service to his music; but perhaps it was no hindrance to the development of the art that it was so, for, instead of adhering to the stereotyped forms of Italian music, which a youth so susceptible as he was must have been forced to adopt, he not only found a voice of his own, but was led by his researches into the science of music to the system of harmony which is of almost supreme importance for the later developments of the art. This side of Rameau's work will be treated in greater detail in the succeeding volume of this series; for the present it is only necessary to speak of his compositions. Before obtaining admission to the Académie Royale he wrote *L'Endriague* 1723, *L'Enrôlement d'Arlequin* 1726, and *Samson*, the libretto of which last was procured from Voltaire through the interest of Rameau's patron, La Popelinière. The performance was forbidden, apparently on the ground of its biblical subject, but the objection must have been a mere excuse, for Montéclair's *Jephté* was given in 1732. Rameau's first appearance at the opera was with *Hippolyte et Aricie*, in 1733; he had to contend with many difficulties, for the newness of his style provoked loud opposition from a part of the audience; and if we may believe the evidence of Rousseau in the 'lettre d'un Symphoniste à ses Camarades de l'Opéra' (1753), the members of the orchestra took care to produce an unfavourable impression against the work by playing wrong notes, and by other means. The followers of Lully declared it to be ' bizarre, baroque, et dépourvu de mélodie,' and it took a good many years to conquer the entire approbation of the public. Campra had the discrimination that was wanting in the rest of his countrymen, for he prophesied that the opera had stuff in it for ten ordinary operas, and that the composer would eclipse all his contemporaries. The ballet, *Les Indes galantes* (1735), had another doubtful reception, as the composer admits in the preface to the 'four concerts' in which it was arranged for publication. It is rather surprising to find an Italian song introduced by one who was afterwards to stand as the champion of French music. With *Castor et Pollux* (1737) the tide began to turn in his favour; and if it be not quite accurate to say, with Pougin[1], that it 'ferma la bouche aux détracteurs,' it was from this point that he began to be accepted alike by the public at large and by the educated musicians. It would take too long to give a complete catalogue

[1] Arthur Pougin, *Rameau : Essai sur sa vie et ses œuvres*, 1876.

of all the ballets and fêtes provided by Rameau for the Académie or for his various patrons[1]; his principal works were *Dardanus* (1739), *Zaïs* (1748), *Pygmalion* (1748), an act taken from an earlier opera, *Platée*, *Naïs*, and *Zoroastre* (1749), the last of which contains much of the music intended for *Samson*. *La Princesse de Navarre*, written to a libretto by Voltaire on the occasion of the Dauphin's marriage, was given at Versailles with wonderful success in 1745, and its music was afterwards used in other works of the same kind. *Les Surprises de l'Amour* was first given by Mme. de Pompadour and other notabilities at Versailles in 1748, and at the Académie in 1757. Rameau's last work for the stage was *Les Paladins*, 1760. Besides his operas and ballets, Rameau attained a reputation which he has never lost as a composer of harpsichord music; his two books of 'pièces de clavecin' published in 1706 and 1741 respectively contain things that rival Couperin himself; the gavotte in A minor with variations, the pieces called 'La Poule,' 'Le Rappel des Oiseaux,' and 'Les Trois Mains,' are excellent compositions; the pretty 'Tambourin' in E minor, one of his best-known pieces, is taken from a rather more elaborate version in *Les Fêtes d'Hébé*, a ballet of 1739. The set of 'concertos' or chamber trios, for a harpsichord with violin or flute and bass, which appeared in 1741, show a genuine feeling for characteristic chamber-music effect. In Rameau, first among the Frenchmen, we find a decided instinct for instrumental colouring; throughout his operas, nothing is more remarkable than the way he uses his accompanying instruments, and in many ways he shows himself a strong opponent of the various conventions that had been started by Lully and kept up by his followers. For instance, his overtures differ from those of all the earlier men in that they sometimes begin with, a fast movement, not of the regular 'dotted' type; as an unusually perceptive piece of

---

[1] The reader may be referred to Pougin's interesting essay just mentioned, and to Grove's *Dictionary of Music and Musicians*, art. 'Rameau'.

criticism may be quoted a sentence from the notice of
Hippolyte et Aricie in ' Le Mercure ' (quoted in Pougin's
Essay): ' il a donné une musique mâle et harmonieuse, d'un
caractère neuf.' Nothing could sum up Rameau better than
this. In his search for appropriate musical expression, he
did not always avoid harshness of melodic movement, and
his airs may often seem to fall short of the grace of Lully's,
for example; but his ballet airs are always deliciously fresh,
and his treatment of the resources of the orchestra is masterly.

While in early life he had to appear as an opponent of the
old school, in his later years he became the champion of French
music in the famous ' Guerre des Bouffons,' which raged for
some years after the production of Pergolesi's *Serva Padrona*
in 1752. War was declared in a letter by the Baron von
Grimm, referring directly to Destouches's *Omphale* and attack-
ing the whole school of French opera; pamphlets were distributed in the opera-house from the ' coin du roi ' and the
' coin de la reine ' respectively, for Mme. de Pompadour was
on the side of the French music, so that the queen was
naturally a supporter of the Italian comedians. The most
remarkable utterance of the whole dispute was deferred for
a year; Rousseau's *Lettre sur la Musique Française*, published
in 1753, culminated in the often-quoted final sentence:—

' Je crois avoir fait voir qu'il n'y a ni mesure ni mélodie
dans la Musique Française, parce que la langue n'en est pas
susceptible ; que le chant Français n'est qu'un aboyement
continu, insupportable à toute oreille non prévenue ; que
l'harmonie en est brute, sans expression et sentant uniquement
son remplissage d'écolier; que les airs Français ne sont point
des airs, que le récitatif Français n'est point du récitatif. D'où
je conclus que les Français n'ont point de Musique, et n'en
peuvent avoir; ou que si jamais ils en ont une, ce sera tant
pis pour eux.'

There are many side references to the short-comings of the
Paris opera, which are of considerable value. We learn that
the instruments were of bad quality, that the conductor was

placed with his instruments behind him instead of in front, that it was customary to make a loud tapping with the bâton throughout the performance, that the harmonies are badly filled up, that the number of double-basses relatively to the violoncellos was too small, and that the actor dominated the orchestra too much, instead of the orchestra dominating the actor and determining the time of the measure.

These objections, like much else in the famous letter, must be taken with some hesitation, for it is abundantly clear that Rousseau was not a very accomplished musician from a technical point of view. His articles in the *Encyclopédie* were so full of errors that Rameau wrote a pamphlet, *Erreurs sur la musique dans l'Encyclopédie* (1755), following it up by a continuation to which Rousseau responded by collecting his articles, with considerable emendations, into a *Dictionnaire de la Musique*, published in 1764. The articles on the various points in dispute at the time are naturally very interesting, as, for example, that on 'Ouverture,' in which the ordinary French overtures are severely blamed because they have no character in common with what they usher in. Under 'Orchestre' Rousseau repeats what has already been referred to in speaking of his letter, that the Paris orchestra was one of the least effective. The other writings on music fall outside the period of which this volume treats; and for the same reason the only one of Rousseau's musical works which can be discussed here is *Le Devin du Village* (produced just at the time of the Guerre des Bouffons in 1752 at Fontainebleau, and in Paris in the following year). Rousseau, like all ill-equipped musicians, clamoured for greater simplicity than was in vogue; all elaboration was distasteful to him, and he went so far as to maintain that the ear was not capable of receiving two melodies simultaneously; so that, as a natural consequence, everything in the nature of fugue was out of the question. His opera certainly realizes his own theories perfectly. It has charming melodies, and proceeds along the

simplest possible lines; if there is no very great degree of
dramatic power or of emotional expression, in such a subject
these were perhaps not required.   In his *Pygmalion,* produced 1775, he tried the experiment of letting the speaking
voice of the actors carry on the action, with instrumental
interludes between the speeches.   Fragments of an opera
Daphnis et Chloé were published in 1780, and the charming
album of songs, *Les Consolations des Misères de ma Vie*
(1781), shows him in some ways at his best.   Even here
there are unmistakable signs of his technical shortcomings;
in the graceful setting of Rolli's *Se tu m'ami,* the opening
strain is obviously in $\frac{9}{8}$ time, but he writes it out in $\frac{6}{8}$, thus
disguising it altogether until the attempt is made to play
it, when its real rhythm is plain.

As a figure of some prominence in the Guerre des
Bouffons mention must be made of J. J. Cassanea de
Mondonville (c. 1711–1773), whose opera *Titon et l'Aurore*
(1753) attained a great success, the partisans of the 'Bouffons'
being almost crowded out of the theatre.   Before this he had
given two less successful works, *Isbé* (1742), and *Le Carnaval
de Parnasse* (1749).   He wrote afterwards a pastoral in the
dialect of Languedoc, *Daphnis et Alcimadura* (1754, in French
1768), by means of which he seems to have obtained the post
of director of the Concerts Spirituels.   Before describing this
important institution, it may be mentioned that Mondonville
deserves to be remembered if only for his most amusing and
successful *jeu d'esprit,* a musical setting of the long-winded
form in which the 'Privilège du Roi' appears in the publications of the period.   It is all gravely set out in the form of
a cantata, and was duly published in 1760, with parts for two
violins, alto, bass, two oboes, and two horns.

The Concert Spirituel was an important factor in the
musical life of Paris during the eighteenth century; it was
founded by Anne Danican-Philidor (b. 1681), the eldest of
the four brothers of whom the most celebrated was Francois

André, the famous composer and chess player (1726–1795), whose music lies outside the range of this volume. The concerts were given in the Salle des Suisses of the Tuileries on twenty-four fixed days in the year, when operas were forbidden, owing to church festivals. The first took place on March 18, 1725, and Anne Philidor conducted them, and for two years more. The motets of Lalande were in high favour at these concerts, as Burney notices in 1755. By an agreement with Francine, the impresario of the opera, Philidor bound himself to give neither operatic nor French music, the latter no doubt meaning music with French words. In 1728 this restriction was removed, and Mouret was appointed musical director. The 'Académie Royale' took over the concerts in 1734, and Mondonville, who succeeded Royer as manager and general director in 1755, was identified with the concerts until 1762; the concerts went on till 1791. The famous players on oboe and bassoon, the Besozzis, father and son, are familiar figures to the reader of Burney's tours; they made a furore in 1735 at these concerts, and the organist Balbâtre (b. 1729) was a prominent figure among the performers. Another eminent organist was named Calvière (1695–1755), who held the appointment of organist to the Chapelle du Roi from 1738. Although the fame of François Couperin, 'le Grand' (1668–1733), remains to us as a composer for the harpsichord, he was a most eminent player of the organ, though he wrote nothing for the latter instrument. His father and two uncles held the post of organist to the church of St. Gervais, Paris, in succession, and he himself was appointed to the same place in 1698, being given the post of organist of the Chapelle du Roi in 1701, when he was also made 'Claveciniste de la chambre du Roi.'

Another famous organist and harpsichord player, Louis Claude Daquin, or d'Aquin (1694–1772), deserves a word of notice, if only on account of the characteristically conceited speech of Marchand, who, when retiring from the post of organist of the Cordeliers, said to his organ: 'Adieu, chère veuve! d'Aquin seul est digne de toi.' Daquin wrote a number of graceful pieces for the harpsichord, among which 'Le Coucou' alone keeps its place in concert-programmes; some 'Noëls,' a cantata, and other works are mentioned.

In connexion with the introduction of opéra comique into France, the name of Antoine or Antonio d'Auvergne deserves mention. He was born in 1713, played the violin at the Concert Spirituel in 1740, and led the opera orchestra in 1751. At the outbreak of the revolution he retired to Lyons, and died there 1797. It was in 1753 that he wrote the first genuine French opéra comique, *Les Troqueurs*, a piece resembling the Italian intermezzi rather than the productions of the vaudeville type. Among the more obscure composers of operas, etc. the names of Bourgeois (d. 1750), the writer of two pieces; J.-B. de Bousset (1662–1725); Lalouette, a pupil of Lully who died in 1728; Brassac (called Brissac in Burney's *History*, iv. 607), who wrote *L'Empire de l'Amour* in 1733, and *Léandre et Héro* in 1750, are to be found in Jean Benjamin de Laborde's *Essai sur la Musique Ancienne et Moderne*, published in four volumes in 1780, a book which throws a good deal of light on contemporary French music, although it is of no very wonderful worth as a piece of permanent musical literature. Like his famous collection of 'Chansons,' the essay is adorned with very beautiful engravings.

The 'Opéra Comique' as a theatrical institution, if not as a recognized form of musical art, began in 1716 under that name, deriving the nature of its entertainment from what were called the 'spectacles de la foire.' Its popularity soon became so great that in 1721 the Italian and French comedians united in obtaining its suppression, but it began again in 1724. From 1745 to 1752 it was again prohibited, but after that date it increased in dignity, and throughout modern times it has been the more important of the two opera-houses from an artistic point of view.

The famous ' 24 Violons du Roi,' which, through Charles II's wish to copy everything French, were the originals of the 'four-and-twenty blackbirds,' or 'fiddlers,' familiar to every English child, endured as an institution and part of the royal household until 1761. Of violin soloists, by far the greatest was Jean-Marie Léclair (1697-1764), who began his career as a dancer at Rouen, and subsequently went as ballet-master to Turin, where he had the great advantage of studying under Somis. He was never a very great success in Paris, partly owing, it may be, to his Italian training ; among his works, which include four books of solo sonatas, two of violin duets, four of trios, and two of concerti, are many delightful move-ments, besides the hackneyed 'sarabande' and 'tambourin' by which his name is preserved in the memory of concert-goers. Senaillé (1687-1730) and Guignon (1702-1774) are among the most prominent names of French violinists; the latter used to play duets with Mondonville at the Concerts Spirituels, and a quarrel with him about the leadership of the second violins in the opera band was the cause of Léclair's retirement and journey to Holland, on the return from which he was assassinated. With them must be mentioned the ex-cellent flautist, Blavet (1700-1768), who was moreover the composer of a number of 'spectacles' of small value.

None of the French singers of the time made a name for themselves outside France, and very few vocal soloists of merit are even mentioned in the books that describe the other con-ditions of music so minutely. Burney is of course not an unprejudiced judge, as he was so hotly in favour of everything Italian ; but we may guess that there was a good deal of truth in his observation that 'the French voice never comes further than from the throat; there is no *voce di petto*, no true *porta-mento*, or direction of the voice, on any of the stages[1].' He speaks also of the process of deterioration through which the Italian singers pass after long residence in France.

[1] *Tour in France*, p. 18.

From what has gone before, it is quite clear that the French at this period were a distinctly musical nation, and that it was by their own personal and national characteristics, and by their maintenance of ideals of their own, that their music had so little hold upon the rest of Europe. During the first half of the century some of the operas of Lully, Cambert, Desmarets, and Rameau were played at various German theatres, and the Germans seem to have enjoyed the simplicity and charm of Rameau before his style made its way in other countries. The foregoing sketch has been treated in some detail in order to explain the kind of musical atmosphere which had so strong and important effect upon the work of Gluck, and through him upon music in general.

CHAPTER XIV

THE STATE OF MUSIC IN ENGLAND

IT is a more or less humiliating process for Englishmen to turn from the musical condition of the continent to that of their own country in the time of Handel. No Englishman of the period bore the smallest share in the main stream of musical development which we have watched in its course in Germany, Italy, and France. While France stood apart from the central current, so to speak, there was an active school of music within her frontiers; interest in things musical was exhibited by the educated classes, the discussion of musical questions was carried on no less eagerly than in Germany or Italy; and her composers had the chance of making themselves famous, if only in their own land, and enjoying the recognition of their contemporaries. The primary cause of England's sterility in music of her own was undoubtedly the obsession of Handel. From the day of his arrival to seek his fortune in the opera, he sat down (no less homely similitude will serve) upon what had been a musical nation, and he acted as a repressing influence on the art of his adopted country until more than a century after his death. To state this fact is in no way to impugn his greatness, any more than to refer to the bulk of the elephant is to underrate its sagacity. This kind of obsession must be carefully distinguished from the whole-hearted yet judicious admiration of a great man, such as a nation may often exhibit; it has not seldom been found possible to admire a great artist's

work without imposing upon all who follow him the fatal
alternative of either slavishly imitating him, and reaping a
measure of success, or of gaining artistic independence at the
risk of sacrificing every chance of worldly advantage. Such
a condition was, no doubt unconsciously, imposed upon the
English musicians of Handel's time and long afterwards; and
no one who understands the facts can wonder that our claim
to be numbered among the musical nations of the world has
been almost universally denied by the modern continental
historians. The foreign musicians who in successive generations have won fame and money in England have never
hesitated to repeat the same sort of sneers that were in fashion
when Mattheson wrote his *Neu-eröffnetes Orchester*, and said :
' He who in the present time wants to make a profit out of
his music betakes himself to England.' In another part of
the same book he has a comparison of the four principal
nations in regard to their musical peculiarities. ' The Italians,'
he says, ' exalt music ; the French enliven it ; the Germans
strive after it ; and the English pay for it well. The Italians
serve music ; the French make it into a companion, the
Germans anatomize it, and the English compel it to serve
them.' It is fair to say, however, that he admits in the
English a critical faculty, remarking that ' the Italians are
the best executants, the French get most amusement out of
music ; the Germans are the best composers and workers, and
the English the best judges.' The first he calls admirable
and ingenious, the second amiable and witty, the third indefatigable and thorough, and the fourth equitable and delicate.
It has before been pointed out that the English were considered
to appreciate the music that was brought to them from abroad,
and to be something better than mere stupid dispensers of
large salaries to musicians. Still, the fact remains that the
English music of this period counts for very little in a
historical record.

It stands to reason that even a Handel could not have

imposed himself upon the public as he did, or attained the
supreme position he held so long, if there had been a flourishing English school of composers at the time of his arrival
which could have held its own. There are many proofs that
this was not the case. The environment was most favourable
for his reception, since in the very year after his arrival, and
at a time when it would be absurd to attribute to him any
repressing influence whatever, the decay of the great English
school was commented on in Arthur Bedford's famous tract,
The Great Abuse of Musick[1]. The author loses no opportunity of pointing out the gross immorality of the words of
fashionable songs, of operatic librettos, of catches, and in
short of all vocal music whatever. As he gives ample quotations from the passages to which he most strongly objects,
the reader is often in doubt whether his motives were quite
as pure as he makes out. But although we may not be able
to agree with him that all references to Greek or Roman
divinities are necessarily blasphemous, or that the commonest
phrases of love-songs are indecent in intention, his evidence
concerning the decline of music is very valuable. He naturally
views it as a ' judgement' that ' Purcell was taken away in the
prime of his age, and Dr. Blow soon after,' and though he
does not perhaps succeed in convincing us that these great
men were removed as a punishment for the nation's wickedness,
we may believe him when he says that ' *Musick* declines as
fast as it did improve before.' His objections to the style
of music that was coming into vogue at the beginning of the
eighteenth century are better founded, and his estimate of
the number of secondary English composers is a guide for
which we may well be grateful. ' In these eight Years past
there are about fifty Composers of Musick : none of these are
equal to the other two [Purcell and Blow]. About ten of
them may be reckon'd of a second Rank ; the rest are generally

[1] *The Great Abuse of Musick*, by the Rev. Arthur Bedford, Chaplain to the Duke
of Bedford, 1711.

flat and mean, their *Movement* forc'd, their Fancy strain'd, and their natural Genius seems sometimes fitter for the *Church,* but compell'd to serve the *Play-house.*' Bedford is an enthusiastic admirer of the old school of English cathedral composers. 'Our antient *Church Musick* is lost, and that solid grave *Harmony* fit for a Martyr to delight in, and an Angel to hear, is now chang'd into a Diversion for *Atheists* and *Libertines,* and that which *Good Men* cannot but lament. Everything which is serious, is call'd in *Derision, The old Cow Path,* and reputed as *dull* and heavy.' In an earlier part of his book, the author tries to persuade us that it is with the definite object of making the 'antient musick' seem dull and heavy that the shorter notes have been brought into common use in other music; 'The *common Notes* in our *Church Musick* are *Minims* and *Semibreves*; instead of these we have *Crotchets, Quavers, and Semiquavers*; And as the quicker Notes increase, so the Design of the *Composer* is that the other may be sung so much the slower, and consequently make the *Antient Musick* seem dull and heavy, which of itself is of a far different Nature.'

The struggle between the old ideals and the new is forcibly illustrated in the cathedral music of the period, the only serious branch of the art which was cultivated to any important extent by the English composers after Purcell's death. It is by their anthems and services that we can best gauge the amount of real musical ability in the country; for in this alone had a strong and genuine English tradition been handed down from the past. Operatic music, before the arrival of Handel, was in so uncertain a condition in England, that in order to make a great sensation on the stage a far stronger man was needed than was to be found among the Englishmen of the early eighteenth century. The few instrumental compositions that were of native origin were confessedly modelled on Italian patterns; the early harpsichord suites were but a somewhat faint reflection of Purcell and Blow, until the Handelian

suites on the one hand, and the 'sonatas' of Domenico
Scarlatti on the other, were introduced to the public. Cantatas,
or successions of airs divided by short recitatives, there were,
but they owed their origin to the country from which they
took their title; and the single songs that were issued month
by month in the various magazines devoted to them, were, for
the most part, of extremely small value. In church music
alone England had an independent voice, and the noble traditions of the past were adhered to for a considerable time,
although in various hands it passed through stages of gradual
modification and was brought more and more into conformity
with the weaker Italian types of sacred music. Of the Catch
and the Glee, two forms of music that were peculiar to
England, a few words must be said later; in almost all periods
they were employed by the same men who reached fame in
their church music.

The name of Jeremiah Clarke is mainly connected in most
people's minds with the fact that he shot himself, it is said
for love, in December, 1707. He had been a pupil of Blow,
and he seems to have imbibed more of the Purcellian manner
than any other composer of his time. He was successively
Organist of Winchester College Chapel, Almoner, Master of
the Choristers, Vicar Choral, and finally Organist at St. Paul's,
a Gentleman of the Chapel Royal, and Organist, jointly with
Croft, of the Chapel. In a volume of harpsichord pieces, in
which he collaborated with Blow, Francis Piggott, and Croft
(published 1700), he is styled 'Organist of St. Paul's Cathedral,
and Composer of the Musick used in the Theatre Royal.' His
first great success was in connexion with the theatre, for he
wrote incidental songs for a large number of pieces, and among
the songs are some of which the names are known at the
present day, though the plays in which they were sung have
long been forgotten. 'Could a man be secure,' which comes
from a piece called *The Committee*, is a capital song of its
kind, and while 'The bonny grey-eyed morn' from *The Fond*

Husband (included in *The Beggar's Opera*), and 'Lord, what's come to my mother,' from *The Bath*, have lovely tunes of great individuality, he excelled in the composition of more vigorous tunes that are well worth being restored to popular vogue. A stirring song in honour of St. George, 'Twelve hundred years at least,' and 'A Health to the Imperialists, or an Invective Ode on the treachery of the Elector of Bavaria' evidently were considered good enough to reappear in the 1700 collection as a 'Serenade' and 'March' respectively. The latter has so fresh a rhythm, and beauty of so distinctively English a cast, that no apology is needed for introducing it here; the vocal version, which may have appeared later than the instrumental, is printed without any bass, and presents various minor alterations; only its first half is here given, but the march is given entire :—

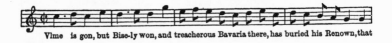

Vlme is gon, but Bise-ly won, and treacherous Bavaria there, has buried his Renown, that

strolling Prince, who few years since was cram'd with Wil - liam's   gold. &c.

A MARCHE.

Another set of *Choice Lessons for the Harpsichord*, printed,
after Clarke's death in 1711, contains a number of pieces
making up several suites ; but there is little or nothing to
distinguish them among collections of the kind. Clarke's
anthems show no great power of sustained invention, and his
choral numbers are of comparatively slight interest; the 'verse'
portions, more especially those for alto, tenor, and bass, are
for the most part expressive, masterly in design, and sincere
in expression. In ' I will love thee, O Lord, my strength,' first
printed in the second edition of Playford's *Harmonia. Sacra*,
one of the three included by Boyce in his *Cathedral Music*,
he introduces the wavy line above the voice-parts, at the words
' The earth trembled,' which Purcell had in time past borrowed
from Lully. ' Bow down thine ear' and ' The Lord is full
of compassion,' though not chosen by Boyce, are finer than
anything he gives; in both the voices are handled with a good
deal of effect of a characteristic kind.

It is interesting to watch the gradually increasing frequency
with which the composers of this period employ the very
meagre expedient of letting two highly pitched voices sing in
unvarying successions of thirds above a bass; if Clarke is not
entirely free from the habit, at least he seldom lets his thirds
be sung by voices higher than an alto and a tenor, so that
the gulf between the two florid parts and the bass is not as

wide as with the Italians, who started the practice. In William
Croft (1678-1727), who was Clarke's colleague at the Chapel
Royal, another contributor with him to the set of harpsichord
pieces already mentioned, the first Organist of Saint Anne's,
Westminster, and Blow's successor as Organist of Westminster
Abbey and Master of the Children of the Chapel Royal,
passages of this kind are found far more often than in Clarke's
works; they disfigure many of the beautiful anthems which
were written for the various state ceremonies for which he
had to compose music during the reigns of Anne and George I.
In the fine eight-part anthem for the thanksgiving after
Blenheim, ' I will give thanks,' he does no more than Clarke
had done; and the eight-part chorus at the end of the work
is of imposing effect.   In 'Praise the Lord, O my soul'
two little organ interludes occur in which the full-blown convention is seen in all its bareness.   The effect of the fine fugal
opening of ' We will rejoice in Thy salvation' (1718), and
the massive closing chorus, are oddly at variance with the
style of the 'verse,' although the inevitable thirds are not quite
continuous, and are given to the alto and tenor.   In one of
his latest anthems, ' Give the King Thy judgements' (1727),
the five-part chorus at the end—a number of great dignity in
other respects—is full of these meaningless twitterings in thirds,
which occur between every possible pair of voices.   One of
Croft's noblest works is the chorus 'Where, mighty Anna,
will thy glories end?' in the first of two odes on the peace of
Utrecht, which were written by way of exercise for his degree
of Mus. D., which he took at Oxford in 1713.   The overtures
to the two odes are more or less on the French pattern, having
a fugal allegro for their main attraction; both are scored with
some knowledge of orchestral effect, and were published
together, as *Musicus Apparatus Academicus*.   In 1724 he
published two volumes of sacred music, containing thirty
anthems and his famous 'Burial Service'; part of the latter
is by Purcell, and in a characteristic preface Croft takes it for

granted that the reason why Purcell's setting of the sentences
has been retained 'will be obvious to every Artist.' In the same
preface it is stated that the book is the first full score engraved
on plates. Two of the anthems have orchestral accompaniment; some, such as 'O Lord, rebuke me not,' 'O Lord God
of my salvation,' and 'Hear my prayer,' show little or no
influence but that of the most dignified school of the past,
while in many of the others appear the incongruities to which
reference has already been repeatedly made[1]. At one point
in his career Croft seems to have come near to touch the main
stream of European music, although quite unconsciously. The
hymn-tune called 'St. Anne's,' which appeared with Croft's
name as author in a collection published 1708, has so remarkable an identity in its first line with the theme of Bach's
great organ fugue in E flat, published in the third part of the
Clavierübung about 1739, that the fugue is known to all
English organists as 'St. Anne's fugue.' No attempt seems
to have been made to discover whether the English hymn-tune
or the book in which it appeared was known to Bach, but as
it is only comparatively recently that the origin of the name
'Suites anglaises' was made clear, there is good reason to
hope that some evidence on a point of at least equal interest
may some day be found.

As compared with the more dignified strains of Clarke and
Croft, the church music of John Weldon (1676–1736) must
appear as 'flimsy' to the reader of the present day as it did
to Burney; a vein of rather sugary melody runs through it,
the choral portions are reduced to a minimum, and it is clear
that he liked nothing better than to give an accomplished
singer passages to show off his execution, whether in such
solo anthems as were published under the title of 'Divine
Harmony' and intended for a singer named Elford, or in the
various songs written in plays, or to be 'performed att his

---

[1] See a long notice of these anthems in Burney's *History of Music*, iii. 605–611.

Consort in York Buildings.' A four-part anthem, 'In Thee, O Lord,' in Boyce's collection is the most solid piece of his writing that is extant; and it is curious to think that such a man should have been a pupil of Purcell, and should have won the first prize in the celebrated competition for the setting of Congreve's masque, *The Judgement of Paris.* Weldon was a Gentleman of the Chapel Royal, succeeded Blow as Organist of the Chapel, was the Organist of St. Bride's, Fleet Street, and St. Martin's-in-the-Fields.

James Goldwin, or Golding (d. 1719) is known to modern students of cathedral music by his six-part anthem, 'I have set God always before me,' printed in Boyce's collection, and by two anthems in the collections of Page and Arnold, but many more are extant in MS. such as those in the library of Christ Church, Oxford; the Fitzwilliam Museum, Cambridge; and the Tudway collection in the British Museum. He was a pupil of Dr. William Child, whom he succeeded as Organist of St. George's Chapel, Windsor, in 1697. Boyce's opinion is fully endorsed by Burney, that Goldwin had remarkable courage in harmonic transitions, anticipating the effects of a later time.

The one English composer of the period who undoubtedly deserves the honour of being mentioned in the same breath with the great masters of the continent is Dr. Maurice Greene (c. 1696-1755), a man who, in more favourable surroundings, would have attained an European celebrity. With more individuality than any of his English contemporaries, he possessed a true and practical admiration for the style of the older church composers, and contrived to solve the problem of combining it with the more modern modes of expression with more success than might have been expected. Such a combination, to our ears, cannot fail to convey some hint of incongruity, and Greene's very eclecticism may have been a subsidiary reason for the brevity of his fame. A pupil of Charles King and Richard Brind, he was successively Organist of St. Dunstan's-in-the-West, St. Andrew's Holborn, and St. Paul's (1718). His later appointments were those of Organist and Composer of the Chapel Royal, Professor of Music at Cambridge, and Master of the King's Band of Music. He thus united in himself all the most important musical offices of the country. From all contemporary accounts, Greene's character had traits in it that were less than wholly admirable. He was strongly attracted to Handel and his music at the time of that master's arrival in England; and, even before he got the appointment of Organist of St. Paul's, used his influence to get permission for Handel to play upon the organ there. Not seeing any necessity for taking sides in the famous rivalry between Handel and Bononcini, Greene kept up an intimacy with the latter which naturally made Handel furious. So far there was nothing blameworthy in Greene's conduct; but when it came to helping Bononcini to palm off Lotti's madrigal upon the Academy of Ancient Music as his own, Greene lost much of his influence with the musicians. He founded a concert society with the boys of the Cathedral Choir, at the Devil Tavern in Fleet Street; and it is a small proof of the idolatry paid to Handel, that his obvious and singularly undiverting witticism on the circumstance that 'Dr. Greene has gone to the Devil' should have been preserved and handed down with the utmost reverence, as if it were something worthy of the honour. Not many years afterwards, in 1738, he helped to found the Royal Society of Musicians, a charitable institution which is still carrying on a good work. The small fortune he received in 1750, in the shape of an estate in Essex, was indirectly of great advantage to English music, for he spent his later years in collecting and editing the large number of services and anthems which, after his death, were brought out by Boyce as *Cathedral Music* (1760–1778), and in which, by his own desire, nothing of his own appears. Greene's most important works are, first, a setting of Pope's

Ode on St. Cecilia's Day, written for the occasion when, being appointed Professor at Cambridge, he accumulated the degrees of bachelor and doctor of music. A duet from this, given in score in Hawkins's *History*, is a good example of the flowing style of the composer's earlier writings. In various collections of organ voluntaries and harpsichord lessons the author's skill in the solid style of the past is clearly displayed; his paraphrase, the 'Song of Deborah' is stated on good authority to have suggested the subject of Handel's oratorio, and it is not impossible that his 'Jephtha' (1737), may have been honoured in the same way, though in this case Handel's work did not appear till fourteen years after Greene's. Though such beautiful songs as 'Go, Rose' (printed in the *Harmonicon*, vol. iv.) and the various other solos and cantatas, tell of fine musical invention, Greene's greatest work is undoubtedly his collection of *Forty Select Anthems in Score*, published 1743. Of these, the fine 'God is our hope and strength' and some others, keep their place in modern use in the comparatively few cathedrals where solid church music is still loved and practised; 'I will sing of Thy power,' 'O clap your hands,' and 'Lord, let me know mine end,' are more or less familiar to the student of our cathedral music, and the splendid 'Lord, how long wilt Thou be angry' shows how thoroughly Greene had assimilated the best traditions of the past, even if he sometimes allowed himself a certain harmonic freedom which no doubt provoked the remark that he knew but little of the theory of music. In his 'Lord, let me know mine end,' a solemn march measure of four crotchets in common time is kept up without cessation throughout, with splendid effect. Instances are only too common in which he adopts the practice spoken of above of letting two voices wander about in thirds above an uninteresting bass; perhaps the worst specimen of his work in this way is the Christmas anthem, 'Behold, I bring you glad tidings,' in which the two soprano parts seldom move in any other intervals than thirds. The other conventional trick of the Italian vocal composers, that to which Scarlatti's name has been generally attached, and which consists of giving to the voice the first part of the strain, as it were in the introduction, has evidently become a recognized tradition in England by this time; in the anthem ʻThou, O God, art praised in Sion,ʼ the alto solo ʻBlessed is the manʼ has an asterisk at the end of the second bar of the prelude, indicating a point from which a repeat is to be made after the first phrase—a fragment of less than three bars—has been sung. Greene, it is worth noting, is the one English organist of the time who was thought worthy of the signal honour of being mentioned by Mattheson; see his *Vollkommener Capellmeister*, p. 479.

Greene's sometime apprentice, William Boyce (1710–1779), claims notice in this place, out of chronological order, because he continued Greene's work as a collector of the glorious compositions of the English church. He was Organist of St. Peter's, Vere Street (as it is now called), and subsequently of St. Michael's Cornhill, succeeding Kelway who had gained the post in a competition in which Boyce was one of the candidates. He conducted the Festivals of the Three Choirs from 1737 for several years; in 1755 he succeeded Greene as Master of the King's Band of Musicians and Conductor of the Festivals of the Sons of the Clergy. He was made Organist of the Chapel Royal in 1758, and in the same year was compelled to retire from public life, owing to increased deafness. His career extends beyond the limits of this volume, but his earlier and more important works come just within its scope. His best-known anthem at the present day is the solid and dignified ʻO where shall wisdom be foundʼ; in his full anthem for eight voices, ʻO give thanks,ʼ occur the fashionable flourishes in thirds between each pair of voices. Scarcely less famous in its own time was the anthem ʻBlessed is he that considereth the sick,ʼ written for the Festival of the

Sons of the Clergy, and regularly performed there for many years. The celebrated duet 'Here shall soft charity' was originally part of an ode written for the benefit of the Leicester Infirmary, it was always introduced into the anthem, and was its most popular portion; it has very little real interest, but is smoothly and flowingly written. The fugal chorus at the beginning, and the treatment of the overture, on a pattern copied from the French, deserve mention. This, and the ode and anthem performed at Cambridge for the installation of the Duke of Newcastle as Chancellor, in 1749, show some skill in orchestral writing, and some feeling for colour. His twelve sonatas for two violins printed in 1745 were popular for many years, and some of the overtures to his odes, &c., were included in the *Eight Symphonies* that were issued after his death. Among his regular anthems for ordinary use, by far the finest is 'By the waters of Babylon,' a noble piece of work, in the 'verse' portions of which the composer seems to have resisted with great success the prevailing fashion for writing in thirds. The serenata 'Solomon' was brought out in 1743, and was very successful and popular for a long time. A less creditable performance was the addition of various 'improvements' to the celebrated *Te Deum* and *Jubilate* of Purcell, the beauty and dignity of which was obscured by them for many years.

The last anthem-writer of any note who belongs to this period, James Nares (1715–1783), would seem to have been oppressed by the prevailing taste in church music, for his fugues with introductory voluntaries show considerable contrapuntal skill, though meaningless flourishes are too often brought in at the end. *The Royal Pastoral*, a work which from internal evidence must have been written to celebrate the sixth anniversary of the marriage of Frederick, Prince of Wales, and is therefore pretty accurately dated 1742, has a fine five-part chorus in solid style at the end of the first part. One of his anthems, 'Call to remembrance,' in five parts has some dignity, but his treatment of the solo voices, as for example, the two sopranos in 'By the waters of Babylon' and the three sopranos in 'God is our hope,' shows how far he had gone in practice from the ideals of the older days. As a man of mediocre attainments may sometimes, as though by accident, light upon a fine idea and carry it out with an ability that is vainly sought for in the rest of his productions, Nares would have had a claim to the veneration of all who have an ear for musical beauty, if he had written nothing but the catch, 'Wilt thou lend me thy mare,' and the following 'lesson' for the harpsichord. The poignant expression of the first movement and the delicious freshness and gaiety of the second, are almost worthy of Bach.

JAMES NARES.

* The proper phrasing of this passage would be more accurately indicated thus:—

His organ voluntaries conform to a type familiar at the
time, one employed by a few composers who deserve to be
mentioned; though the *Whole Book of Psalms* of John
Travers (d. 1758) is nothing but a set of short and very
poor anthems, set to a paraphrase, his *XII Voluntaries for
organ or harpsichord,* published after his death, contains some
good work, and exhibits the usual arrangement with regard to
stops in vogue at the time. Each voluntary sets out with
a movement of more or less solemn character, headed 'dia-
pason,' and most of them have a brisk section labelled
'Cornet,' followed by a flourish for 'Trumpet.' Travers's
name has been preserved less by these than by his canzonets,
of which several, such as 'I, like a bee,' 'Haste, my Nanette,'
and 'When Bibo thought fit from the world to depart,'
remained in vogue for convivial use for many years. They
show much skill in the interweaving of the parts, which are
generally two. Joseph Kelway (d. 1782) was so skilful an
extemporaneous player that Handel was much struck by his
performances; his published sonatas for harpsichord have
no great merit, and generally consist of two quick movements
divided by a slow section, which almost always ends with
a flourish. The organ pieces of his pupil, John Keeble (1711-
1786), are rather more solid in style than his own; they have

similar directions for diapasons, 'eccho' stops, &c., and the
frequent passage of imitation are elaborately explained to the
player by a system of numbers. John Stanley (1714–1786),
remembered as the 'blind organist of St. Andrew's, Holborn,'
published a number of voluntaries of very good style, with the
usual directions as to stops; No. VIII is very much in the
style of Handel's organ concertos, but the rest show no
special leaning to the Handelian manner. In a book of six
'Cantatas' there is a preface in which the use of the English
language in such songs is warmly advocated, on the ground
that it is as expressive as the Italian. The later part of his
career, during which he endeavoured to carry on the oratorio
performances instituted by Handel, does not belong to this
period. Though some voluntaries for the organ or harpsichord were published by Thomas Roseingrave (d. about 1755),
his chief claim to remembrance is that he was what Burney
calls 'the head of the Scarlatti sect'; his admiration for the
sonatas of Domenico Scarlatti, formed during an early visit
to Italy, led him to issue the valuable set of '42 Suits' (sic)
to which he prefixed a piece of his own, of some merit. In
1720 he conducted the performance of his friend's opera,
Narciso. A book of 'Eight Suits' of his own for harpsichord contains some interesting pieces, one a chaconne of
very free construction. George Hayden's name must just
be mentioned, since his duet, 'As I saw fair Clora,' attained
a wide and lasting popularity; his cantatas for solo voice are
singularly weak, and but for this really pretty duet his name
would not have been preserved.

It is necessary in the next place to refer to the work of
some foreign musicians other than Handel, whose influence
on English music was not inconsiderable. First, John
Christopher Pepusch (1667–1752) came to England about
1700, and was engaged in the orchestra of Drury Lane
Theatre. He had a hand in preparing many of the adaptations from Italian operas that were in fashion before Handel's

advent, such as *Thomyris* and others; and one of a set of
cantatas published about 1712 was the famous 'Alexis,' the
fame of which lasted for many years after his death.   In
this volume was a preface containing the usual defence of the
English language as a vehicle for music.   A number of
masques, &c. were composed by him for Lincoln's Inn Fields
Theatre, in the direction of which he was at first a humble,
and subsequently a very dangerous rival to Handel.   It was
not till the date of *The Beggars' Opera* (1727), that the public
taste was so far attracted as to portend a financial risk for
Handel's enterprise; but that it did so to a very serious extent
cannot be doubted.   The humours of Gay's libretto were somewhat highly spiced (he outdid them so far in a second attempt,
Polly, that the performance was forbidden), but the feature
of the work was the happy thought of arranging traditional
and other popular tunes to the words.   Even in the present
day no one can deny the simple charm which the old tunes
have in their somewhat artless setting, and we need not be
surprised at the vogue of the piece, even without taking into
account the welcome contrast from the stilted personages
who stalked through most of Handel's operas.   Throughout
his life Pepusch was a great theorist, and a strong advocate
for restoring the system of solmisation by the hexachords; his
system was embodied in the anonymous *Treatise on Harmony*,
published in 1730, and among his pupils were many of the
best of those whose names have lately been mentioned, such
as Boyce and Travers.

The fashion of the so-called 'ballad operas,' which began
with Pepusch's delightful pasticcio, remained until a much
later period, in fact until the days of Shield and Storace; a
remarkably successful burlesque opera, *The Dragon of Wantley*,
written by Henry Carey, was set by John Frederick Lampe
(c. 1703–1751), who, in spite of his satirical vein, exhibited also
in other pieces of the same kind, managed to endear himself
to the best musicians of the time.

The oratorio of *Judith*, by a Flemish musician, William Defesch, obtained considerable popularity in 1733; the author wrote various other works, and was a good violinist, dying about 1758.

In the adaptations from Italian operas, Nicolo Francesco Haym played an important part: it is difficult to say exactly what share he had in the composition of the additional numbers in *Camilla*, *Thomyris*, and other things, as he seems generally to have claimed more than was actually his. The advent of Handel had the effect of changing Haym from a composer into a poet, for his name appears as the librettist of many of Handel's operas; two letters signed by him, jointly with Clayton and Dieupart, appeared in *The Spectator* in December, 1711, and January, 1712 (Nos. 258 and 278, see p. 239). An air by him is printed in Hawkins's *History* (chap. 174), and two sets of sonatas for two violins and bass have considerable merit. Of the more meritorious of the other signatories of these two letters, Charles Dieupart (d. about 1740), it is only necessary to say that his name will be long preserved in an unexpected way; it has been shown that the 'English suites' of Bach are in several cases adaptations of movements from a book of suites by Dieupart, which are proved to have been in Bach's possession, and which, from the accident of Dieupart's living in England, may well have been known in Bach's family as the 'English Suites.'

In connexion with these Anglo-Italian operas, it is worth remark that the miserable poverty of Thomas Clayton as a composer may be easily gauged by a glance at the overture to his opera *Rosamond*, set to a libretto by Addison, which is given in Hawkins's *History* (ed. 1853, p. 811). Here the practice of writing in thirds is carried to a pitch that is actually ludicrous.

John Ernest Galliard (c. 1687-1749), first appeared in London as an oboist, being appointed chamber musician to Prince George of Denmark about 1706. In the first few years of his residence in England, he learnt enough English to set three anthems, which were performed on occasions of national rejoicing. An opera to words by Hughes, *Calypso and Telemachus*, was brought out in 1712, and Rich, the manager, employed him to provide the music for a kind of nondescript entertainments he got up under the name of pantomimes. His setting of Milton's 'Morning Hymn of Adam and Eve' for two voices obtained a wide celebrity in 1728 and was afterwards expanded into a work of larger proportions by Dr. Benjamin Cooke. Galliard's translation of Tosi's treatise on singing has already been mentioned (see p. 186 ff.); in one of the 'musical entertainments' called *The Royal Chace* occurs the song, 'With early horn,' which became known all over England through the singing of Beard the tenor. The violinist, Michael Christian Festing (d. 1752), deserves mention, not only for the share he had in founding the Royal Society of Musicians, but on account of his solos for violin, which are admirable in their way. His 'Ode upon the return of the Duke of Cumberland from Scotland' (after the rising of 1745), is unusually elaborate, considering that only a soprano solo is employed; it is accompanied with trumpets, two horns, drums, two oboes, two violins and horns.

It is curious that in a country which historians are so very fond of calling unmusical, the public concert should have been a recognized institution for a very long time before such a thing was established, or even known, on the continent. The first regular concerts, to which the public were admitted by payment, were those given in his own house by John Banister, from a date somewhere between 1672 and 1678. They were given every day, and the price of admission was one shilling. After Banister's death the concerts were kept on by the famous 'small-coal man,' Thomas Britton (d. 1714), and at these, which were given weekly, at first with no charge for admission, but afterwards at a yearly subscription of ten shillings, Handel and Pepusch were among the regular performers.

The 'Academy of Ancient Music' flourished from about 1710 till 1792, and here too Dr. Pepusch was a prominent figure; the secession of Greene from this undertaking has been already mentioned. On the death of Britton, some of those who frequented his concerts started similar enterprises with varying success: a painter named Woolaston, a good player on violin and flute, started a meeting of the same kind as Britton's, and another venture was organized at the Angel and Crown Tavern in Whitechapel. The concerts given by an enthusiastic letter-founder, William Caslon, took place only once a month, on the Thursday nearest the full moon, for the convenience of his patrons' return to their homes. These latter seem to have been more in the nature of private concerts, or musical clubs—analogous to the Italian 'accademia,' than regular public concerts; but of the latter there had been instances in the 'great room' in York Buildings, from 1700 to 1720. The 'Castle concert,' which had a successful career of many years, at the Castle in Paternoster Row, from 1724, began a few years before that in the house of one Talbot Young. From 1728 until a disastrous fire in 1748, concerts were given in the Swan Tavern, afterwards the King's Arms, in Exchange Alley, Cornhill. This building, like York Buildings, where Thomas Clayton started concerts in 1711, and 'Hickford's rooms' are frequently mentioned in contemporary accounts. The still famous 'Gentlemen's Concerts' in Manchester were started some time before 1749.

The famous Festival of the Three Choirs, held in rotation at Gloucester, Worcester, and Hereford, began in the city first-named in 1724; the Madrigal Society was founded in 1741, the year of *The Messiah*, by John Immyns, the enthusiastic amanuensis of Dr. Pepusch, and both these undertakings are in a most flourishing condition at the present day. The 'Catch Club' which existed from 1761 till late in the nineteenth century leads us to the consideration of one of the few forms of music which were indigenous to England.

From the days of Shakespeare, the practice of singing catches
at convivial gatherings had been kept up in England; and
few of the composers who have been mentioned in this chapter
failed to exercise their contrapuntal skill in the composition of
the particular form of canon which the word indicates. The
'round,' which is sometimes treated as the equivalent of
the catch, is nothing but a canon such as many of the
greatest composers of Europe have practised from the time
when music as an art was in its infancy; but the catch de-
pends for its point upon the placing of the syllables in such
a way that while one set of words is being sung, other words
are presented or suggested to the hearers' ears. As was only
natural, so convenient a vehicle for the conveyance of ideas
it was better not to print was eagerly enjoyed by singers
and hearers alike, and throughout the history of English
music, the words of too many of the best catches would not
bear a very minute scrutiny by a severe moralist. There are
specimens, mostly of a date later than this period, such as
Webbe's 'Would you know my Celia's charms,' or Callcott's
'How, Sophia,' in which the fun of the form is preserved without any touch of indecency. A bare mention must suffice of
the glee, another musical form peculiar to England; although
the name is of extreme antiquity, and of no slight age as
appended to a musical form (since it occurs in Playford's
Musical Companion, 1672), it lay almost dormant during this
period, and enjoyed its chief vogue immediately after its close.
It preserved in fashion the disposition of voices to which such
frequent reference has been made in the foregoing pages, the
meagre device of letting two voices sing in thirds far above
a bass, with no middle parts to give solidity to the structure;
for a favourite combination with the glee-writers was that of
two sopranos and a bass. Another peculiarity of English
music, which, though far less important artistically, has
remained in vogue down to the present day, is the Anglican
double chant. The single chant was adapted in quite early

times from the type of the ecclesiastical tones, by cutting off
the 'intonation' and confining the free outline of the plain-song
within a scheme of seven bars, only the first and fourth of
which could be extended to accommodate the words at the
beginning of each half-verse. The modern scales were sub-
stituted for the ancient modes, and composers were free to
exercise their melodic invention to any extent within the
narrow limits of the form. The constant repetition of one
short melodic phrase, with one unchanging set of harmonies,
and the inflexible rhythm that has already been referred to,
naturally became very monotonous after a time, and it was
no doubt first for the sake of variety that two single chants
were tacked together to form a double chant, the first of them
being made to end in the dominant, the second to return
to the tonic. For certain psalms, in which the verses go
in pairs, the double chant may be suitable ; but like its more
barbarous descendant, the 'quadruple chant,' it is by no means
in such universal favour at the present day as it once enjoyed,
mainly owing to the revived interest in the true plain-song
of the church, and to the increased knowledge with which
the difficult art of accompanying ancient music properly is
now practised. It is difficult to say at exactly what date
the first 'double chant' made its appearance, but though
arrangements for the purpose have been made from works by
Henry Lawes and Purcell, there is no evidence of an original
composition in this form before the period under consideration :
in Boyce's *Cathedral Music* there is a page of double chants,
but it would seem that by the time this publication appeared,
the form was too familiar to need explanation.

Among English performers who won more than a transitory
success may be mentioned William Babell (c. 1690–1723),
a skilful harpsichord and violin player, whose transcriptions
of airs from Handel's operas were the first examples of the
vulgar pot-pourris that were in fashion through the nineteenth
century (see p. 178) : another eminent violinist, William

Corbett (c. 1669–1748), whose chief work, the concertos styled *Universal Bizzarries* have been mentioned above (see p. 285); while among English singers the most famous were Mrs. Tofts, who was a successful rival of the Italian singers from 1703 to 1709; Mrs. Barbier, whose career began with an attack of nervousness so severe and so charming that it provoked a graceful letter in *The Spectator*, No. 231, made her last appearance in 1729; Kitty Clive (1711–1785) who sang the part of Delilah in Handel's *Samson*; Mrs. Anastasia Robinson, who sang in many of Handel's operas from 1715 until her marriage with the Earl of Peterborough in 1723; and Lavinia Fenton, whose performance of Polly Peachum in *The Beggars' Opera* was the crowning-point of her short career; she married the Duke of Bolton and died in 1760. The bass, Richard Leveridge (1670–1758); and the tenor, John Beard (c. 1717–1791), were the most eminent of English male singers.

Besides the various translations, such as that of Geminiani's works, and Tosi's treatise on singing, which have been already referred to, there were a few books which serve to illustrate the amount of interest taken in musical things by the British public. In 1721 Alexander Malcolm published a *Treatise of Music, speculative, practical, and historical*, at Edinburgh, in which the facts of just intonation, and the necessity for establishing equal temperament, were explained a year before the appearance of Bach's *Wohltemperirtes Clavier*; the interesting *Essay on Musical Expression*, by Charles Avison, organist of Newcastle (c. 1710–1770) appeared in 1752, and the scholarly *Harmonics, or the Philosophy of Sound*, by the Rev. Robert Smith (1689–1768), master of Trinity College, Cambridge, was brought out in 1758.

If the age of Bach and Handel was comparatively barren as far as English music goes, it must be remembered to the nation's credit that a good many of its best national tunes had their origin at this time. 'Heart of Oak' won the applause of the nation in Boyce's *Harlequin's Invasion* (1759), a piece set to a libretto by Garrick; though the career of Thomas Augustine Arne belongs to a period later than that covered in this volume, it must be mentioned that his *Alfred*, containing the immortal 'Rule, Britannia,' appeared in 1740.

For the vexed question of "God save the King," which was published in the *Gentleman's Magazine* for October 1745, the reader is referred to the new edition of Grove's *Dictionary*, vol. iii, pp. 406–8, and to the Preface to the second edition of the present volume. It was long attributed to Henry Carey, who is said to have sung it at a banquet in 1740 in honour of the taking of Portobello; but it has been proved to have been in existence as a national expression of loyalty at a very much earlier date, since Purcell quotes it as a well-known song. Though it appears to have been first intended for the House of Stuart, it became widely popular in the eighteenth century in celebration of the House of Hanover, and was adopted by Germany as her national anthem in 1793.

With these few words about a tune in which Englishmen take a pardonable pride, our survey of the age of Bach and Handel may appropriately conclude.

INDEX